# Arm of Eve

# Arm of Eve

## INVESTIGATING THE THAMES TORSO MURDERS

**Sarah Bax Horton**

First published 2024

The History Press
97 St George's Place, Cheltenham,
Gloucestershire, GL50 3QB
www.thehistorypress.co.uk

© Sarah Bax Horton, 2024

The right of Sarah Bax Horton to be identified as the Author
of this work has been asserted in accordance with the
Copyright, Designs and Patents Act 1988.

All rights reserved. No part of this book may be reprinted
or reproduced or utilised in any form or by any electronic,
mechanical or other means, now known or hereafter invented,
including photocopying and recording, or in any information
storage or retrieval system, without the permission in writing
from the Publishers.

British Library Cataloguing in Publication Data.
A catalogue record for this book is available from the British Library.

ISBN 978 1 80399 748 3

Typesetting and origination by The History Press
Printed and bound in Great Britain by TJ Books Limited, Padstow, Cornwall

Trees for L*Y*fe

This book is dedicated to Detective Inspector John Regan of the Metropolitan Police Thames Division, also known as the river police

# Contents

| | | |
|---|---|---|
| Introduction | | 9 |
| 1 | The first murder: Rainham, May 1887 | 17 |
| 2 | The Whitehall murder, September 1888 | 33 |
| 3 | The Battersea murder, Monday, 3 June 1889 | 53 |
| 4 | A suspect called 'Lancashire Jack' | 72 |
| 5 | The Pinchin Street murder, Whitechapel, where a woman's torso was discovered at 5.25 a.m. on Tuesday, 10 September 1889 | 88 |
| 6 | Profiling the Thames Torso Killer | 109 |
| 7 | The non-fatal attack on Jessie Miller, Monday, 1 July 1889 | 126 |
| 8 | The non-fatal attack on Elizabeth Sarah Warburton, Wednesday, 23 October 1889 | 142 |
| 9 | The Salamanca Place murder, Vauxhall, where a woman's dismembered body was discovered on Sunday, 8 June 1902 | 165 |
| 10 | A parallel case: the murder of Julia Martha Thomas in 1879, and a reconstruction of the Salamanca Place murder | 181 |
| 11 | Why not Jack the Ripper? | 202 |
| 12 | A final analysis of the Torso Killer | 223 |

| | |
|---|---|
| Conclusion and true crime reconstructions of the Thames Torso Murders | 241 |
| Epilogue | 253 |
| Acknowledgements | 255 |
| Timeline | 257 |
| Map | 260 |
| Select bibliography | 263 |
| Notes | 265 |
| Index | 283 |

# Introduction

The Thames Torso Killer should, by rights, take precedence over Jack the Ripper as the world's first unidentified modern serial killer. He started to kill in early 1887, over a year before the Ripper, and his last murder was in autumn 1889, almost ten months after that of the Ripper's last victim, Mary Jane Kelly. The Torso Killer murdered and dismembered at least four women, in addition to the unborn child of the only victim who was identified. The police surgeons of the day pieced together the headless remains and provided best-guess descriptions of each woman, while Metropolitan Police officers worked through lists of missing persons. Despite their best endeavours, all but one went nameless to their graves. This book is named *Arm of Eve* after a sketch by Albrecht Dürer of Eve's idealised left arm, its hand curled around the forbidden apple, representing the universal woman.

The Metropolitan Police Whitechapel Murders files cover the deaths of eleven women between 1888 and 1891. Those women were similar to each other in their destitution and dependence on street-hawking and soliciting. At least five were casual sex workers killed by Jack the Ripper: Polly Nichols, Annie Chapman, Elisabeth Stride, Catherine Eddowes and Mary Jane Kelly. A sixth, Martha Tabram, was probably the Ripper's first kill. Emma Smith, who died twenty-four hours after being attacked, said she was assaulted by a gang of men. Scotland Yard assessed Rose Mylett's demise to be an accident. The murders of street walkers Alice Kinsey, or McKenzie, and Frances Coles also remained unsolved. Some commentators add Kinsey to the canon of women killed by Jack the Ripper, as her abdominal injuries were similar to the type of posthumous mutilations which he inflicted for his own gratification.

One of the last murders on those files was that of an unidentified woman referred to as the Pinchin Street trunk, whose dismembered torso was discovered under an East End railway arch. Like the other cases, it has long been considered a possible Ripper crime. But the Pinchin Street victim was killed by the Thames Torso Killer. The police of the day classified it as such, attributing it to a second serial killer active at the same time who was believed to have committed four murders. While the Ripper killed between August and November 1888, the Torso Killer started his attacks in April 1887 and probably stopped after the Pinchin Street murder in September 1889.

Extraordinarily, the Torso Killer operated at the same place and time as the Ripper, with whom he shared notable similarities. Like the Ripper, this killer picked his victims through chance sightings of women who fitted his ideal victim type. Mostly dark-haired and busty, they were of a similar age to his wife, and happened to be alone when he spotted them. A few of them, low on funds, might have occasionally sold their bodies for sex. Unlike the Ripper, who did not sexually assault his victims, the Torso Killer was a rapist turned killer; his approach based on the classic rapist's mantra: isolate – inebriate – penetrate. His frustration with women manifested itself through violence, gaining control through brute force. It is clear from their injuries that his victims put up a vigorous defence. He was brutal, physical, under-educated, clever enough to develop a repeatable crime, but not so intelligent to grasp that his methods created a pattern that could be deciphered.

Unlike his notorious counterpart, the Torso Killer did not simply abandon his victims' bodies. He cut them up and deposited the pieces at locations around Central London; not only in the River Thames and Regent's Canal, but also in Battersea Park, a private garden, under a railway arch and, notably, in the foundations of New Scotland Yard. Mutilation and dismemberment are two distinct 'signatures' of murder.

## INTRODUCTION

The Ripper's primary objective was to open his victims' abdomens and remove their organs. In extreme cases, he cut their faces and other body parts. The Torso Killer dismembered his victims' bodies, both for gratification and disposal. This difference alone is sufficiently significant to indicate not one, but two serial killers, as defined by the police of the day.

The four murders typically attributed to the Torso Killer occurred in close sequence and are named after locations where body parts were found: Rainham in May 1887; Whitehall in September 1888, at the first peak of the Ripper scare; Battersea and Pinchin Street in 1889. The police surgeons of the day used scientific techniques to deduce the age, height and defining characteristics of each woman, while Scotland Yard's Criminal Investigation Department (CID) and divisional police officers appealed for information from the public to make a match. Only the 'Battersea' victim was ever identified, a pregnant 24-year-old from Chelsea named Elizabeth Jackson, demonstrating that the historical names were misnomers. They do not represent the locations where each woman was accosted or killed, frustrating the police investigation. As in any murder series, each subsequent case reveals something new about its perpetrator and confirms something consistent in his operational method.

The Metropolitan Police District covered a 15-mile radius of Charing Cross and was divided into four districts, sub-divided into divisions. Police from up to a dozen divisions investigated the Torso cases, reflecting the diverse locations where body parts were found. Ripper veterans from Whitechapel's H Division worked on the Pinchin Street murder, as did divisional police surgeons led by early forensic expert Mr Thomas Bond and his assistant at Westminster Hospital, Doctor Charles Hebbert. Bond was the real powerhouse of the duo, being 'probably the expert of his day, esteemed by his colleagues, often brought in when other medical evidence was in dispute'.[1] Both men were also involved in the Ripper post-mortems, notably that of Mary Jane Kelly, after which Bond produced the world's first profile of a serial killer.

The senior police officers involved in the Torso investigations also had Ripper experience. They included Metropolitan Police Commissioners Sir Charles Warren and his successor James Monro, CID Chiefs Robert Anderson and Melville 'Mac' Macnaghten, Chief Constable Colonel Bolton Monsell, H Division Superintendent Thomas Arnold, Chief

Inspectors Henry Moore and John West, Detective Inspectors Donald Swanson, Frederick Abberline and John Shore, and Inspectors Charles Pinhorn and Edmund Reid. The author's great-great-grandfather Harry Garrett was an H Division sergeant based at Leman Street police station, and was previously a constable in Greenwich's R Division. Like his seniors, he worked in some capacity on the Ripper murders, as did Detective Sergeant Frank Froest, who was directly involved in the Pinchin Street Torso case owing to its East End location.

Several more police surgeons and officials were involved in both the Thames Torso and the Whitechapel Murders investigations. Doctor George Bagster Phillips, a stalwart of the Ripper case, was called out alongside his assistant Doctor Percy Clark, as was Doctor Frederick Gordon Brown, the City Police surgeon who had conducted the post-mortem examination of Ripper victim Catherine Eddowes. And one of the coroners was, again, Wynne Edwin Baxter.

The officers of Thames Division, the river police, were instrumental in bringing my proposed perpetrator of the Thames Torso Murders to an approximation of justice. The river police force numbered 200 men, with a chief inspector, seven inspectors, forty sub-inspectors, five detectives and 147 constables. Policemen patrolled the Thames in six-hour shifts, using twenty rowing boats and two steam launches.[2] Their headquarters was at Wapping, in a building still in use today, although in this instance their police station at Waterloo Bridge was the scene of the action.

In ensuring the conviction of this perpetrator, Detective Inspector John Regan drew on his considerable local knowledge of the river's smugglers, thieves and miscreants. Described in police records as precisely 5ft 6⅜ inches tall, with blue eyes and greying hair, Regan was born just north of the river in St George-in-the-East. A year older than my police ancestor Harry Garrett, he was his contemporary and, in 1891, his near-neighbour on Stepney's Oxford Street, today's Stepney Way.

A key document for any researcher into the Thames Torso Murders is a report in two parts written by Doctor Charles Hebbert with input from his senior colleague Bond. The report was compiled from lecture notes for students of forensic science, and was prefaced as being for their future guidance, should they be required to report the results of a post-mortem examination to the authorities:

> When a medical man is called upon by the coroner or the police to examine such cases, he often is at a loss to know how much or how little to report, so in the following pages I have indicated the usual procedure, hoping that they may interest some students of forensic medicine, and perhaps aid them in framing a report if ever they are requested to make one.[3]

In it, Hebbert demonstrated how the post-mortem examination of a murder victim could assist in identifying the body, where possible state the cause of death, and deduce characteristics about the victim and perpetrator to direct the police investigation.

The Hebbert report definitively unites the four crimes committed in the period 1887–89:

> The mode of dismemberment and mutilation was in all similar, and showed very considerable skill in execution, and it is a fair presumption from the facts, that the same man committed all the four murders.[4]

It makes two vitally important points: 'the golden rule, as quoted by [forensic scientist Alfred Swaine] Taylor, is "that a medical man, when he sees a dead body, should notice everything"'[5] and chillingly, that:

> the cases taken as a whole are valuable as illustrating the difficulties we labour under in describing a person from such imperfect data, and as showing how a skilful, determined individual can murder and dispose of four bodies without detection.[6]

In the author's hypothesis, although the killer evaded being charged with multiple murders, he was convicted of a serious lesser offence, putting him out of action for several years.

This series of crimes appears impossible to solve. The Torso Murders present several difficulties which at first sight seem intractable: where the perpetrator operated; how and where he accosted his victims if they were strangers; if not, how he knew them; where he killed them and secreted their body parts before disposal; even where he dumped their remains, as the tide took them far from that spot. Perhaps owing to the case's impenetrability, the few writers who have written book-length examinations of the Thames Torso Killer have relied heavily on Ripper suspects in their theories about his identity. In the author's analysis, the Torso and Ripper series are distinctly separate. In 2020, I made the startling discovery that, in the closing days of 1889, the Torso Murders might have been partly avenged by the river police. A search against my own profile of the killer uncovered a man with a criminal record, which documented his prosecution and subsequent custodial sentence for just one of his crimes.

My prime suspect is James Crick, a waterman and lighterman based at Horsleydown[7] on the south bank of the River Thames adjacent to today's Tower Bridge. Watermen rowed skiffs or wherries to transport passengers, or ships' crews, along or across the river. They were licensed to carry a specific number of passengers depending on the size of their skiff, and a later chapter cites the limit of eight. Lightermen transported goods using a range of craft including the London lighter, also known as a Thames or dumb barge as it was not powered by sail or engine. Heavily reliant on the tides, it was manoeuvrable by a single man with a pair of large oars, or by a man and a boy, and if 'above 50 tons burden' by 'at least two competent men'.[8] Whilst lighting was a year-round trade, driven by traffic to and from the docks, watermen mainly plied their passenger trade in the fair-weather months between April and October.

James Crick fits the type of criminal profile that was applied to Jack the Ripper, of having an absent father, a dominant mother, and being a risk-taker whose frustration and aggression were often targeted against women. Like Hyam Hyams, named by the author as Jack the Ripper in *One-Armed Jack: Uncovering the Real Jack the Ripper*, the first victim of his violence was his wife. Later charged with rape and attempted murder in two separate incidents, Crick was convicted of a single charge of rape and sentenced to fifteen years' imprisonment. After his early release from jail, a further murder suggested a possible match to the series, as a sackful of human remains was discovered in June 1902 at Vauxhall's Salamanca Place. James Crick could have been the Torso Killer, and his victim type, method of violent assault and mobility on water fit that criminal profile. Unlike Jack the Ripper, there are no eyewitness accounts that link the killer to his victims, no link between his lodgings or relatives' premises and the murder locations, and no distinctive physical or psychological characteristics that serve to identify him.

The Torso Killer was an opportunist, roving across much of Central London to solicit his victims. Like Jack the Ripper, he picked out a series of women who were solitary and vulnerable. She could have been anyone who fitted those criteria, whom he found attractive. He felt confident that he could intimidate each one into doing what he wanted, and that any offered resistance would be futile. Aged between 20 and 40, she was the sort of woman who was willing to have a laugh and a drink, and take up his chance offer of a free ride.

# 1

# The first murder: Rainham, May 1887

You are now
In London, that great sea, whose ebb and flow
At once is deaf and loud, and on the shore
Vomits its wrecks, and still howls on for more.

From Percy Bysshe Shelley's 'Letter to Maria Gisborne'

The Queen's Golden Jubilee took place in the glorious year of 1887, when every borough offered its own tribute to their monarch in the form of a statue, municipal improvement or personal gift. A year when, after fifteen years in the force, my police ancestor Harry Garrett was made acting sergeant at Lee Green police station in South East London, swiftly followed by his well-earned promotion to sergeant. But before the summer celebrations, on Wednesday, 11 May, a boatman fished a sackful of human remains from the River Thames at Rainham in Essex.

Accounts of what became known as 'The Rainham Mystery' begin at the same time and place: the morning of Wednesday, 11 May 1887, when the River Thames's equivalent of a delivery driver, Essex lighterman Edward Hughes, spotted a bundle on the foreshore at Rainham Ferry. He jumped out of his craft, walked over and picked it up, looking for something of value. Even a corpse attracted a finder's fee of 5 shillings paid by the local parish. The bundle gaped open to reveal a part of a human torso comprising a woman's pelvis below the third lumbar vertebra. Named after the first place where a body part was washed up, Rainham marked the start of a series of murders sharing the same method of killing, dismemberment and disposal, and committed by the same hand.

The investigation united officers from the Essex Constabulary, the river police of Thames Division, and Scotland Yard, which was represented by Superintendent John Shore and Detective Inspector Arthur Hare. An officer of nearly thirty years' experience, Shore would later work on the Ripper investigation, to which Hare was also connected as a personal friend of one its leading officers, Inspector Frederick Abberline. Hare and Abberline were initiated into the same Freemason's Lodge, Zetland, on the same day in 1889.[1] A high-flyer, Hare would retire in 1906 as a CID superintendent.[2]

The Rainham murder instantly presents two red herrings, as its stated time and place were both misapprehensions. The investigating police deduced that the body part had been washed by the tide 15 miles downstream from London, where the murder had occurred several weeks previously. On being alerted to Hughes's find, the police immediately launched a search for the remaining body parts, starting with a small bight close to the spot where the bundle was discovered, as flotsam usually gathered there, in addition to other creeks and bays. Despite significant effort, they found nothing.

On Saturday, 14 May at Rainham's Phoenix Hotel, 54-year-old Charles Carne Lewis, the highly experienced Coroner for South Essex, opened the inquest into the death of an unknown woman. The jury viewed the body part in an adjoining shed, where it 'presented a very horrible appearance, there being only a portion of the body, and that in an advanced state of decomposition'.[3]

The first witness was Hughes, aged 24, a licensed lighterman who transported goods to and from the docks along the River Thames. A pen-and-ink drawing in the *Illustrated Police News* shows the fresh-faced Hughes staring in shock at what was an inaccurate depiction of a full-length, headless and armless torso.[4] As the murders continued over the next eighteen months, equally gruesome sights would be depicted in the press, their sensationalism generating sales.

Hughes testified in detail about finding the remains:

> At about 11.30 on Wednesday morning [11 May] he was on his barge at Rainham Ferry; the barge was lying alongside the jetty at Mr. Hempleman's factory; the tide was flowing; he saw what appeared to be a bag, which the tide was washing up; the bag was about 30 feet from his barge; he went to it and brought it ashore; as he was picking the bag up it partially came undone, and he saw it contained part of the body of a woman; he told a man who was coming up into Rainham to inform the police; he left the body on the shore in charge of another lighterman [George Crook];[5] he did not see any papers or any linen in the bag; he saw nothing but the body of the woman.[6]

Hempleman's was a chemical and manure manufacturer employing eighty men. Described in the press as a 'blood and bone factory on the marshes',[7] it was a suitably grisly location for that discovery. In a possible conflict of interest, its wealthy owner, Frederick Seband Hempleman, was the jury foreman.

Constable Stock, who was stationed at Rainham, took up the story:

> [At] about 12.30 on Wednesday morning he received information which induced him to proceed to Rainham Ferry; on the shore near Mr. Hempleman's factory he found a piece of sacking, tied up with cord; it was partially undone, and he could see it was part of the body of a woman; it was at once taken to a shed at the Ferry public-house, and then removed to the Phoenix Hotel; Dr. Calloway [sic] saw it the next day ...[8]

Stock gave the following replies to questions from the coroner. He confirmed that there was no linen or paper in the bag, no letters or mark of any kind on the sacking, and nothing peculiar in the cord with which the sack was tied.[9] He added, 'The knot was an ordinary one which anyone could tie, and had no distinctive character about it, such as a sailor's knot [presumed to be a bowline or hitch knot] or a slip knot.'[10] Both of the latter types of knot were more complex than the standard overhand knot.

The next witness was general practitioner and surgeon Doctor Edward Callaway, aged 51, who was based at Barking. Doctor Callaway provided the results of his post-mortem examination of the remains:

> On the 12th ... he was shown part of the body of a female, which consisted of the last two bones and a half of the lumbar vertebrae above the trunk, which had been sawn through completely straight by a fine sharp saw. The integuments [skin and related structures] surrounding the vertebrae were cut by a very sharp instrument, which had also passed through the abdominal wall.
>
> There was neither head nor legs, and the thighs had been taken clean out of the socket of the pelvis, the muscles of the thigh being cut obliquely from the inside to the outside. These were also clean cut, and must have been done by a sharp instrument. There was no jaggedness in any of the cuts, which had evidently been done by some one expert in the use of the knife.
>
> He could not detect any particular mark of violence to the body, which had been dead probably about a fortnight. The viscera [intestines] in the body had been removed, the pelvis was empty, and there was neither bladder, womb nor rectum.

And in response to a set of questions from the coroner:

> Although death had taken place fourteen days [previously], still the body might not have been in the water for so long a period. He should judge that the age of the deceased would be from 27 to 29, and the body was in a very well nourished condition. There were no evidences of maternity. It would be contrary to the Anatomical Act to part with the body from a hospital ...

The Anatomy Act of 1832 regulated the anatomical examination of donated bodies, and ensured that they were 'decently interred'[11] within eight weeks of receipt. Callaway continued:

> It look[ed] as though some one were attempting to get rid of the body piecemeal. He was quite sure, however, that a very skilful person had cut up the body, the part of the spine offering least obstacles to

severance having been selected for the operation. The way in which the thighs had been cut proved conclusively that the person who operated was thoroughly acquainted with anatomy.[12]

The doctor added in response to further questioning that, in his opinion, the body was cut up for the purpose of lessening its bulk for disposal. There were no marks or moles on the remains that could lead to the victim's identification.[13] Although not stated in court, the most likely explanation for removing the body's organs was to render it less buoyant in the water, otherwise it would 'float, often, because of intestinal putrefactive gases, belly upwards'.[14]

The final witness of the day was Superintendent John Dobson, of the Essex County Constabulary. At his retirement six years later, he was described as one of the sharpest officers in the force.[15]

> He saw the body on Wednesday in a shed at Rainham Ferry, and on Thursday, he examined the body in company with Dr. Calloway [sic], and then proceeded to Scotland Yard, and saw Superintendent Shore, who stated that there was no information in the office of any woman being missing. Notices of the finding of the body were immediately telegraphed all over the metropolitan district, with instructions to look out for the missing portions of the body ...
> 
> Superintendent Shore stated that the hospitals were very careful and particular, and ... this was [not] part of a dissected body.[16]

The coroner adjourned the hearing until 3 June, to allow the police to search for the missing body parts 'if they had been got rid of in the same way'.[17] Through the press, the particulars would be ventilated, and watermen, who ferried passengers along the Thames, and other river workers would be on the lookout. He added that it was quite possible that this was another Wainwright case.

Lewis was referring to a notorious case of 1874, in which brush maker Henry Wainwright shot his lover Harriet Lane and buried her body in a shallow grave under the floorboards of his warehouse in Whitechapel Road. A year later, when he went bankrupt and needed to vacate the premises, he disinterred the corpse, and dismembered it for disposal. He persuaded one of his workers to join him in carrying the two heavy parcels, wrapped in black American canvas, to a street corner, where he hailed a cab. His companion, suspicious of their putrefying contents, alerted the police, and Wainwright was arrested shortly after his arrival at Southwark.[18] Wainwright's motive for dismemberment was purely practical, to enable him to move the decomposed body parts to another place of concealment without arousing suspicion.

On Friday, 3 June, when the Rainham inquest resumed, Doctor Callaway was recalled to state the cause of death as far as he could:

> From a close inspection of the body, there was nothing whatever which would give any indication as to the manner in which the deceased came by her death, or the cause of such death. All he could say was that the body had been dismembered very shortly after death ... [19]

Superintendent Dobson was also recalled, and testified that a Mrs Cross of Albany Terrace, Richmond Upon Thames, had written to him giving information about her daughter, who had disappeared from home on 20 January. Richmond was in South-West London, 25 miles away from Rainham. A description of Miss Cross circulated by the police read: 'Age 28, height 5ft 8in, complexion dark, pencilled eyebrows, short curly black hair, and exceedingly handsome face.'[20] The water was muddied by the fact that she regularly went missing, as Dobson explained to the court:

> The young woman was of weak intellect, and in the habit of absenting herself from home for a few days, when she would wander to the side of the river and get upon any barges, boats, or yachts which might happen to be moored alongside the towing path. [She] had never been heard of, although the police had made every endeavour to discover her whereabouts.[21]

The police interest in Miss Cross demonstrates their awareness that the Rainham victim could have been picked up anywhere in the Metropolitan area, transported alive or dead on a boat, put into the Thames at any spot, and her body taken by the tide to its discovery location. River workers were interviewed regarding Cross's disappearance.

A proportion of bargemen and lightermen, who transported cargoes on the Thames in different vessels, were also watermen, the riverine equivalent of taxi drivers. Watermen often worked as lightermen over winter, when poor weather deterred their passengers. The Watermen's Company licensed all watermen and lightermen on the River Thames and, it was claimed, did not cancel the licences of men convicted of felonies, mainly theft from cargoes.

A case of gang rape and robbery dating from the autumn of 1886, the year before the Rainham murder, suggested that a minority of river workers could pose a danger to women. Its victim was a 23-year-old inmate of Chelsea Workhouse, Sarah Ann King, who was described as having an unspecified intellectual disability. One September morning, she was found wandering the streets by a local police constable and returned to the workhouse. The medical superintendent Doctor Moore, having heard her account and examined her, concluded that she 'had been subjected to a very gross outrage'.[22]

King claimed to have been accosted by a man on Chelsea Embankment, and taken by him on a rowing boat onto a barge on the Thames, where she was held overnight and raped by five men. The main suspect allegedly threatened to kill her. He also took payment from the rest of the men for having sexual intercourse with King, and stole 17 shillings from her pocket.[23] Three of them were tried for rape at the Central Criminal Court, colloquially known as the Old Bailey, and acquitted. No evidence was offered upon other charges of robbery with violence, and another charge of rape on an unspecified victim four days after the attack on King.[24] It is possible that King's intellectual disability disadvantaged her, and at an earlier police court hearing of the case, her evidence was described as 'highly unreliable, contradictory, and improbable'.[25] She was certified for admission to Caterham Lunatic Asylum before her case came to court.[26] None of the identifiable suspects had any later criminal charges brought against them.

At the Rainham hearing, Superintendent Dobson also reported the disappearance of a Mrs Carter, of Vauxhall, in August 1886, who had not been heard of since, 'notwithstanding diligent enquiries'.[27] Those two names were the nearest the police came to any identification of the victim. Both women had gone missing considerably earlier than the date of the murder. The coroner summed up, saying that he saw no benefit in any further adjournment, and that although the deceased had no doubt been the victim of foul play, 'nothing leading to a clue to the incriminated parties had been discovered'.[28] He advised the jury to return an open verdict, which they did.

Only two days after the verdict was returned, several more body parts surfaced. Their various discoveries again raised questions about the timing and location of the murder, and the additional problem of whether they were disposed of at the same time or on staggered dates. On Sunday, 5 June, close to Temple Pier in central London, pierman John Morris retrieved a floating right human thigh including the patella (kneecap), wrapped in coarse canvas and tied with cord. It was examined by Doctor George Hamerton, police surgeon for Holborn's E Division.[29] The Coroner for the City of London, Samuel Langham, refused to conduct an inquest on the lone thigh, because it was not 'a vital part',[30] and it was buried at the City of London Cemetery at Ilford.[31]

On the same day, the victim's lower thorax and upper abdomen were discovered as a single piece on the south bank of the Thames near Battersea Pier. That finding triggered a meeting on 11 June between the Battersea district coroner Braxton Hicks, Doctors Callaway and Kempster, the police surgeons for Rainham and Battersea respectively, who had both examined the body part, and officers Shore and Ayre of Scotland Yard. Previously, Doctor Callaway had confirmed that the remains fitted with the lower abdomen and pelvis found at Rainham and that the piece of sacking was exactly similar to that used to wrap the Rainham and Temple Pier bundles. It was decided not to hold an inquest at once, but to preserve the Battersea remains in a glass jar filled with spirits of wine, and await further developments.[32]

Over the next three weeks, body parts continued to emerge north of the river at St Pancras Lock and the Regent's Canal. The canal ran for 8.6 miles between Paddington in West London and the Limehouse Basin in the east, where it joined the River Thames. The police had the canal dredged for approximately 2 miles, from the Midland Railway Goods Station at St Pancras as far as Primrose Hill.[33] Doctor Callaway and Inspector Hare examined the pieces of limbs at St Pancras Mortuary and confirmed that they belonged to the same body.[34]

Another meeting was held, this time of the four coroners in whose districts the various body parts had been found: Samuel Langham (City of London); Charles Carne Lewis (South Essex); Athelstan Braxton Hicks (Battersea); and Doctor George Danford Thomas (Central Middlesex). It was agreed that Danford Thomas would hold a single inquest at the Crowndale Hall in Camden Town. A qualified doctor and lawyer, he was 'a man of very unostentatious and retiring disposition'.[35] Shortly before his death in August 1910, Danford Thomas conducted the first hearing of the inquest into the discovery of human remains at the notorious American Doctor Crippen's house in Holloway, North London.[36] Hawley Harvey Crippen murdered his wife Cora in January of that year. Chief Inspector Walter Dew, who had served on the Jack the Ripper investigation as a young constable, was alerted by ship's telegram to Crippen's escape and effected his extraordinary arrest during an Atlantic crossing to Canada.[37] Dew's CID chain of command included further personalities from the Ripper investigation, Assistant Commissioner Macnaghten and Frank Froest, by then promoted to superintendent.[38]

Mirroring the first inquest, the second had two hearings, this time with an adjournment of nearly four weeks between them. On the afternoon of Monday, 11 July, Danford Thomas opened the inquest into the discovery in the Regent's Canal of two arms and two lower legs with feet. The left lower leg also had the left kneecap attached. He introduced the case by stating that other portions of the body of a female had been found in different parts of the metropolis, and that an inquest, with an open verdict on the cause of death, had been held on the portion of the trunk found at Rainham Ferry.

Danford Thomas went on to observe:

All these parts were believed to belong to the same corpse. The head had not yet been picked up, and all the internal organs were missing. There was no proof of identity thus far.

It was imagined that a body must have been dissected by some skilled person, and it was suggested that some medical students might have become possessed of a body, and scattered its mutilated parts about as a grim joke. On the other hand, it was possible that a murder had been committed. The police were still pursuing their investigations into the case.[39]

The four men who had made discoveries within his district testified about the dates and locations of their finds, which had all occurred in or near waterways in North London. Frank Hurle, keeper of the St Pancras locks, testified that he had discovered the right arm in the waters of the Regent's Canal near the coal dock of the Midland Railway. James Berry testified that he found the other arm inside the coal dock. George Monkford and Charles Rodwell stated they found two legs on the same day in the waters of the Regent's Canal between the St Mark's and Gloucester bridges.[40] The press reported that both legs were wrapped in canvas and tied with cord. The feet were described as 'small and well formed' and a further distinguishing feature was mentioned, but not in court: 'in the front of both legs are evidences of some kind of congestion, such as varicose veins ...'[41]

Inspector Hare testified about the discovery of other parts of the body: on 11 May, the lower part of the trunk at Rainham; on 5 June, the right thigh on the north bank of the River Thames opposite Waterloo Pier (meaning Temple Pier); and on 8 June, part of the thorax at Battersea.[42] Doctor Callaway confirmed that he had examined all of the body parts, with the following results:

> The portion of the trunk found at Rainham Ferry ... belonged to a female who he thought was about 27 or 28 years old. When he saw it first he thought it had then been in the water a fortnight. The internal contents [organs] were missing. The spine had been sawn through. The thighs had been cleverly dissected out of the joints [by a skilled person] ...
> The right thigh, found in the Thames, corresponded with the trunk. The thorax, too, found at Battersea, corresponded with the trunk. The collarbones and breast[s] were absent. The sacking in which all the remains were wrapped corresponded, save that in which the thigh was placed, which was of a slightly coarser texture.[43]

In response to questions from the coroner, Callaway confirmed that he thought the deceased had died at the beginning of May, or end of April.

As far as he could possibly gather, the arms and legs also corresponded with the torso, although the left thigh was missing. There was nothing to guide him as to the cause of death. He finished by stating, 'It is my conviction that the body has been thus cut up in order the more readily to get rid of it – to dispose of its parts.'[44] The coroner commented that it was a very grave matter indeed. As Home Secretary Henry Matthews had ordered a further surgical examination of the remains to be made, he adjourned the proceedings.[45]

On the afternoon of Saturday, 6 August, Danford Thomas resumed the inquest, stating that, since the last sitting, the left thigh had been found. The first witness, William Cope, a labourer, testified about his discovery:

> On Saturday July 16th, whilst he was at work at the Camden Town locks, he noticed in the waters of the Regent's Canal, between two barges, a piece of flesh, which on getting out he found was a left thigh. He called a police-constable, who took it away.[46]

The next witness was Detective Inspector Arthur Hare. He reported that since the adjournment, every inquiry had been made, but without finding any clue about the victim's identity. Mr Thomas Bond then took the stand. An anatomical lecturer at Westminster Hospital, and experienced police surgeon, he would become the leading medical expert on the Torso Murders. At the behest of Assistant Commissioner James Monro, Bond provided his expert opinion on this unusual case.[47]

Bond testified as follows:

> He had examined the different parts, and he found that the whole of them corresponded, and were certainly parts of the same body. He searched the body, but could not find any marks likely to lead to identification.
>
> From a measurement of the different parts he was of opinion that the female was 5 ft. 2 [inches] to 5 ft. 4 [inches] in height. He concluded that the age of the woman was from 25 to 35 years. The body was that of a well-nourished, stout woman, and she had dark hair.
>
> The different parts had been divided by some persons having a knowledge of anatomy. He was certain that the body had not been

divided for dissecting purposes. The parts had been in the water for about three months, and he had no doubt that they were put in at the same time. There was no evidence as to how the deceased came by her death.[48]

His final statement commented on the actions of the killer or killers to prevent the body from being identified:

The head and shoulders were absent, and, in his opinion, would never be found. In the first place, the perpetration of the crime, if crime it was, would make this unrecognisable; and, in the second place, if thrown into the water, the weight of the bones would keep the skull at the bottom of the water.[49]

Bond's statement that the head and shoulders were missing makes it clear that the torso was cut into three parts. The word 'shoulders' referred to the upper thorax and collarbones. It was not possible to discern whether the head and neck had been separated from the collarbones and shoulders.

Bond's description of the victim's hair was based on her black pubic hair. To estimate the victim's height, Bond's colleague Hebbert dismissed as unreliable the 'figure carré des ancients', a method which measured a square around a man with outstretched arms and legs, as seen in Leonardo da Vinci's *Vitruvian Man*. Instead, he took an average of three measurements. The first placed the top of the pubes at the centre of the body; the others followed 'the ancient Egyptian canon' that the length of the middle finger as measured down from the root of the thumb-nail at right angles to the axis of the middle finger when the hand was laid flat on a table was 1/19th of the height; and that the forearm from the tip of the olecranon (elbow) to the end of the middle finger was 5/19ths of the height.[50] Based on 'a number of observations', Hebbert considered the latter to be 'the only measurement which gives anything like an accurate result'.[51]

The coroner summed up briefly before the jury returned the verdict, 'That the remains found were those of a woman between twenty-five and thirty-five years of age; but there was not sufficient evidence to show by what means the said woman came by her death.'[52] The police investigation continued with little to work on. The press speculated that the body was not that of Miss Cross, the woman who disappeared in January from Richmond Upon Thames, as 'her feet were abnormally large' compared to the 'remarkably small' feet of the victim.[53]

Another article quoted an unnamed woman with a missing sister in the continued efforts to identify the body:

> For some time during last year her sister had been keeping company with a young doctor, and she knew that the latter had seduced her. Both parties lived in South London, but last year the doctor obtained possession of a practice in a northern suburb, and went to live there, being followed shortly afterwards by the young woman, who insisted much against his will in living with him.
>
> They led the neighbours to believe that she was his housekeeper, but she suddenly disappeared about two months ago, and has not since been heard of. Her age and general description answers that of the body found in the Thames, and inquiries are being made with the view of ascertaining whether the young woman is still alive.[54]

In the lack of any further information or discoveries, the investigation petered out. What is left are the conclusions of the Hebbert report, with the following stated objectives when examining the eight parts of the Rainham victim:

> In the inquiry we had to determine the following points: whether they were human and belonged to the same body, the race, age, sex, height, complexion, and condition of life, and, if possible, the cause of death, and the skill or ignorance of the operator.[55]

Hebbert analysed the victim's 'condition of life' meaning her likely occupation, marital status, childbearing status and social class. He also made detailed observations about the perpetrator's method of cutting up her body:

> The skin of the hands and feet was too much decomposed to show whether she had led a life of hard manual work. There was no mark made by a wedding ring. The uterus was that of a virgin, but the vulva

was too decomposed to give indication with regard to old or recent injury. ... There were circular slightly depressed marks, about half an inch deep, just below the knees. ... The mark round the leg showed that garters were worn below the knee, a custom, I believe, more common among the lower than the upper classes, who either wear garters above the knee or suspenders. She had recently menstruated.

The cuts on the surfaces of the vertebrae were such as would be made by a saw, and the long sweeping incisions through the skin showed that a very sharp knife had been used. The disarticulations were neatly and cleanly done, in each case the joint being exactly opened. The absence of ecchymosis [bruising] showed that all the cuts were made after death.

It was obvious, from the direction and manner of the cuts, that no ordinary surgical or dissecting-room operation had been carried out. Although no special knowledge of anatomy was shown, the cuts indicated a practical skill in amputating limbs at joints, and making clean sweeping skin cuts. It may be argued that such skill would be gained by a hunter or a butcher, as either of these are in the habit of rapidly and skilfully separating limbs, and of cutting up a trunk into several parts.

I do not think that any surgeon or anatomist could have done the work so well, as they are not *constantly* operating, while a butcher is almost daily cutting up carcases [*sic*]. Moreover, the limbs were separated in almost precisely the way a butcher or hunter would adopt, i.e. making a series of cuts round the flexure of the joint, and then by a strong twist wrenching out the head from the joint and cutting the capsule.

The condition of the skin showed that each part had been lying and decomposing in water, and that several months had elapsed since the date of death.

The summary was that the remains were those of an adult female of Caucasian origin and dark complexion, from twenty-five to thirty-five years old, and about 5 ft. 3 in. high, that she had not borne a child, and in fact, from the small size of the *os uteri* [mouth of the uterus] was unlikely to conceive; that the body had been mutilated *after* death by some person who, though not necessarily a skilled anatomist, yet had some knowledge of joints, and the readiest mode of separating limbs, and by inference a butcher or hunter; that decomposition had taken place in water, and some months elapsed since death.[56]

Hebbert and Bond were consistent in their analysis that no medical professional or student was involved in this case. The perpetrator's knife skills came from a trade or side-line similar to that of a butcher or hunter. Although he was less clear about the date of death, at an inquest hearing Doctor Callaway was specific that the Rainham torso had been in the water for approximately a fortnight before 11 May. A press article quoting an interview with Callaway provided further information and reduced that fortnight to nearer a week: 'there is tolerably good circumstantial evidence that the murder was committed on May 1, or, at any rate, not later than the second of that month'.[57]

According to the published tide tables, on Monday, 2 May 1887, high water at London Bridge was at 8.20 a.m. and 9 p.m. On the following day, it was one hour and twenty-two minutes later.[58] Alternatively, if the time lapse of a fortnight were correct, the tides were more favourable on Wednesday, 27 April 1887, when high water at London Bridge was at 4.13 a.m. and 4.31 p.m. Sunrise was at 4.42 a.m and sunset at 7.13 p.m.[59] An article dated 23 April reported a spring tide, meaning an exceptionally high water level: 'the evening tides have been at their worse for [rowing] practice, the water at that time having been nearly out of the river'.[60]

With a very high tide occurring at 4.13 a.m., the perpetrator could have killed on the previous night and put the body parts into the tidal Thames at a central location such as London Bridge before his working day began. A strong ebb tide, with unusually high and fast-flowing waters, would take the remains eastwards past the sinuous U-bend of the Thames to the other side of the Isle of Dogs, at Rainham. A flood tide would take them westwards to Battersea. In the tideless Regent's Canal, the body parts would hardly move, directly placing the killer at the spots where they were found. In late April and early May, the weather was consistently cold, slowing down the decomposition of the remains. The relative darkness of a new moon afforded him additional protection.

Dismemberment was an extreme option for the killer to take, requiring skills, time, effort and implements. In the Thames Torso Murders, it always occurred after death and was not the cause of death. Criminology classifies the act of dismemberment as either offensive, in which it is the perpetrator's main objective, or defensive, with its motive being to render the victim unrecognisable and destroy evidence relating to, for example, fatal injuries. If its purpose was to prevent police from identifying his victim, she might be connected to him as his wife or partner. Alternatively, she might have been an acquaintance or stranger accosted by chance yet seen socialising with him. The body was stripped of all clothing and footwear, representing items with an intrinsic financial value if sold or pawned.

The killer's method of dismemberment revealed semi-proficient knife skills and the type of tools available to him. His approach was not wholly methodical, as the right patella was attached to the right thigh, whereas the left patella was attached to the left lower leg and foot. The rough sacking, canvas and cord he used to tie up the remains revealed the materials he had to hand every day for his trade. Canvas sacks were breathable, used for foodstuffs that tended to 'sweat', releasing moisture into the air. He arguably left the expression of his criminal fantasy, or distinctive 'signature', in extensive dismemberment and any superfluous mutilations of his victims' bodies. His acts of dismemberment were therefore both defensive, to conceal the body and identity of his victims, and offensive, meaning sexually motivated.

The first murder in a series is likely to be committed close to the killer's home, in circumstances where he feels comfortable. In his immaturity, he may make discernible mistakes before he learns from experience to cover his traces and conceal his techniques. And in this particular case, the Torso Killer did make mistakes, although none of sufficient magnitude to betray himself. By leaving body parts in multiple locations, and possibly even on different dates, he exposed his mobility on water and his links to specific geographical locations on the industrial Regent's Canal. The next murder increased the probability that its perpetrator worked on the river.

# 2

# The Whitehall murder, September 1888

> Man is not truly one, but truly two ... the unjust might go his way, delivered from the aspirations and remorse of his more upright twin.
>
> From *The Strange Case of Dr Jekyll and Mr Hyde* by Robert Louis Stevenson

On Tuesday, 11 September 1888, a year and half after the Rainham murder, a woman's severed arm was found on the Thames foreshore at Pimlico in Westminster, Central London. The exact location of that discovery was the riverside of Ward's Deal Wharf, a wholesale timber business at 113 Grosvenor Road, and its date was hugely significant to the police and the anxious public. The second of the 'canonical five' Ripper killings, the murder and evisceration of Annie Chapman in a Spitalfields backyard, had taken place only three days earlier.

As in the Rainham case, the authorities waited for more body parts to be found, issuing instructions to the police and river workers to search along the Thames. On Friday, 28 September, a boy walking along Lambeth Road saw 'a curiously-shaped paper parcel' in the garden of the Blind Asylum.[1] Being enterprising enough to fish it out between the railings, assisted by a passing bricklayer and the local shoeblack, its contents were found to be 'the arm of a woman which had been cut from the body. It was decomposed, and had been laid in lime. The fingers were clutched.'[2] What became known as the 'Lambeth arm' was taken to Kennington Lane police station.

In the early hours of Sunday, 30 September, the Ripper killed two women in separate attacks in Whitechapel and the City of London. Elisabeth Stride had her throat cut, while Catherine Eddowes's face and body were subject to significant posthumous mutilations including the cropping of the tip of her nose and part of one ear.

The capital's police forces were already stretched to their limits when, on the following Tuesday, 2 October, a woman's torso was discovered in a dark corner of New Scotland's Yard's vaulted basement. It was 2 miles north-east of the discovery of the first arm, on the Victoria Embankment, where over a hundred labourers were working at a prime location near the Houses of Parliament. Nobody knew whether this was an act of deliberate audacity, defiling the new headquarters that the police were already calling 'our Palace',[3] or simply one of convenient disposal among the rubble and rubbish of a building site.

Hebbert reported:

> The trunk is that of a female, the breasts being present. It comprises the thorax and upper part of the abdomen, the head having been separated at the sixth cervical vertebra, and the pelvis and lower part of the abdomen at the fourth lumbar vertebra.[4]

Whereas Bond and Hebbert fitted the right arm found on the riverbank to the torso and declared it a match, the second was quickly discounted from the investigation. It is lost to history whether the Lambeth arm was the left or right limb, how much of it was intact, and whether it was in fact female. The press reported that medical students had removed it from a dissected corpse, and placed it where it was found as a hoax.[5]

Even at the height of the Ripper scare, the press reported that the murders were not undertaken by the same man. It was at a critical point when Jack the Ripper had killed at least four victims, and the Torso Killer two, with the coincidence of timings intensifying the capital's shock and distress:

Although there is no reason whatever for connecting the murder, whose victim was discovered in the buildings at the Whitehall end of the Embankment, with the terrible series of assassinations that have appalled the metropolis, there can be no doubt that it has added to the existing excitement and dismay. The fact, too, that mutilation, although not of the same character, has been practised, and that the head and limbs of the victim have been cut off, adds to the resemblance.

There is, however, no similarity in the circumstances under which the crime must have been committed. The victim in the present [Whitehall] case was not felled and murdered upon the spot where the remains were discovered; indeed, it may be at once accepted as a fact that she met her death inside a house. The ghastly process of dismemberment and packing up must have taken a considerable time, and could not have been carried on in the open air, where there was a risk of discovery …

Never was the air more full of horrors than it is at present; it would almost seem that we had an epidemic of murder among us.[6]

On the afternoon of Monday, 8 October, the Coroner for the City and Liberty of Westminster, John Troutbeck, opened the inquest into the death of an unknown woman at the Sessions House on Broad Sanctuary. Troutbeck was described by his contemporaries as a man who 'well knew his own mind, and in the conduct of his court was very careful to preserve his authority'.[7] On the same afternoon, the funeral of Ripper victim Catherine Eddowes was held at the City of London Cemetery at Ilford. It was a busy day for Londoners, as thousands of people lined the route of the funeral procession from the City eastwards, while in Westminster large crowds manifesting 'the greatest interest' gathered in Westminster outside the Millbank Street mortuary and the Sessions House.[8]

Before the inquest hearing began, the jury were sworn in at the mortuary, where they viewed the body parts 'through a window, for fear of contagion. It was on a table propped up, and the arm recently found was placed in the socket. The body was a dark brown colour.'[9] The first witness was 45-year-old Frederick Wildbore, who described himself as a carpenter employed by Messrs Grover and Sons at the New Central Police Office at Westminster. He saw what he called 'the parcel', meaning the bundle containing the torso, three times on two consecutive days, starting at 6 a.m. on Monday, 1 October:

> I had occasion to go to the vaults to find my tools, my labourer having taken them there on the Saturday. I then noticed what I took to be an old coat thrown on one side. It was lying in the corner of a recess. It was very dark there, even in the middle of the day. I could not find my tools – my labourer having, in fact, already removed them.
>
> In the evening at 5.30 I went once more to the vaults, and I then noticed the parcel again. There was no smell, not in the least. I drew my mate's attention to the parcel, and struck a wax vesta [match] to look at it.[10]

Wildbore stated that he saw the parcel again on the next morning. He only reported it at lunchtime:

> About one o'clock Mr Brown, the assistant foreman, came down to where I was at work, and I then informed him of what I had seen. We both went and looked at the parcel, and we thought it seemed curious ...
>
> I heard of the discovery of a body about three-quarters of an hour after Mr Brown had seen the parcel ... When I lit the match was the first time I had noticed anything particular. There was some debris in the place ... When I saw the parcel first I thought it was a workman's old coat.[11]

In a reversal of the parlour game 'pass the parcel', neither the foreman Charles Brown nor Wildbore fancied touching it, delegating that task to a workman called George Cheney, who told bricklayer's labourer George Budgen to examine it. Budgen testified:

> I looked at it, and found that the top was bare, and the rest wrapped in some old cloth, but could make nothing of it. I thought it was some old bacon at first. I took hold of the strings around it, and dragged it into the light and cut the strings, three or four in

number. On opening the old wrappers I saw that the parcel contained part of a human body ... The police afterwards took charge of the remains.[12]

The next witness was A Division's Detective Sergeant Thomas Hawkins, who stated that he went to the site after Brown reported the discovery at King Street police station:

> I saw lying in the vaults of the new police buildings an open parcel in dress material, which had been tied round, and a body of a woman in it. I looked further along the recess where it had been and saw a piece more dress material. I saw the place where it had stood. The wall was very black, and the place full of maggots. I left the body in charge of a constable, and sent to the medical officer, Mr Bond.
>
> [In response to a question from the coroner] The vault ... was very dark, and the recess was across a trench, which was also in the dark. A person to go to the recess would have to cross the trench on a plank; the trench could not be seen without a light.[13]

Hawkins's testimony implied that the torso had been propped up against the wall rather than buried.

Frederick Moore, a deal, or timber porter, testified that he found a woman's right arm on 11 September, on the foreshore at Pimlico:

> I was standing outside the gate at 113, Grosvenor-road, where I work. My attention was called by other workmen to the arm where it lay in the mud. It was underneath the sluice, which comes out of the [Millbank] distillery there ... I said it was no arm. I tried to reach it, but could not. One of my fellow workmen got a ladder.
>
> I then found it was an arm. It was quite bare. There was a string tied tightly round the top. I could see nothing more [on the foreshore]. I gave the arm to a policeman on the Embankment ... [The tide was] low, running down fast.[14]

Constable William James testified that he took the arm from Moore and took it to the police station, where it was examined by Westminster police surgeon Doctor Thomas Neville. It was then taken to the mortuary at Ebury Bridge. He added that he was placed on special patrol on the Embankment for a week afterwards, but saw nothing else on the mud.[15]

The next witness testimony covered the question of access to the building site at New Scotland Yard. Charles Brown, the assistant foreman to whom the find was first reported, described the site's layout as follows, answering questions from the coroner. The supposition that the remains were deposited on site over the weekend immediately prior to their discovery was later proved false:

**Brown:** The works are shut off from the surrounding streets by a hoarding about 7ft. high.
**Coroner:** How many entrances are there?
**Brown:** Three; two in Cannon Row [today's Canon Row, facing west] and one on the Embankment [facing east]. There are gates at the entrances as high as the hoardings.[16]

The main entrance of New Scotland Yard, when completed, was on its south elevation. The South Building was later extended by the addition of the North Building. It is adjacent to today's New Scotland Yard.

**Coroner:** How long is it since the vaults referred to have been completed?
**Brown:** About three months [dating back to the first half of July].
**Coroner:** Who was admitted besides the workmen?
**Brown:** No one, unless they had business with the clerk of the works.
**Coroner:** Was any one [meaning a guard] kept at the gates?
**Brown:** No; there were 'no admittance' boards up.
**Coroner:** How are the works left on Saturday?
**Brown:** Locked up, except one small gate in Cannon Row. There is no watchman there. No one is left on the premises at night. There is a latch on the small gate. The latch is let down. No one could open it unless he knew how to do it. It is opened by a small knot of string close to the top of the door.
**Coroner:** What are the approaches to the vaults?

**Brown:** Planks laid crossways down the road. At the bottom of the planks it is very dark. The floors and drains have to be laid in the vaults yet. The carpenters were at work in them a week before the remains were found.
**Coroner:** Was there any appearance of any locks having been forced?
**Brown:** No.
**Coroner:** Do you think it would require a previous knowledge of the building to get to the vaults?
**Brown:** Yes ... because no one would think of going to the place where the parcel was found unless he knew something about it.[17]

In response to a question from the jury, Brown replied that there had been one theft of tools from the building since work began. In response to a further jury question about access from an adjoining building to the north, he said, 'I do not think it possible that anyone could have lowered the parcel from Richmond-mews [at its north-western corner].'[18]

The witness testimony, supplemented by information from press reports, indicated that the remains were found in the south-western corner of the New Scotland Yard basement, where Derby Street met Cannon Row. The main entrance to the building was also on the south elevation, nearer the south-eastern corner. The fact that the remains were found lying across a trench next to the wall on the Cannon Row side of the building suggested that the perpetrator had entered from the unlocked gate or over the hoarding on that side. The site was, however, highly visible from the embankment and river, where it received deliveries of building supplies from Westminster Pier.

The next witness, labourer Ernest Hedge, was the last man at the building site at close of business on the Saturday. Several journalists misreported his name as 'Edge', having heard him announce it in a strong Cockney accent. The court looked to Hedge to determine the timeframe when the body was supposedly deposited:

He was in the vault on Saturday (the 29th of September), at half-past 5 in the afternoon, to fetch a hammer, and there was no parcel there then. He struck a light to go across the trench and looked round. The vault led to nowhere ...

He was the last on the works on that Saturday and locked up the works. He left the place all secure. He did not open the works on Monday. He locked up all the doors [meaning gates] except one, which was on the latch ... No one unconnected with the works would be likely to notice from the outside the means of entering this door.[19]

Hedge's testimony stood in direct contradiction to that of the eminent police surgeon Thomas Bond, who considered that the body had been *in situ* for weeks, and rotted away there. Bond's theory ruled out any link to the date of the Ripper's double killing on that Saturday night. However, his statement about the method of killing by cutting the victim's throat did suggest a possible connection. Bond testified that, on the day the body was found, shortly before 4 p.m., he was called to the building site to see the decomposed trunk of a woman:

It was then lying in the basement, having been removed from the dark vault where it was found. The strings which had tied it had been cut, and it was partially unwrapped. I visited the place where it was found, and I saw the wall against which it had been lying. The wall was stained black at the place where the parcel had rested against it. I thought the body must have been there several days from the state of the wall; but I could form no definite opinion as to how long it had been there. I directed the detectives to take charge of the trunk and of the wrapper, and to remove them to the mortuary ... [The torso] arrived there in the evening, and I superintended its disinfection and the placing of it in spirits [to preserve it].

On the next morning I made a *post-mortem* examination, assisted by Mr Hibbert [*sic*: Hebbert]. The trunk was that of a woman of considerable stature, and well nourished. The head had been separated from the trunk at the sixth cervical vertebra, which had been sawn through. The lower part of the body and the pelvis had been removed, and the fourth lumbar vertebra had been sawn through in the same way as in the removal of the head, by long, sweeping cuts.

The length of the trunk was 17 in., the circumference of the chest was 35½ in., and the circumference of the waist was 28½ in. It was all very much decomposed, but the skin was not so much decomposed as the cut parts, and I examined it for wounds. I found none on the body. The skin was light. The arms had been removed at the shoulder joints by several incisions, which had been made apparently obliquely, and then downwards around the arms. The joints had been removed straight through the joint — that is, disarticulated through the joint. Over the body were clearly-defined marks, where string had been tightly tied. The body appeared to have been wrapped up in a very skilful manner.

On close examination we could not find the *linea alba* [abdominal connective tissue] which would indicate that the woman had borne children. It was impossible to ascertain, owing to the decomposed condition of the remains, whether there had been any wound inflicted on the neck in life. The neck had been divided by several incisions and sawn through below the larynx [voice box].

On opening the chest, we found that the rib cartilages were not ossified; that one lung was healthy, but the other lung was adherent [inflamed], showing that for some time the woman had suffered from severe pleurisy [a lung disease] ... The heart was healthy, but there was no blood in it, and no staining of the organ with blood. That, to my mind, is an indication that the woman did not die from suffocation or by drowning.

The liver was in a normal condition, and the stomach contained about one ounce of partly-digested food. There was no appearance of inflammation. The kidneys were normal, and the spleen also. The small intestines and the part which attaches the intestines to the body were in place, and were healthy. The lower part of the large bowel, and all the contents of the pelvis, were absent.

We found that the woman was of mature age, and over 24 or 25 years of age. She was ... a large and well-nourished person, with fair skin and dark hair ... The date of death, as far as we could judge, would have been six weeks or two months before the discovery, and the decomposition occurred in air, and not in water.

I subsequently examined the arm ... from Pimlico ... I found that the arm accurately fitted the trunk. The cuts corresponded, and the general contour of the arm corresponded to the body. It was a fleshy, rounded arm. The hand was long, the fingers tapering, and the nails very well shaped. It was the hand of a person who had not been used to manual labour ...

I am satisfied that it was not a death by suffocation. It was more likely death from hemorrhage, for the heart was pale, and free from clots …

She was a very tall, big woman – at least 5 ft. 8 in. high.[20]

It was not stated in court that the probable cause of a death from bleeding was a cut throat. The next medical witness, Doctor Hebbert, testified that on 16 September, he had assisted Bond in examining the victim's arm found at Pimlico, approximately 1 mile away from New Scotland Yard. He confirmed that the arm matched that torso:

> It was the right arm, which had been separated from the trunk at the shoulder joint by a cut which passed obliquely round … The arm was surrounded in the upper part by a piece of string, and this made an impression upon the skin of the arm. When the string was loosened, it was found that there was a great deal of blood in the arm.
>
> The skin of the arm was in a fair condition, and was not very much decomposed, but the skin of the hand was very thin, white, and corrugated through immersion in the water … There were no scars or marks of any kind, and there were no bruises.
>
> There were a few dark brown hairs left under the arm … I was enabled to examine the arm at the same time as the trunk, and found they exactly fitted. The skin cuts corresponded, and the bones and the hair corresponded. The hair was precisely the same, and when the two lots were mixed together they could not be separated …
>
> For a surgical motive, the cut [at the shoulder] would have been so made to leave the skin outside. In this case the skin was cut through by several long cuts, and then the bone was sawn through. The pieces of paper produced [in court], which were found near the body, are stained by some animal blood [meaning mammalian and possibly human] … There is no mark of a ring on the finger of the hand.[21]

A match was made between hairs found on the arm and 'a few dark brown hairs' in the torso's armpit. The Hebbert report stated: 'The hair taken off the arm and the hair from the axilla of the trunk are identical,' without specifying whether both samples were taken from a dissected armpit.[22]

The final witness of the day was 39-year-old Detective Inspector Henry Marshall, who had charge of the case. Marshall confirmed that at 5 p.m. on 2 October, he went to the site and took possession of some pieces of newspaper, two pieces of material and the 'miscellaneous lot' of string with which the parcel was tied. He explained that the lengths of different cords comprised 'one piece ... of sash-cord, and the rest is of different sizes, and there is also a piece of black tape'.[23]

Marshall provided the following details about the newspapers and dress fabric:

> With regard to the [larger] piece of [news]paper, I have made inquiry, and find it is a piece of the *Echo*, dated the 24th of August, 1888 ... A number of small pieces of paper ... found on the body ... are pieces of the *Daily Chronicle*. They are not pieces of any paper issued from that office this year.
>
> The dress is a broché [brocaded] satin cloth, of Bradford manufacture, but an old pattern, probably of three years ago. It is rather common material. There is a flounce in it six inches from the bottom. The material probably cost [six and a half pence] a yard.[24]

An eyewitness described the fabric as a black flowered sateen (a patterned cotton fabric in satin weave).[25] Marshall concluded by stating that the all-important task was to find the woman's head, and that the police would like to question one or two more of the workmen. The coroner agreed to adjourn the inquiry for a fortnight.

Marshall's searches were without result, as the police were looking for items that had been dumped and failed to look for anything buried. With the permission of the police and the building contractor, on Wednesday, 17 October, an enterprising journalist, Jasper Waring, took a Spitzbergen dog called Smoker into the New Scotland Yard basement to rootle out any further body parts. The dog, being told to 'find it', started to scratch at a heap of earth. The labourer Ernest Hedge helpfully brought over a spade, and dug out 4 or 5 inches of earth mixed with stones and pieces of brick. He unearthed a 'well-shaped' left foot and leg, cut above the knee.[26] Its discovery was covered in the next inquest hearing on Monday, 22 October.

Questions addressed to the first witnesses attempted to establish when the torso had been left in the vault. Assistant foreman Charles Brown was recalled to state that, on Friday, 28 September, he had been in the vault with a light, measuring up for a surveyor. However, he did not examine the recess and it was possible that the torso might have been in the corner without him seeing it. Clerk of the works George Eraut had the same experience on his Saturday shift, when he 'saw nothing ... but a few rags which the men had used on brickwork'.[27]

Carpenter's labourer Richard Lawrence testified that he left a basket of workmen's tools on a mortar board at the end of the vault shortly after noon on the Saturday. He went back to fetch it at 6.10 a.m. on the morning of Monday, 1 October, and it had not been disturbed. His workmate Alfred Young gave similar evidence, saying that he noticed 'nothing particular ... [and] there was no light or lamp.'[28]

Surveyor Arthur Franklin, who was in the vault with Brown on the Friday, provided equally inconclusive information:

> He had been to the vault measuring work. He did not actually go into the corner where the remains were found, and he noticed nothing in that direction beyond rubbish and some old bricks and stones. If there had been a parcel there he certainly thought he should have noticed it, especially if any bad smell pervaded the place.[29]

Jasper Waring was then called to explain how he found the left leg and foot using the canine sleuth Smoker. William Angle, a journalist who had accompanied Waring, added the following information: 'He considered the corner where the leg and foot were found was higher than the rest of the ground, but not conspicuously so. The ground there had evidently been trodden upon'.[30]

Workman Hedge was recalled, as was Thomas Bond, the latter to testify about his on-site examination of the leg and foot on 17 October. As with the arm, in a macabre jigsaw puzzle, he was obliged to prove that the body parts belonged to the same corpse:

> I went into the recess of the vault where the body was found, and I found there a human leg partially buried. It was uncovered; but it had not been removed from the place where it was found. I examined

the earth which had covered it, and I found that this gave unmistakable evidence of having covered the leg for several weeks – that the leg had been there for several weeks. Decomposition had taken place there, and it was not decomposed when placed there.

The upper part of the leg was in a good state of preservation; but the foot had decomposed, and the skin and nails had peeled off. The limb was removed, and next morning it was examined by Mr Hibbert [sic] and myself. We found that the leg had been divided at the knee joint by free incisions, and very cleverly disarticulated without injury to the cartilages.

The limb and foot agreed with the arm and hand in general character – in general contour and in size. We had no doubt that the leg belonged to the body and to the arm. I took the opportunity, I may say, while in the vault to examine the spot where the body was found, and I am quite sure that the last witness is wrong as to the body not having been there a few days before. The body must have lain there for weeks, and it had decomposed there ...

The decomposition was of a character of a body only partially exposed to the air. The brickwork against which it had leant was deeply covered with the decomposed fluid of the human body turned black, and it could not have done that in a day or two. The stain is not superficial, but the brick work is quite saturated. I should think it must have been there quite six weeks when found – from August. There was no mark of a garter on the leg, and there were no corns on the foot, which was well shaped.[31]

Bond overruled the workmen's well-intentioned belief that they did not miss the parcel and exposed as false the idea that the remains were dumped over the weekend of 29 to 30 September. The body parts must have been taken there, possibly in two trips, close to the time of the victim's death in August.

Doctor Hebbert was recalled to confirm the size of the leg which, as the body and the arm, suggested that the woman was 5ft 8 or 8½ inches tall. He added:

The leg and foot were bruised in two places ... He thought that death was probably as early as the middle of August. There were two bruises on the leg, one inside and the other outside, each about the size of a shilling. In his view death took place about the middle of August.[32]

In his report he described the bruises as occurring before death, and described them as 'dark purple … and the tissues beneath contained clotted blood … The marks were ante-mortem bruises.'[33] The outer bruise was larger than the one on the inside of the leg. It was the first mention of signs of violence to the body in life.

Constable Thomas Bowden, who was guarding the site, said that, having asked his inspector's advice, he allowed the two journalists Waring and Angle into the vault. Inspector Joseph Peters thought the police had no right to stop the gentlemen after they had received the authority of the builder.[34] The next police witness, Sergeant George Rose, happened to know Coroner John Troutbeck and his family well, as they lived near one another within the precincts of Westminster Abbey, at numbers 2 and 4 Dean's Yard respectively.[35] Rose testified that, after it had been examined by Mr Bond, he wrapped the leg in a brown paper parcel, which he tied up, sealed, and placed on a board. He took it to the mortuary in a cab.[36] Subsequent to that date, he had taken several dogs – bloodhounds and terriers – to the vault, but they had found nothing.[37]

The final witness, Inspector Marshall, stated that this was all the evidence he had to offer and that the police were still pursuing their enquiries. Although unstated, a key question was whether this murder formed a series with the Rainham case. The coroner summed up as follows:

> There was not, in his opinion, any evidence of identity beyond the fact established by the surgical testimony, that the remains were those of a well-developed female, over 20 years of age, unaccustomed to manual labour, and who had probably never been a mother. How the deceased came by her death there was no evidence to show, but much pointed to the probability of a violent death …
>
> Probably the main object of the person who put the body in the vault was to get rid of it, and not to permanently conceal it, which he must have known to be extremely difficult. It was for the jury to say whether, in their opinion, a crime had been committed, or whether

they thought that the evidence did not warrant them in doing more than return an open verdict.[38]

After a few minutes' consultation, in the absence of any cause of death, the jury took the coroner's advice and returned the open verdict of 'Found dead'.

The victim's clothing might have led to her identification. Her torso was wrapped in part of a black brocade-effect skirt, a budget version of a style which was in vogue three years previously. Found with it was a steel dress improver, a semi-circular cage of steel wires padded to form a bustle that would emphasise her shapely rear. That fashion had ended before 1888,[39] and was satirised as impractical in the press: '"Spring time's come again," sang the poetess, as she journeyed heavenward in consequence of sitting down too suddenly upon her new steel dress improver.'[40]

According to the press, the police did manage to find a lead to that type of skirt, which was made in central London:

> One officer states that the maker of the silk skirt in which the body was found has been discovered. The maker is the proprietor of a West-end establishment. Having discovered so much, it is probable the person who ordered and received the skirt will be reached.[41]

The paragraph concluded, 'Thus some sensational development of the case is anticipated.' According to the fashion of the day, she would also have worn a small, light hat on the top of her head. Disappointingly, the skirt did not lead to the victim, although clothing did help to identify the third woman killed by the Thames Torso murderer, Chelsea prostitute Elizabeth Jackson.

Bond and Hebbert considered that the woman was of a different class to the Rainham victim. All accounts were consistent 'that the deceased was a very fine woman, and that the body was exceedingly well nourished'.[42] Her clothing indicated that, although not a trend-setter, she followed fashion. If she were from a higher social class, why was she not missed? The press speculated that her friends thought this lady had gone abroad for the sake of her weak lungs.[43] There are other possibilities. She might have been what the Victorians called an excursionist, or day-tripper, who disappeared on a jaunt away from home. Alternatively, she could have been a ladies' maid, believed to have moved on suddenly to another position. Whoever she was, the Whitehall victim was not an 'unfortunate' like the Ripper victims, a street walker wearing threadbare clothes and selling her body for a few pennies a go.

As the police advertised for information about women who were missing from Westminster and nearby areas, a remarkable number of people came forward with the names of family and friends. The police actively investigated at least two named individuals as the possible victim: Emma Potter and Lily Vass. Both were working class and, at the age of 17, too young to match the police profile. Potter was found by an A Division inspector, possibly at Fulham Road Workhouse, and taken back to her mother, who had reported her missing.[44]

On 19 July, Lily Vass had left her parents' home in Chelsea, ostensibly to return to her work as a maid at a house on Wandsworth Common. In fact, she had left her situation, and could not be traced. Her father Robert went to Millbank Street mortuary, where he failed to identify the body parts as his daughter, her mother having only felt able to view the black sateen skirt fabric, which she did not recognise.[45] Online records reveal Vass's marriage in 1890, placing her firmly in the land of the living.[46]

At the end of October, the body parts were photographed in the continuing hope of an identification, before being buried at Woking Cemetery. A reporter who saw the 'curious photograph' described it as representing 'the remains of the woman found in Whitehall with the arm picked up previously in the Thames attached to the shoulder':

> The trunk has been made to stand on what looks like a fig box placed upon a barrel. The arm ... obviously belongs to the body, which is that of a woman of remarkable stature.
>
> The left breast is emaciated from a surgical operation, presumably for cancer, but this operation, coupled to the colossal proportions of the figure, offers a starting point of the investigation into the identity of the deceased that the police might have followed with probable advantage ...
>
> Three copies only of the photograph are extant ... [47]

The newspaper article's repeated exclamations about the woman's size emphasise that she was tall by late Victorian standards, and so well-built as to be memorable. The Hebbert report makes no mention of any particular damage to, or decomposition of, the left breast. It states the measurement of the 'circumference of thorax at level of nipple line', later adding, 'There are no scars nor wounds …' In his desire for a scoop, the reporter might have exaggerated, or invented, an identifiable attribute. The photographs in question cannot be located, nor is there any applicable reference in Metropolitan Police records to the photography or display of body parts, as opposed to intact corpses.[48]

After the burial, an old woman called at the mortuary. She said that she 'thought she recognised in the photograph … some trace of her daughter, who has been missing since August, but she could not be positive upon that point'.[49] Their names are lost to history, but the police must have investigated her claim. It seems certain that August was the month of the murder. It is possible that the victim came from another part of London or beyond, and the police needed to look further afield for her family and friends than in Westminster and its immediate environs.

The police had established the date of the scrap of paper from the *Echo*, which was only 6 inches long by 4 inches wide. An examination of back-copies at the newspaper's office fixed it as 24 August 1888.[50] If not the exact date of the murder, it represents a date on or after which the torso was wrapped for disposal. The piece from the *Daily Chronicle* could not be dated to any issue published in that year, and no further mention was made of other papers found near, but not attached to, the severed arm. The only other wrapping on the torso was fabric from the victim's own skirt. The left leg and foot were unwrapped, but better preserved than the torso, having been 'sufficiently covered by earth to exclude the air'.[51]

String was used to tie up the end of the arm, and what the police called 'sash cord' was wound expertly around the torso as if securing a package. Inspector Marshall reported that black tape and different types of string were also used to bind the wrappings to the torso. The Hebbert report described how this was done and the condition of the surface of the skin:

The skin is fair and not much decomposed. The breasts are large and prominent, with small, well-shaped nipples. There are no scars or wounds, but there are impressions made by the string with which the trunk was tied. These are four in number, two running down obliquely from the shoulder and two crossing the chest, one at the level of the nipples and one across the upper part of the sternum [breastbone]. The divided surfaces are much decomposed, and the parts full of maggots.[52]

Hebbert appeared to contradict himself regarding the condition of the skin, as the torso displayed varying states of decomposition, its cut or divided edges being 'much decomposed'. Its wrappings were more sophisticated than the coarse canvas and string used to wrap the Rainham remains. In comparison to the Rainham case, the fact that the Whitehall head was separated from the torso at the bottom of the neck suggests that the Rainham victim's head was removed from the same place at the top of the missing collarbones and shoulders.

When examining the arm, Hebbert was categorical that a medically qualified person had not removed it from the body. He was seeking to argue that it had not been excised in an amputation and was not medical waste:

The limb is clearly not separated by the ordinary surgical operation at the shoulder-joint for the following reasons:

1st. The incision of an ordinary operation by transfixion [cutting through tissues] has the lowest part outside and the highest inside for the formation of the flap, and if by the double flap methods, the longest piece of skin is taken from the outside of the arm.

2nd. The entire absence of disease, either of joint or limb, such as would warrant an operation.

3rd. The separation took place *after death*.

It certainly shows no trace of having been prepared for the dissecting room, as there is no inject in the vessels, nor sign of preservation by antiseptics.[53]

Bond and Hebbert were clear that the same person dismembered both bodies, stating of the Whitehall arm, 'The manner in which the limb had been separated was exactly the same as in the first case, and similar arguments as to the occupation of the operator will apply in this case ... [It was] a person with some knowledge of anatomy.'[54] They again thought that the killer must be a hunter or butcher.

A press reporter said of the torso that: 'The flesh had a dark reddish hue, as if it had been plentifully sprinkled with antiseptic, such as Condy's fluid.'[55] Condy's fluid was a household disinfectant that was also used by mortuary staff to preserve dead bodies and minimise their odours. The same eyewitness observed, 'The remains might have weighed over 50 lbs. [3½ stone or 23kg], no light load for even a strong man to carry any distance.' The police surgeons actually weighed the torso, proving that it was almost 5 stone. Even if he did not carry the torso for any appreciable distance, the perpetrator must have been physically strong enough to manoeuvre it, and conduct its dismemberment.

How did the Torso Killer transport the remains? The largest and most difficult item to move was the torso, with or without the left calf and foot. After bundling it up, if carried in a sack on his back, he cannot have travelled far carrying a weight of nearly 5 stone, and heavier if including the leg and foot. He could have used a barrow, or even public transport: bus, tram or train. The distance between the wharf where the arm was found and New Scotland Yard spanned a twenty-minute walk from Lambeth Bridge to the far side of Westminster Bridge. Both riverside locations, he could have used a barge or boat to travel between them. Building supplies were transported to the site by river, including granite blocks supplied by Dartmoor Prison's convict labourers.

The next question was how the killer gained access to the site. There were three gates: two on Cannon Row, one of which was only secured by a latch, and one on Victoria Embankment. If he did not use a gate, he could have scaled the 7ft-high wooden hoarding at either side. The hoarding facing the river had a pile of cement stacked behind it, which would ease any descent.

The embankment entrance was more accessible to a passing stranger. That gate was open all day, explaining how a stranger might survey the site or even gain access by daylight. A policeman was stationed at the junction of the embankment with Westminster Bridge Road, 150 yards away from the hoarding. There was no night watchman on the premises, but even so, depositing a human torso inside the vaulted cellar was high-risk.

Part of Wildbore's testimony stated that he did not access the vaults via the pathway formed by two planks abreast, but 'by means ... of a compo floor'.[56] Whatever that composite floor was made of, it suggests that the perpetrator could have accessed the corner where he left the remains more easily than might be thought. He must have lit his way with a candle or lamp.

Archival Metropolitan Police files show that work on the foundations was well advanced in October 1887. Architect Richard Norman Shaw found it impossible to report to what extent he would be able to use the existing foundations of an uncompleted opera building, 'as each day reveals a new state of things'. He remarked that after digging 35ft, they had come to 'what seems to be a good bottom'.[57]

The same correspondence contains cross-section sketches of the trenches in the foundations of the west elevation, including one of the north end, precisely the area where the body parts were found. The actual surface of the foundations was 10ft below pavement level. Trenches were then excavated to a further 13–14ft deeper, to explore the composition beneath. The sketches depict the depth of a top layer of Thames mud followed by layers of clay and sand, followed by sand and gravel, water and lastly gravel.[58]

It is highly likely that the Torso Killer was aware of the New Scotland Yard building site before he deposited the remains there. He might have worked in a trade that introduced him to the site directly as a contractor, or indirectly as a goods delivery man. He was a man who was able to store body parts for a period of days, possessed an appreciable level of knife skills and was dextrous in wrapping packages. Leading a double life, was the Thames Torso Killer masquerading as an ordinary tradesman? After a gap of eight months, the next body parts surfaced on the south side of the river at Battersea, 3 miles upriver from Westminster. The police launched a massive murder investigation, and in a significant advance, they succeeded in identifying the victim.

## 3

# The Battersea murder, Monday, 3 June 1889

>How art thou lost, how on a sudden lost,
>Defaced, deflow'red, and now to Death devote?
>
>Adam addressing Eve after she took the forbidden fruit, from
>*Paradise Lost* by John Milton

The so-called Thames, or Battersea, Mystery represented significant police progress, as its victim was identified, and her former partner John Faircloth, who was known as 'Jack', briefly considered its prime suspect. A young woman with strawberry blonde hair disappeared on home territory, heavily pregnant, and wearing distinctive clothing that had already passed through many hands. Remnants of those clothes were used to wrap her mutilated remains for disposal, and their itemisation in a press report, alongside a personal description of the victim, was read by a quick-witted neighbour. The police investigation was extensive, revealing considerable information about the perpetrator and his methodology. As in the Rainham case, almost all of the victim's body parts were found except the head.

The case began in the early morning of Tuesday, 4 June 1889, when three lads bathing near Albert Bridge, on the south side of the River Thames abutting Battersea Park, saw an object on the foreshore, being washed by the tide. It was a human thigh separated at the knee joint, covered by a white cloth, later identified as half of a pair of women's drawers. Isaac Brett, aged 14, was advised by a passer-by to take it to the nearest police station on Battersea Bridge Road.[1]

Less than three hours later, John Albert Regan, a dockworker unrelated to Inspector John Regan, saw some children playing with a parcel washed up on the south bank, near George's Stairs, Horsleydown. It contained two large flaps of skin with a woman's uterus (womb) and placenta (afterbirth), wrapped in what was described as an apron. Hebbert described the flaps of skin as follows:

> The flaps of skin and subcutaneous tissues consisted of two long, irregular slips taken from the abdominal walls. The left piece included the umbilicus, the greater part of the mons Veneris [pubic mound], the left labium majus [the outer fold of the vulva] and labium minus [the inner fold of the vulva]. The right piece included the rest of the mons Veneris, the right labium majus and minus, and part of the skin of the right buttock. These flaps accurately fitted together in the mid-line, and laterally corresponded to the incisions in the two lower pieces of the trunk. The skin was fair, and the mons Veneris was covered with light sandy hair.[2]

Press reports quoted:

> the generally accepted theory that the two parcels ... were thrown into the water from the Surrey side of Albert Bridge, between six and nine o'clock in the morning. The bundle containing a portion of a leg sank, and was discovered on the foreshore when the tide receded; while the other package, being lighter and more buoyant, was carried to Horsleydown by the tide.[3]

Detective Inspector John Bennett Tunbridge of Scotland Yard was put in charge of the case. In 1892, Tunbridge would be involved in the successful prosecution of Thomas Neill Cream as the Lambeth Poisoner. Assistant Police Commissioner and CID Chief Robert Anderson called in Bond to examine the body parts. He confirmed that they belonged to the same woman, who had been dead for less than forty-eight hours, and that her abdomen showed signs of 'an unlawful operation', meaning an abortion.[4] Bond later corrected himself on this point.

On the afternoon of Thursday, 5 June, at Wapping, the Coroner for the Eastern District of Middlesex, Wynne Edwin Baxter, held an inquest into the remains found at Horsleydown. Baxter was a colourful character, who had already held inquests into the deaths of three of the Ripper victims and publicly stated his opinion that the Ripper's objective was to acquire his victims' uteri, as indicated by the murders of Nichols and Chapman, and later of Eddowes and Kelly. A coroner was responsible for carrying out an inquest into human remains stored within their jurisdiction, hence the Battersea remains did not come within Baxter's remit.

The hearing was held at Wapping Vestry Hall, a few minutes' walk along the High Street from the Thames Police headquarters. Its only two witnesses were John Albert Regan, who had found the remains, and the Thames policeman who received them from him. Regan testified that he was on the shore at George's Stairs, waiting for employment at the local dock, when he saw six or seven boys throwing stones at something in the river. The boys picked up what appeared to be a parcel wrapped in a white apron and emptied its contents onto the mud. They called out to Regan, saying it was full of 'guts'. Recognising pieces of flesh, he called out to some Thames policemen who were passing in a boat. Although not believing the remains to be human, the police accepted the parcel from Regan and took it to their headquarters.

Alfred George Day, a ferryman at George's Stairs, who was with Regan when he picked up the parcel, provided additional information to a reporter. He said that he believed the flesh had not been in the water long, as blood was flowing from it. It was wrapped in a child's white apron, which was dirty from the river mud, and tied at the four corners. The 'apron' was later found to be the missing half of the undergarment found at Battersea, which was stained with blood. The inquest was adjourned until Wednesday, 3 July, to give the police more time to pursue their investigation.[5]

Twenty minutes before Baxter's inquest was about to open for its first session, a gardener employed at Battersea Park, Joseph Evan Davies, found a bundle in one of its shrubberies. It was near to the wall of the frame-ground, where several cold frames protected ornamental plants. Suspicious of its smell, he fetched a policeman to take the bundle away. Multiple findings on the Friday, Saturday and following Monday brought the body parts to a total of twelve.

Based on medical and police reports, the following description of the dead woman was issued to the press:

> The remains are those of a woman, age from 24 to 25 years, height 5 ft. 4 in. to 5 ft. 6 in.; well built and fleshy; very fair skin; hair light brown or sandy; well shaped hands and feet; bruise on ring finger, probably caused by wearing a ring, nails on both hands bitten down to the quick, four good vaccination marks about the size of a three-penny piece on left arm, skin on palms does not indicate that deceased did hard work, considerably advanced in pregnancy.[6]

That description was constructed by Bond and Hebbert, with the latter commenting in the second part of his report, which covered the Battersea and Pinchin Street victims:

> The chief point of interest is that in the third case the victim was identified, and the deductions as to sex, age, height, &c., argued from the anatomical examination, proved correct, and it may be fairly claimed that the identification was in great measure due to the description given by these means.[7]

The same article enumerated the pieces of clothing 'in which the remains were enclosed':

> The skirt of an old brown linsey dress [made of a mixed cloth combining linen with wool], red selvage [border], two flounces round bottom, waist band made of small blue and white check material, similar to duster cloth, a piece of canvas roughly sewn on end of band, a large brass pin in skirt, and a black dress button (about the size of a threepenny-piece), with lines across, in pocket;
>   a piece of the right front, two pieces of the back, the right sleeve, and collar (about 4½ in. wide), of a lady's ulster [an overcoat with a waist-length cape over long sleeves], grey ground, with narrow cross

stripes of a darker colour, forming a check of about three quarter-inch square, ticket pocket with outside lap on cuff, upon which there is also sewn a large black button, the material of good quality, but much worn,

a light-blue flannelette bag about 13 inches square, top edge unhemmed,

a pair of women's drawers (old), square patch on both knees, originally of a good material, band formed of several pieces joined, L. E. Fisher in black ink at right end of band. A piece of tape sewn on with black cotton to each end of band to tie round body,

the various parcels tied up with black mohair bootlaces, piece of Venetian blind cord, and ordinary string.

The various articles described can be seen between 10 a.m. and 4 p.m. daily at Battersea police station by persons who have missing female relatives. The clothes may not have been worn by the deceased.[8]

Despite its slightly off-putting final sentence, several people did attend the police station to view the clothing. In a burst of public-spirited activity, 'an army of riverside men' helped the authorities to search the local area for further evidence.[9]

The name of L.E. Fisher marked on the drawers found at Battersea was universally considered a valuable clue to the woman's identity. Police issued to the press a photographic facsimile of the marking, written in black ink and 'in a clear clerkly hand'.[10] Two possible identifications were reported to the police: a young woman who had gone missing in Oxford, and the sister of a constable in the Hertfordshire Constabulary, of whom nothing had been heard since she eloped with a plasterer. Disappointingly, neither of the leads proved positive. The first Laura Fisher was found alive and well and working at a hotel in Ramsgate,[11] while Constable Fisher was taken to Battersea Bridge Road police station, where he was unable to identify the body parts, 'nor could certain physical peculiarities of his relative be traced in the remains'.[12]

On Friday, 7 June, an inquest was held at Pimlico on the death of an infant child, whose body was found by some boys on the evening of Tuesday, 4 June, near Ebury Bridge. Ebury Bridge crossed the non-tidal Grosvenor Canal a short stretch inland from where the Battersea victim's arm was found. In a possible parallel to the Rainham case, a lighterman making those drops could have transited from the River Thames to the canal in order to make an onshore trade delivery. Given the paucity of available information, the jury returned a verdict of 'Found dead'. Despite press speculation that there was 'some reason' to suspect the child might belong to the Battersea victim,[13] it appears certain that her baby was never found.

On Saturday, 15 June, Coroner Athelstan Braxton Hicks opened an inquest regarding the body parts stored within his jurisdiction at Battersea. It was held at the Star and Garter Hotel, opposite the church of St Mary by the River. Braxton Hicks and the local police surgeon, Doctor Felix Kempster, who would be called as a witness, had been introduced to the Rainham case with the examination of a body part found at Battersea. A man of great kindness, Braxton Hicks funded a poor box and clothes box, and let no act of bravery go unrewarded.[14]

After the jury viewed the remains, Braxton Hicks called twenty-three witnesses, starting with Thomas Bond. Bond testified that on 4 June, he was requested by police to examine some human remains at Battersea and Wapping. He had since examined other remains. Bond handed the coroner a lengthy report, which he himself read to the jury:

> All the remains were those of the same woman. The deceased would be about twenty or thirty years of age, and she was fair and plump. She would be about 5 ft. 4 in. or 5 ft. 6 in. in height. The head had been separated from the neck at the sixth cervical vertebrae, the tissues having been divided by a series of sweeping cuts. The legs and arms had been very neatly disarticulated. As a result of his examination of the abdomen, [he] was of opinion that the woman was about eight months advanced in pregnancy, and that her death probably took place within twenty-four hours of the first portion of the body being discovered.
>
> The condition of the ring finger [on her left hand] showed that a ring had been forcibly removed either just before or immediately after death. The palms of the hands denoted that the deceased was not accustomed to manual labour.

> The system of cutting up the body showed skill and design – not the anatomical skill of a surgeon, but the technical skill of a butcher or horse-knacker, or any other person accustomed to deal with dead animals. There was a similarity of design in the cutting up in this case with that of the Rainham mystery and the more recent case in Whitehall.[15]

Importantly, Bond validated this murder as the third in the Thames Torso series. He confirmed the coroner's observation that the head was never found in either of the other cases.

The coroner then raised the delicate question of whether the woman had died in the process of an unlawful process, meaning an abortion, asking: 'There is no evidence of an instrument having been used?'

Bond replied:

> No. An instrument had not been used. We could not say whether she had drugs administered to her, as the intestines were missing, nor could we tell whether death had been caused by suffocation, since the heart and lungs were missing. She might have had her throat cut, but as the head is missing there is nothing to show.[16]

Braxton Hicks questioned him further:

> Was [it] possible that the parts were missing by design, in order to conceal the cause of death[?] ... For instance, might an abortionist have adopted the course?[17]

Bond replied in the negative, before adding that the following body parts were still missing: 'The head and upper part of the neck, the lungs and intestines, and the foetus, which had been removed after death.'[18] The Hebbert report stated that 'the foetus had evidently been removed through the incision in the left walls of the womb'.[19] The foreman of the jury asked, 'If Mr Bond did not think it was a medical gentleman who had done this, who did?' He was silenced by interventions from another member of the jury and the coroner himself.[20]

Doctor Felix Kempster corroborated Bond's evidence, producing a report he had prepared:

He believed that death had taken place within 24 hours when he saw the thigh on the 4th ... All the remains had apparently been distributed upon the same day. When he examined the left hand on the 8th ... he could not see any bruise on the ring finger, and it was only by subsequently cutting into the finger that a bruise was noticed.[21]

The implication was that a wedding ring had been removed from the woman's hand, as had happened to Ripper victim Annie Chapman. Jackson's thigh displayed visible bruising, most likely from her attacker's grasp: 'There are four bruises on it, as if from fingers; and these, there is no doubt, were caused during life.'[22] The Hebbert report also described 'a small bruise over the internal condyle (crook of the elbow) of the left arm, and another one just below the right internal condyle'.[23]

A series of finders were called, to trace the movements of the remains from their discovery to their removal to Battersea mortuary in the grounds of St Mary by the River Church. The first finder, 15-year-old Isaac Brett, testified about sighting a parcel against a barge on the foreshore under Albert Bridge.[24] He handed it in to Detective Sergeant William Briggs. The second finder was 11-year-old Patrick M'Carthy, who might have appeared instead of the docker Regan to save him from losing a day's pay,[25] and who stated that he had found another parcel near George's Stairs in Horsleydown and passed it to Alfred Freshwater of the Thames Police. Freshwater told the court that the portion found could have been brought down on a single tide, suggesting a short time lapse between the murder and the disposal of the remains. Gardener Joseph Evan Davies testified about finding a parcel in Battersea Park, 200 yards away from its wicket gate close to Albert Bridge, and showing it to Constable Walter Angier.[26]

Newspaper reporter Claude Mellor testified that at noon on Saturday, 8 June, he alighted from a steamer and spotted a parcel lying in the narrow front garden of Shelley House at number 1, Chelsea Embankment. Mellor added, 'The parcel must have been thrown over the railings, because, in falling, some branches of a bush beneath which the parcel lay had been broken off.'[27] A police inspector came up and removed it. Shelley House was owned by the poet's son Sir Percy Florence Shelley, whose tenant was the current resident. In a connection to the Torso Murders spotted by other researchers, his mother

Mary Shelley was the author of the novel *Frankenstein*,[28] in which a giant human-like creature is constructed from dead body parts.

Charles Marlow, a Battersea barge builder, testified that on Thursday, 6 June, at about 4 p.m., he saw a parcel floating in the river, near the London, Brighton and South Eastern Railway Goods Depot on the south bank of the Thames. He secured it and brought it ashore. The parcel contained the upper portion of a human body. By coincidence, that location was opposite Ward's Deal Wharf on Grosvenor Road, where the Whitehall victim's right arm was found.

Edward Stanton, a waterman from Limehouse, stated that on Friday, 7 June, at about half-past nine in the morning, he found the left thigh and foot floating in the Thames, near the West India Dock Buoy. He handed it over to the river police. The Hebbert report stated that the left thigh had the patella (kneecap) attached.[29]

Solomon Hearne, a gipsy tinman and brazier, drew laughter by stating his address as 'living in a tent near a dust-heap on Lammas-land, Townmead-road, Fulham'.[30] He deposed that, at half-past four on the afternoon of Friday, 7 June, he found a woman's right calf and foot lying on the foreshore of the Thames on the Fulham side, near Wandsworth Bridge. It was barely wrapped in the collar torn from an ulster with a dark check pattern, and tied by a piece of string below the knee. T Division's Constable Frederick Chinn took it from him.

William John Chudley, a Southwark lighterman, testified that at about a quarter to eight in the morning on Saturday, 8 June, he saw a bundle floating off Phoenix Wharf at Bankside. He recovered the left arm and hand of a woman, which was doubled up and tied tightly together with a piece of common string, and wrapped in brown paper. He passed it to Inspector Knight of Thames Division, who passed it on to Inspector Denness. When examined by Doctor Kempster, it was found to have four vaccination scars on the upper part of the arm, and light auburn armpit hair.[31]

The next finder, Inspector Churcher, had been out in a police boat actively looking for more body parts. At lunchtime on the same day, he saw some human remains floating in the mid-channel between Albert Bridge and Battersea Park Pier. Joseph Squires, a Westminster lighterman, said that on Whit Monday, 10 June, at about half-past twelve, he found the right arm of a body floating in the river near Newton's

Wharf, Bankside, east of Blackfriars Bridge.[32] The arm was doubled up and its wrist and shoulder were tied tightly together by a piece of string. It was reported more colourfully in the press that the hand was tightly clenched, as if the woman had died in agony.[33]

David King, an engineer, testified that on Thursday, 6 June, he found some remains floating in the river off Palace Wharf near Nine Elms Pier, which he passed to Thames Division Constable Bransgrove. Labourer Joseph Goodman found human remains in the same location an hour and a half later, which were taken to the mortuary by Constable Hall.

Detective Sergeant Briggs identified the fragments of clothing produced in court as being those found with the various remains brought to Battersea mortuary. He said that the loose buttons in the dress pocket did not correspond with the buttons found on the ulster, but all of the other materials corresponded, as though they had been worn by the same individual. Inspector Tunbridge stated that the police were still pursuing their enquiries and he had no further evidence ready that day.[34] The coroner thanked the witnesses 'who had been instrumental in finding the remains and conveying them to the different mortuaries', adding that:

> [although] the Act of Parliament allowed him to pay only 5s. for the recovery of a dead body, he felt it would be ludicrous to offer them so small a sum to divide between them … seeing the very unpleasant nature of the duties which the witnesses in question had so very properly performed, he should certainly ask the London County Council to grant him permission to remunerate each witness for what he had done.[35]

The inquest was adjourned until 1 July.

On the following day, Sunday, 16 June, Detective Sergeant Briggs took Jasper Waring and Smoker, the journalist and dog who had found the Whitehall leg, to search Battersea Park. The police were keen to find the victim's head, as they had been informed of a missing Chelsea woman whose description exactly matched the remains. The search concentrated on the area around the thicket and nursery where the gardener had found the parcel or bundle, but after an hour and a half, the attempt was abandoned.[36] Nevertheless, within days, the police conclusively identified the dead woman as Elizabeth Jackson, an 'unfortunate' touting for trade, who walked the streets on both sides of Battersea Bridge. Her parents, John and Catherine,[37] were both long-term inmates at Chelsea Workhouse, at the corner of Arthur Street (today's Dovehouse Street) and Britten Street. It was the same workhouse that had housed Sarah Ann King, the alleged victim of a multiple rape on a barge in 1886.

Learning of the active police inquiry into the whereabouts of Elizabeth Jackson, an enterprising journalist located both of her parents at the workhouse. Catherine Jackson related how her daughter's absence had been noted by a mutual friend:

> On Wednesday, June 5th, I called upon Joanna Keife [*sic*: Keefe], 3 Cheyne Row, Chelsea, who was a friend of hers. She asked me if I had heard anything of Lizzie. I said, 'No.' Joanna then read an account in a newspaper about remains being picked up, and that made me feel uneasy. I had a bad knee, and could not go to the Police-station. I went into the Workhouse the same evening. We talked about the matter there, but I did not think of informing the police.[38]

In terms of her possible identification, Jackson added that her daughter had four vaccination marks on one arm. Elizabeth Jackson's state of pregnancy and her distinctive hair colour and clothing, in particular the grey-and-black checked ulster, prompted women who knew her, and who had passed on the second-hand clothing to her, to come forward to the police. By Saturday, 15 June, her father John wrote to another of his daughters, Annie, to say that he thought the victim was their 'Lida', as he called her, echoing a child's lisp.[39] On approximately Tuesday, 25 June, her family also having reported an old scar on her left wrist, the body was conclusively identified as Elizabeth Jackson.

The first witness at the resumed inquest on Monday, 1 July, was Elizabeth's mother, Catherine Jackson. Originally from County Cork, she was described as 'a very respectable-looking woman' and testified as follows:

She had had a daughter named Elizabeth, who would now be twenty-four years of age. She last saw her in May. Elizabeth was about 5ft. 5in. in height, well made and plump. When [she] last saw her she had not been doing much work, so her hands were in good condition. Her teeth were perfect; her complexion and hair fair.

On May 31 [she] met her daughter by accident in the Queen's-road, Chelsea, when she tried to run away, but [she] stopped her. [Elizabeth] explained that she was ashamed to meet her mother ... [She] saw the deceased was *enceinte* [pregnant], and asked her as to her condition, and she replied that she expected her confinement early in September. She also said the father of the child was a stone-mason, with whom she was living, whose name she believed was Jack Fairclough, or something similar. They had been in Ipswich, then they came to [Millwall in] Poplar, and eventually to Battersea, where he deserted her. This was on May 27. She mentioned the name of no other man with whom she was acquainted.

Deceased had been in service in different situations in Chelsea since she was sixteen. She had never been in trouble until seven months ago [meaning her pregnancy]. The deceased had a scar on one of her arms caused by a cut from a broken vase made about twelve years ago.[40]

She believed her daughter first met Fairclough, whose name was in fact 'Faircloth', on 6 October.[41] Jackson identified part of the ulster produced in court as being of the same pattern, and having the same type of button, that Elizabeth was wearing when she saw her.

The next witness was Mary Jackson, Elizabeth's older sister, who was a domestic servant. Her testimony confirmed and expanded upon that of her mother:

[Mary Jackson] last saw her sister Elizabeth about six weeks ago [at West Brompton] ... She could identify the skirt found with the remains as having belonged to her sister, but she did not recognise the ulster ... The latter came to ask money of her, and she gave her 4*d.* [fourpence] – all she had. [She] knew her sister had a scar on her left wrist ... and that on her last visit she was in the family-way.

Her sister told her that she had picked up the man she had been living with in a common lodging-house she frequented; in fact, she was compelled to, for he would not leave her alone. [Elizabeth] also used to complain of the ill-treatment of this man – Jack Fairclough or Faircloth – or some such name. She never spoke of any other man as being acquainted with her. She used to wear a brass wedding ring 'because she was supposed to be married to Jack'.[42]

A second sister, Annie Jackson, who was also a domestic servant, mentioned Elizabeth's relationship with 'Jack'. She added that her sister had lived with a man named 'Fred' 'for some weeks'.[43]

Madame Marie Gerard de Grival, a French dressmaker, of 16 Lavender Sweep in Battersea, caused amusement by saying that her husband managed *her* as well as a restaurant. She identified the pieces of ulster as belonging to a garment which she gave to a Mrs Minter of Cheyne Row about three months previously.[44]

Doctor Kempster deposed that he had discovered a scar on the left wrist of the deceased, similar to that described by her family. Before adjourning the inquest, the coroner confirmed that the remains would be buried under the name of Elizabeth Jackson, the identification of her remains having been achieved by their retention for as long as a month. He emphasised the requirement for suitable storage facilities in his closing remarks, noting:

> that probably remains had never been preserved so long before, because coroners – save in Surrey – had no discretion, and, if they incurred expense, must pay it out of their own pockets. The result was shown in the interests of justice having been promoted, and he thought that mortuaries ought generally to be provided for the purpose of preserving remains, where their preservation – as in this case – led to their being identified.[45]

Poignantly, Elizabeth Jackson's death certificate contains a miniature account of her fate, the registrar choosing his wording carefully. Under the column headed 'When and where died' he wrote, 'Portions of body found and brought to Battersea between 4th June 1889 and 10th June 1889.'[46]

Although he was not called as a witness, Elizabeth's elderly father, John Jackson, a former stonemason from County Tipperary, gave an interview to the press:

> She came into the Workhouse here on May 12th, but only stayed for one night. Previous to that date I met her several times, and gave her a few pence, sometimes a penny, the most being 2 ½ *d*. [two-and-a-half pence]. She appeared to be in a very distressed condition.
>
> I gave her the address of a Catholic clergyman, and told her to apply to him to get her into a home for women. She promised to do so. I met her a day or two afterwards, when she told me that she had seen him, but he could do nothing for her. He gave her 6*d*. [sixpence] for her night's lodging.[47]

John and Catherine were both Irish Roman Catholics, and had brought up their children in that faith. Elizabeth Jackson's heavily pregnant state probably disqualified her from entering a Catholic home for women, which lodged homeless women of good character, with the last three words underlined. It was a missed opportunity to get her off the streets. She planned to re-enter the workhouse infirmary only when she went into labour.

The inquest resumed on Thursday, 4 July, with six witnesses, who were all female. The police had managed to locate two of Elizabeth Jackson's friends, who had seen her three days later than her mother had, on the evening of 3 June, with a man. The first two witnesses were sisters in their 30s, who knew her well. Margaret Minter, a laundress of 3 Cheyne Row, testified as follows:

> About three months ago she received an ulster from a Madame Gerards [*sic*], for whom she did laundry work. She was certain that the piece of material produced [in court] belonged to the same ulster. After keeping it for a month, she gave it to the deceased Lizzie Jackson, whom she had known about two and a half years as a domestic servant. She then looked very shabby, and tried to avoid her. She … gave her something to eat, at the same time expressing a hope that she had not lost her situation through drink. She

complained that the young man she was living with had been very unkind to her, and had left her. She said she had been sleeping on the Embankment near Battersea-bridge, all night. It was on May 20 that witness gave her the ulster, and she saw her for the last time on the 21st.[48]

Minter's sister Johanna Keefe, who had alerted Catherine Jackson to newspaper reports about the then-unidentified dead woman, confirmed that she knew Elizabeth Jackson, and that the ulster was unmistakably the same one that her sister gave her. She had given Jackson some black cotton to sew a string on an undergarment, and washed it for her. The garment was patched at the knees.

Keefe added a further point of identification, medical reports having already noted the body's bitten or pared-down nails:

> The deceased used to bite her nails very much ... Once [Keefe] remarked what a nice genteel hand she had, and what a pity it was that she bit her nails. [Jackson] laughed, and replied, 'They will be more genteel shortly.' She added that sometimes [Jackson] slept out of doors in the open air and sometimes in lodging-houses.[49]

The Hebbert report noted in Elizabeth Jackson's fingers the common characteristics of the nail biter: 'The nails were short, the edge much below the tip of the finger, with an irregular outline.'[50]

The next witness, Annie Dwyer, was a lodging house owner at 14 Turk's Row, where Elizabeth Jackson and her friends stayed intermittently. She testified that she had run the lodging house for nearly two years, mainly catering for women, and that she knew little of Jackson's life:

> With the exception of two rooms, the house was let entirely to women. She had known the deceased about a year and eight months, and saw her for the last time about three weeks before her remains were found. She had never seen her with a man. She never asked her any questions relative to her circumstances, but she noticed that she was very shabbily dressed.[51]

Two of her lodgers were the next to testify, and they were the last known people to see Jackson alive. Jane or Jenny Lee, 30 years old, was the first to take the stand:

> [She] said she had known the deceased about two years. She believed she was in a situation [working as a servant] down to the time that she went to Ipswich. For the last seven months she had led a loose life. About two months ago she returned to Turk's-row, and then said that 'her man' had left her the day before, and she had no home or anything to do.
>
> Since then she had seen [Jackson] about with other men. She last saw her on Monday, June 3, when she was with a man. She could not describe his features, but he had on light moleskin trousers [made of densely woven cotton], 'a light buff colour, say', dark cloth coat, and a rough cap, such as men wore who worked on the roads, and she should suppose he was a navvy [an unskilled construction labourer]. [Jackson] was wearing the check ulster and skirt. A woman named Elizabeth Pomeroy was with her at the time, so she only just spoke to the deceased and then left her and the man together. [Jackson] told her that she was going to Battersea.[52]

Lee's companion, Elizabeth Pomeroy, also aged 30, had grown up in Battersea. She testified as follows:

> She had known Elizabeth Jackson four years, at the time she was in service. She last saw her on the 31st of May, and the same day she found the ulster [the second one produced in court] ... hanging up in the kitchen [at Turk's Row].
>
> On the 3rd of June she and Jennie [sic] Lee met the deceased outside the Royal Hospital Tavern with a man dressed like a workman. [She] said to [Jackson], 'I suppose you're going to Battersea,' and she replied, 'That's just where I am going.' She was quite sober at that time. The man had a little bit of whiskers. He was wearing a heavy pilot jacket, and looked like a navvy.[53]

A pilot jacket was a heavy weather-resistant garment often made from waterproofed cotton, wool or tweed. Warm, thick and lined, it was often worn by outdoor workers such as navvies, or road-builders, railway engine drivers and seafaring men.

The final witness, 31-year-old Kate Paine, was the landlady at 5 Manilla Street in Millwall, where Jackson had stayed with a man:

> On April 18th she remembered a man and woman coming to her door and asking for lodgings. She let them a room. The man said his name was John Fairclough, and the woman was his wife. They only had a small linen bag with them, and a cardboard box, which had needles and thread in it.
>
> The man left on the 28th, and the woman the next morning. She did not see the woman the worse for drink; and the man treated her badly. As soon as the woman had left, [Paine] missed a counterpane, which she recognised as the one produced [in court], and she also missed an ulster, which she had not since seen.[54]

Paine added that the woman had told her that the man had beaten her, and that she was a month advanced in pregnancy. Faircloth did not work while he was staying there, but said he had been down to the millstone works, presumably on Westferry Road, to try and get work.

Inspector Tunbridge briefed the court that Faircloth was a miller and millstone dresser, a native of Cambridgeshire, who was discharged from the 3rd Battalion Grenadier Guards on 19 April 1887. When out of work, he peddled brooches. As Tunbridge requested more time to pursue the investigation, the coroner adjourned the inquest until the month's end. He commented: 'It [was] clear that within twenty-four hours of these remains being found in the river this poor creature was alive, and seen talking to a man; and ... it was important to trace both that man and Fairclough [*sic*].'[55]

Two days later, on Wednesday, 3 July, Baxter resumed his inquest at Wapping and closed it with alacrity, as 'he thought it useless that two enquiries should be taking place on the same body'. The local assistant police surgeon, Doctor Michael McCoy, testified that on 4 June, he was called to the Thames Police headquarters 'and shown the lower part of a woman's body. They were two parts of the abdomen and the uterus. It appeared to him that the remains were those of a woman who had been pregnant about eight months.'[56]

Inspector Tunbridge gave evidence about how the body parts had been collected and identified as Elizabeth Jackson, a single woman, aged 24, from Chelsea. He added that the medical evidence showed that the body was cut up after death; but the cause of death had not been stated. The jury returned an open verdict of 'Found drowned', stating the name of the victim and concluding that there was no evidence to show how the body part came into the water.[57] Given Baxter's focus on the Ripper's removal of women's wombs in 1888, the authorities might have been relieved that he made no comment on this case. The press reported that 'the police authorities have abandoned the idea that the deceased died from the effects of an operation [meaning an abortion], as Elizabeth Jackson was under no necessity to resort to it, as all her relatives and friends were aware of her state'.[58] A more trenchant journalist observed that 'no professional performer of illegal operations would risk his neck for the sake of a penniless woman'.[59]

In the meantime, the police put the broad reach of the press to good use. Newspapers published a woodcut print of Faircloth, based on a photograph taken of him in Ipswich.[60] It was also sent to every police station in the United Kingdom. The accompanying police description, matching one given in court by landlady Kate Paine, read:

> Age between 37 and 40, height 5ft. 9in., fair, dark brown hair, clean shaven, pock pitted slightly, nose twisted, broad shoulders, and marks on the back of one hand caused by steel chippings.[61]

The image does not represent Faircloth as distinctive looking, but as a man of average height, build and appearance. His nose does not appear to be twisted or broken, nor is any of his skin marked with scars from smallpox or chippings. His clothing, a pea coat, trousers, peaked cap and boots, are unremarkable. He is depicted as clean shaven, despite the fact that people who knew him in Ipswich reported a small moustache. Although not easy to identify and locate, on Friday, 5 July, an enterprising Devon sergeant did precisely that.

Sergeant William Pope was based at the police station at Ottery St Mary. Himself a former soldier of the Grenadier Guards, he had left the regiment several years before Faircloth joined. Having received Faircloth's description, Pope watched 'an individual whose appearance has given rise to suspicions' and:

being satisfied that he was the man wanted in London, wired Scotland-yard on Friday morning. Inspector Tunbridge arrived at Ottery St Mary by ... train on the same day, and with Sergeant Pope arrested Faircloth at the Railway Inn and took him to the police station. Inspector Tunbridge left Ottery on Saturday morning by the 9.44 a.m. train to London, with Faircloth in custody.[62]

# 4

# A suspect called 'Lancashire Jack'

> There are bad, cruel men, who never ought to have a horse or dog to call their own.
>
> From *Black Beauty* by Anna Sewell

On the afternoon of Monday, 8 July, Coroner Braxton Hicks resumed the inquest into the death of Elizabeth Jackson. He explained to the jury that, although the next hearing was scheduled for 25 July, they should take the testimony of John Faircloth while it was available. He complained that 'all through the case the evidence had been anticipated by the newspapers',[1] including the discovery of Faircloth.

Faircloth took the stand to answer questions about his relationship with Jackson and his movements since their split. A broad-shouldered man of medium height, he had brown hair, grey eyes and a fresh complexion. His deafness, possibly noise-induced hearing loss from army guns, did not seem to hinder his testimony. As he gave his evidence, observers noted that he 'bore the appearance of a respectable mechanic', and, 'though uneducated, he evinced marked intelligence, promptly answering all the questions put to him':[2]

> He stated that he was by trade a millstone dresser, and had no fixed place of abode. He was a native of March [south of Wisbech], Cambridgeshire, and was thirty-six years of age. He knew the deceased, Elizabeth Jackson, having made her acquaintance at the end of last November. He met her at a publichouse [sic] at the corner of Turk's Row [probably the Rose and Crown]. She then told him that she had been living with a man named Charlie. It was on a Sunday night that [he] met her, and on the following day she agreed to accompany him to Ipswich, where he was employed for four months.
>
> She was a sober woman, and they only quarrelled now and then. On March 30 they left Ipswich, and took the train for Colchester, from which place they tramped to London. They stayed for five days at a lodging-house in Whitechapel, afterwards taking lodgings at Mrs Payne's [sic], in Manilla-street, Millwall, remaining there until the second Sunday after Good Friday [Sunday, 28 April]. He asked the deceased to go with him to Croydon, but she refused, saying she preferred going to her mother's at Chelsea until after her confinement. He had no money to give the deceased before he left London.[3]

A summary of his onward journey revealed that Faircloth stayed briefly in Greater London before heading northward to Essex and Cambridgeshire, and returned to the Home Counties before taking a westward route that ultimately led to Devon.

> At Croydon he got a few days' work at the Waddon Flour Mills. From there he went to Wandsworth, where he stayed two nights 'near the railway', going from there to Isleworth, and then to Uxbridge, [northbound to] Ware, and Bishop Stortford [sic: meaning Bishop's Stortford]. He also visited Saffron Waldon [sic], Cambridge, St Ives [east of Huntingdon], Huntingdon, St Neots, Biggleswade (where he stayed at the Red Lion), Hitchin, Luton, St Albans, and he reached Harpenden on May 31, the day of the races.
>
> He also went to Watford, where he slept at the Red Lion, a house kept by an army pensioner named Sullivan. On June 3 he was at High Wickham [sic], and he called at Great Marlow on his way to Reading, where he stayed two nights. He subsequently visited Odiham [in

Hampshire], where he was bitten by a dog, and the relieving-officer gave him an order for the parish doctor, who cauterised the wound.

On Whit-Sunday [9 June] he arrived at Bishopstoke, and he continued going west until he arrived at Tipton, near Ottery St Mary, where the police found him on Saturday. From the time he left Jackson at Millwall he had neither seen nor heard anything of her. He never read the newspapers – in fact, he seldom saw one in the parts he had visited. He had not heard of a body being found in the Thames.

[He] bought an undergarment for the deceased at Lowestoft, but he did not know whether the name 'L. E. Fisher' was on it. He did not know of anyone who would have been likely to do the deceased an injury. The linsey dress produced [in court] was one which [he] bought for the deceased at Lowestoft …

[In response to questions from the jury, he added]: He never heard the deceased speak of a man called Fred. He did not think she had any friends in Battersea, but she had in Chelsea. When [he] was at work he generally wore corduroy trousers and a pilot jacket.[4]

Inspector Tunbridge informed the coroner that Faircloth was wearing the same clothes that he wore when he left London. Enquiries were under way to verify the dates and places mentioned by Faircloth. That was the end of the day's hearing, and the police would work hard to check Faircloth's movements over a journey which spanned a minimum of 300 miles, or 482km.

On the subject of the quarrels between Faircloth and Jackson, at least one press article references a serious assault by him with a weapon:

> Their life was a most unhappy one. Their quarrelling was incessant, and in their mutual recriminations the woman persistently maintained that Fairclough [sic] was a deserter, and she would call in the police and have him arrested. This, however, she never attempted to do, although at times she was most unnaturally used, and on one occasion was badly wounded in the arm by a knife thrust from [him].[5]

That attack, if accurately reported, further demonstrates Faircloth's history of violence against women, and moves him towards being a genuine suspect as the Torso Killer. Criminality may have featured throughout Faircloth's life, but there is only one mention of him in the official criminal records. In 1869, aged 18, he was acquitted of larceny (theft) from the person, having taken a silver watch valued at £4 and tobacco pouch from a man named Samuel Cox at Ely. That jury was sympathetic to the fact that Faircloth returned the watch when challenged.[6]

When the inquest resumed on Thursday, 25 July, Inspector Tunbridge provided an overview of the police investigation to date:

> The movements of [Faircloth] … had been traced with great difficulty, and it was shown beyond all doubt that he was miles away from London both for 10 days before and 10 days after the first remains were discovered in the Thames.
>
> The river had been most carefully dragged, the ornamental waters and the shrubberies in Battersea-park had been thoroughly searched, and inquiries had been made in every direction, but without any satisfactory result beyond establishing identification.
>
> The police had travelled through many counties, making inquiries, and had spent a great amount of time on the case.[7]

The coroner summed up, confirming that there was no doubt about the identity of the deceased, nor that she had been alive within twelve hours of the first remains being discovered. He directed the jury to return a verdict that Jackson was wilfully murdered by some person or persons unknown:

> The case was somewhat different from the cases they had had, unfortunately, in Whitechapel. It was a case in which a woman had died under circumstances which in themselves were excessively suspicious, and to the mind of ordinarily reasonable persons it would suggest that whatever the cause of the death it was the result of some unlawful act on the part of someone.[8]

After a short deliberation, the jury returned the suggested verdict. On the day before that hearing, the funeral of Alice Kinsey, a prostitute described in the press as 'the eighth victim of the Whitechapel murderer'[9] took place in the East End.

From the inquest hearings, Elizabeth Jackson emerges as a young woman who lived from hand to mouth. Her immaturity and pregnancy made her reliant on Faircloth and, later, ill-equipped to cope without sources of support. At the casual ward of Britten Street Workhouse in Chelsea, where her parents were long-term residents, she admitted and discharged herself several times in July 1888, staying there overnight close to her death date, on 12 May 1889.[10] A longer admission to that workhouse, or the protection of a Catholic shelter, might have saved her life, and that of her unborn child.

Although the CID discounted Faircloth as a suspect, as he is the only named individual investigated as the possible killer of Elizabeth Jackson, he warrants further investigation. The press claimed that he described himself as an illiterate man and very deaf. The latter may have been true, but not the former. In 1872, when he enlisted in the Grenadier Guards after four years in the Cambridgeshire Militia, he signed his attestation papers. His term of service was twelve years, expiring in 1884,[11] although he served for longer. It was, and is, the most prestigious regiment in the British Army, as the first Regiment of Foot Guards acted as the Queen's bodyguards at St James's Palace, the Windsor Castle Guard and the Tower of London Guard. When not on duty elsewhere, the Third Battalion was quartered at Chelsea barracks.

Faircloth's record of service was not so illustrious. He deserted twice, in 1880 and 1886. After twenty-one days, being Absent Without Leave (AWOL) became desertion. Descriptions of deserters were circulated to the police and the press. If found, the culprit was court-martialled and could be sentenced to a maximum of six months' imprisonment. The alternative was to be dismissed in disgrace without pay or pension. Faircloth narrowly escaped the recently abolished forms of punishment of flogging and branding, but he served two terms of imprisonment, the first at Windsor barracks and the second at Wandsworth Prison. In April 1887, he was discharged from the army without a pension, making him a free man at the time of the Rainham murder. His movements in the summer of 1888, when the Whitehall murder occurred, are unknown.

The press tracked down his and Jackson's fellow lodgers at 115 Prince's Street in Ipswich, and workmates of Faircloth from the stone-works at St Peter's Foundry. Jackson was described in character as 'rather a timid, shy sort of a woman' and in appearance as 'a tall, fairly-developed woman, weighing about nine stone – fair complexion, with what we call "hay" coloured hair, done up in a knot behind. She wore a plaid shawl and a boat-shaped close-fitting hat.'[12] The same article explained the origin of the nickname of 'Lancashire Jack', as Faircloth had 'lived a great many years in Lancashire'. The explanation given was that 'he had deserted from the Grenadier Guards, and dared not go home for fear of being arrested'.

The description of Faircloth was less than favourable:

> The man had a repulsive face, and looked like a pugilist [boxer] – his nose was flattened, his cheek bones were very prominent, and he was clean shaven except for a dark moustache ... He looked like a man who had lived a very fast life, and had been rather a rough character. He worked in the same shop [workshop] with me, and on one occasion he called my attention to the peculiarity of his hair – I passed my hand over it, and it felt like the bristles of a brush.
>
> I recollect on one occasion he did not turn up at his work as usual ... [assumed: days later] he unexpectedly turned up at the works with a couple of black eyes ... I remarked that the bruises were turning green. [He] replied 'Yes, that is my old woman – she threw the handbrush at me and hit me fairly on the bridge of the nose ... I didn't like to come to the shop with two black eyes ...'
>
> Though he was looked upon by his fellow-workmen as a quiet, harmless fellow, he seemed to have quarrelled a good deal with the woman with whom he cohabited, and to have been jealous of her, though she seldom went out even when she had neither fire nor food in the house.
>
> They left very suddenly on the last day of March and have not since been seen in Ipswich, the sheets and other portable property belonging to the landlady having been disposed of.[13]

It was a moonlight flit. As at Millwall, they took what they could and defaulted on a few nights' payment. The same interviewee made much of the fact that Faircloth regretted his prominent position in a photograph taken at the workshop that was later used by police to trace him:

Some photographer came down to the works, and he said, 'Would any of you gentlemen like to get on that rolley [small wagon] to show the machinery off as workmen?' Fairclough [*sic*: Faircloth] and some others jumped up, and the photograph was taken. [Faircloth] was the most prominent of the group, and he took well because he was dark.

When he saw the photographs he wanted to destroy them, and made use of the expression, 'I must have been a ____ fool to have shoved myself forward like that; I am the principal one of the group.' He was a very peculiar man and extremely reserved.[14]

Faircloth's wish to destroy photographs of himself could be construed as suspicious, and this account confirms that police were in possession of a recent image of him.

Reports about Faircloth's movements are inconsistent about the date on which Faircloth conclusively left Jackson in Millwall. In fact, he left her on 28 April, not at a similar date in May, nor in Battersea, with both mistakes originating from her mother. Catherine Jackson was led by her daughter to believe that Faircloth planned to rejoin her in Chelsea, purporting that she had not been abandoned by the father of her child. And Faircloth must have been the father, although the date of their first meeting was fixed differently by Jackson, her mother and Faircloth as variously September, October or November. If her baby were due in early September, Jackson must have conceived before Christmas.

A possible hypothesis is that Faircloth won or stole money at the Harpenden Races on 31 May, and went back to central London by rail, a distance of approximately 30 miles as the crow flies. His motivation might have been to complete his campaign of coercive control by killing his pregnant partner. Yet this theory lacks weight, and contradicts the extensive CID enquiry into his movements. Another possible suspect is the man seen with Jackson hours before her death, whom neither Jenny Lee nor Elizabeth Pomeroy described in detail. Pomeroy made the best attempt, saying he was dressed like a workman, had a little bit of whiskers, was wearing a heavy pilot jacket, and looked like a navvy, or construction worker. As an itinerant labourer, Faircloth wore that type of jacket. Yet the authorities clearly believed that the navvy was not identical to Faircloth. It must be assumed that the two women were shown a photograph of Faircloth by the police, or even viewed him in person, and failed to recognise him.

The killer must have been a man with tools and premises. As his landlady Kate Paine stated, Faircloth did not carry tools, and could not easily have accessed a very sharp knife and fine-toothed saw.[15] He did not have continuing access to secure premises, or to any form of transport. Moreover, the painstaking investigation of the CID placed him outside London for a wide margin of time, a full ten days either side of 3 and 4 June. Faircloth was a wife-beater and a thief, but he did not kill Elizabeth Jackson. By extension, he makes an unlikely suspect for the other Torso Murders, which were demonstrably part of a series.

What of Jackson's putative men-friends known only as Fred, Charlie and the navvy? It is a reasonable assumption that the police were unable to trace any of them, or if they did, eliminated one or more of them from their enquiries. Another lead from the Battersea case arose from the fact that: 'A piece of fine linen about 9½ in. by 8 in. probably a handkerchief was found rolled and pushed into the body.' The press claimed this practice was done to make the pelvis less buoyant in the water, as 'in the case of a death of a person at sea', making it 'probable that the crime may have been perpetrated on board some vessel or by some one possessed of this peculiar knowledge'.[16]

The local bargemen came under suspicion, as 'a dangerous class of men who infest that locality [Battersea], who took advantage of and liberties with unfortunates'. A woman named only as Ginger Nell related that she had seen Jackson on 2 June and warned her against those men, 'and, furthermore, what better spot could be selected than a Thames barge by night'.[17] The local police would have been aware of the alleged assaults on Sarah Ann King less than two years previously.

A bargeman makes an attractive suspect. His barge afforded him a private place where a homeless women like Jackson could be invited to shelter. His mobility enabled him to deposit her body parts and elude police scrutiny. He could have met Jackson within the grounds of Battersea Park, whose wicket gate next to Albert Bridge 'was very much used at night',[18] or ogled her from his barge moored near the wharves on the insalubrious south side of the river. The barge's below-deck cabin would be a secure place to kill and store human remains. Battersea barge-builders and owners Nash and Miller might employ such a man. The watermen who suggested that the remains were thrown from Albert Bridge might have said so out of fear of being accused of murder.

What other type of tradesman might have committed this and the earlier murders? The Whitehall case involved a hundred workmen on site at New Scotland Yard, with additional visitors from several companies. Although not a comprehensive list of suppliers, Messrs John Grover and Sons of Islington were the building contractors; Messrs Henry, Edward and Walter Cattermole of Highbury employed cart drivers and workmen to deliver bricks and remove the rubble; while Messrs Wenham and Waters of Croydon supplied the plumbing and heating.

Grover's Islington yard was handy for the disposal of body parts on the north side of the river. Their Wilton Works were virtually on the Regent's Canal and close to St Pancras Lock. At a similarly convenient location, Cattermole's had a furniture depository on Kilburn High Road. In autumn 1889, in a case called The Great Robbery of Bricks, three Cattermole employees, Francis Rogers, William Head and Henry Boreham, were variously convicted of stealing and receiving 22,000 bricks valued at £33. But none of the men had any charges brought against them for crimes of violence.

Equally, research uncovers no wrongdoing among the witnesses at the Whitehall inquest. Thomas Hickmott, a cart driver employed by Cattermole, made statements to the press but was not called as a witness. Hickmott raised the fact that unemployed workmen visited the site in search of work:

> It is regarded as utterly impossible that any stranger could have recently visited the place. Before the trunk was found some strange workmen came and asked for employment. Whether their object was to inspect the place I don't know. No one of them, as far as I could hear, was ever seen with a parcel.[19]

Setting aside a site workman or visitor as a suspect, the press reported several instances of stinking parcels, carried or deposited by mysterious strangers. The first mention is about the Rainham case, with unsubstantiated origins, coming from a reporter quoting an unnamed gentleman, who allegedly passed it to the authorities:

It is quite true that on the afternoon of the 17th of last month [June 1887] I saw a woman standing on the pavement near Charing-cross railway station, with a rather loose canvas bag or wrapper in her arms, from which the smell of decomposed human flesh emanated strongly. The idea of a woman standing on the pavement in the Strand, with a portion of a murdered corpse under her arm, is not one which would obtain immediate credence with business people. That is just the reason why it actually took place in this instance, and the woman was permitted to go unmolested on her hideous errand. She looked as if she had calculated in this way.

I regret that I did not watch her closer than I did, but I can identify her, and surely she ought to be found without causing much difficulty. She had doubtless come to London by rail to Charing-cross, and was going north, because she had moved some 50 yards eastwards of the station.

Her height is about 5 ft. 5 [inches], age 48, hair thin and dark, regular features, general contour sharp and slightly elongated, complexion pale, suggesting an indoor life. She was dressed in a bonnet trimmed with some velvet stuff, and a shawl, her entire costume being brown and shabby, though not much worn.[20]

The informant possessed a touching conviction in police powers to locate an unknown woman from an unspecified place, using this basic description. She was probably carrying her dinner, or a treat for her dog. Further searches reveal the source of the story to be a self-styled newspaper reporter named James Greville Burns, and demonstrate that it was invented. In the summer of 1887, the owners of the *London Evening News* took Burns to court for having obtained money by false pretences by knowingly supplying them with false intelligence about the Rainham case.[21]

Three mysterious items surfaced in the police investigation into the Whitehall case. The first was reported by a resident of Llanelli in South Wales, who was visiting London:

He happened to be in Cannon-row on the Saturday before the body was found, and at an hour when the place was practically deserted. His attention was directed to a man who climbed over a hoarding into the ground whereon the new police office is being erected, and where afterwards the body was discovered. Two other men were with him who had a barrow on which was a bundle.

The whole proceeding seemed curious, and afterwards, when the remains were found, the South Walian 'put two and two together', handed in his information, and also a description of the man. The result is that a workman has since been interviewed in the vicinity, who admits having been on the spot on the day in question, though his business there is not very clear.[22]

This information, fascinating if true, turned out to have a prosaic explanation. The three men had brought a bag of sand to the site by truck, and one climbed over the fence to open the gate for his workmates.[23]

In late August 1888, Inspector Marshall was summoned to Guildford to pick up the second suspicious item, a brown paper parcel discovered on the railway line near Guildford railway station. It contained a boiled left calf and right foot, presumed human. A doctor had already certified the items as human, and had them buried in a local cemetery. Given that the date of the parcel's finding, 24 August, not only fell within the timeframe of the Whitehall murder but matched the exact date of its *Echo* newspaper fragment, Marshall had the items disinterred and took them to London for examination by Bond and Hebbert. The two surgeons 'discovered conclusively that they are those of a bear, and therefore have no relation to the human remains found at Westminster'.[24]

A third bundle was reported at the time of the Whitehall murder. Edward Deuchar, aged 24, an insurance company inspector, who went on a rather pongy journey on the number 12 tram:

> A little over three weeks ago [in mid-September] he went on a tramcar from Vauxhall station to London Bridge. It is stated that he noticed a man on the car carrying a parcel. He would not have taken particular notice of the parcel but for the fact that there was a terrible smell emanating from it. The olfactory organs of most of the passengers were affected by the extraordinary stench which pervaded the car. A lady gave her husband, who was sitting next to the man, some lavender to hold under his nose.

The parcel seemed to be heavy. The man carried it with extreme care under his arm. It was tied up in brown paper. The top of it was under his arm, while he held the corner end in his hand. Mr Deuchar said the man looked ill at ease and agitated. He described him as a powerfully built man, of rough appearance, with a goatee beard, and rather shabbily dressed. Mr Deuchar is confident that he could recognise him again.

The car went on, and when at the Obelisk, St George's-circus, several persons alighted. Mr Deuchar still remained on the car, but when about thirty yards past the Obelisk, said, 'This stench is awful; I can't stand it any longer,' and proceeded to go out. Just at that moment, the suspicious looking individual with the parcel asked the conductor, 'Have we passed the Obelisk yet?' and then jumped out. Mr Deuchar, when he had descended and walked some distance towards London Bridge, called a policeman's attention to the retreating form of the 'man with the stinking parcel', and told him to 'keep an eye on him'.[25]

Although Deuchar's inconclusive account can have little relevance to the search for the killer, it is a useful reminder that the remains could have been disposed of entirely by land, with parts thrown into the river from the embankment or dropped from a bridge. The concept of the perpetrator carrying body parts on foot to deposit them at inland locations is intrinsic to the next two cases.

Any number of trades could have been plied by this unnamed serial killer. According to Bond and Hebbert, the perpetrator was not a doctor or a rogue medical student. If not a butcher, he could have been a hunter. Butchers, mad or otherwise, formed plausible suspects in the Ripper case, as did slaughterers or mortuary workers. Hunters, whether as a trade or a hobby, are not easy to research, although the perpetrator must have acquired his knife skills by some means.

Further questions follow: *Why was the dismemberment necessary? Was it sheer practicality or a means of gratifying his need for brutality?* He could kill the women with a blow to the skull, above the hairline, or throttle them, and put their bodies in the water in the hope that they did not surface. If they were retrieved, there was every possibility that immersion in water and decomposition would cover the traces of their murders, leading them to be labelled as suicides. And perhaps that is what happened, in additional unknown cases where the killer did not have a knife to hand.

*How did the killer meet his victims?* To render them unidentifiable by removing their heads implies that he must have been seen with them, and was linked to them by association in specific locations, such as pubs. They may have been his sexual partners, whether casual or longer-term. However, in their post-mortem analyses, Bond and Hebbert do not specify whether or not sexual intercourse had taken place, presumably owing to the states of decomposition of the remains, and immersion in water or absence of some of them. By contrast, the medical statements in the Ripper cases explicitly stated that there was no sign of sexual intercourse.

*Where did he kill and dismember them?* The Elizabeth Jackson murder proves that the killer remained in the same location to carry out both of those activities. He must have picked Jackson up in the Battersea area, taken her to a secure location, and from or near that place, disposed of her remains in the river.

Deductions about his motivation suggest that the perpetrator must be an insecure man with a dangerous grudge, who has been rejected by women when he seeks their easy compliance. Frustration drives his violence against them. Bruising was detected on parts of the Whitehall remains, and also in four different areas of Elizabeth Jackson's body. Her left thigh was severely bruised, with four bruises as from fingers on its outer side and back. He may have come away himself with visible scratches, bumps and bruises, taking a week or more to heal, and excused by his physically active trade.

The Hebbert report highlights similarities across the cases, proving beyond reasonable doubt that the women were killed and dismembered by the same hand. All three torsos, in the literal meaning of the word, were cut up into three parts, although the first part of the Rainham torso and the second and third parts of the Whitehall torso were never found.

- The first part was from the 6th cervical to the 7th dorsal or thoracic vertebrae, namely from the bottom of the neck to the middle of the back.

- The second part was from the 8th dorsal (Rainham was the 5th) to the 3rd lumbar vertebrae, namely from the middle of the back near the bottom of the shoulder blades to above the pelvis.

- The third part was from the 3rd lumbar vertebra, the top of the pelvis, to the bottom of the buttocks, excluding the legs which were removed at the thigh sockets.

- Where the lungs and heart were missing, in the Rainham and Battersea cases, the perpetrator had removed them from the top end, leaving the diaphragm intact.

- In the cases of Whitehall and Elizabeth Jackson the uterus was removed, as was Jackson's foetus.

- The arms and legs were removed skilfully from the socket with sweeping circular cuts. The legs were separated at the knee joint, however there was a variation in whether he left the patella, or kneecap, attached to the thigh or lower leg.

The killer's signature of actions performed for his own gratification might extend to the way that the body parts were wrapped and tied. The Hebbert report mentioned the possible use of a ligature on the right arm in the Whitehall case, stating, 'The ligature was either tied round to prevent the bleeding from the veins, or to fix a newspaper wrapper round the limb. In either case it had the result of preventing the draining out of blood.'[26] The report does not mention the improvised tampon used in the Battersea case, which if factually correct, would also have plugged any leakages.

In the Rainham case, the bundles were wrapped in two types of canvas, with one rougher than the other, and tied with cord. There was nothing unusual about the knots. The implication is that the perpetrator used what material he had to hand. In the Whitehall case, the bundles were wrapped in what was presumed to be the woman's own skirt, with her steel dress improver, or bustle, included, alongside fragments of newspaper. They were tied with what might have been Venetian blind or sash cord, a black tape which might have come from her skirt fastening, and assorted pieces of string, and this was done by someone who was skilled in wrapping.

Elizabeth Jackson's body parts were comprehensively bundled up in her own clothes, which were torn. If they were torn up to be used as wrappings, that implies a habit of tearing instead of using implements like scissors or a knife. All of her clothing had been removed and parts of it – her dress, ulster, bag and drawers, were reused as packaging for the remains. Her drawers were marked 'L.E. Fisher', a potentially identifiable clue. Yet the killer did not remove the marking, either because he did not notice it, did not consider it important, or was illiterate.

The bundles were tied with mohair bootlaces which, again, were presumably her own, as well as with a piece of Venetian blind cord, and ordinary string. The Venetian blind cord is a piece of middle-class soft furnishing that seems out of place. Why would the killer use Venetian blind cord and where did he get it from; a warehouse, shop or directly from the window of his place of residence? Were his live victims tied up with the same cord that was later used to secure the bundles of their body parts? It is possible to state that the perpetrator was deeply practical and methodical, characteristics that must have been useful for his trade. Whether or not his murders were planned, his clearing-up operations were well thought through, and effective.

The crucial question returns: *Was the perpetrator based on the river?* The constraints within which the killer operated help to define him. If he used one, his boat must have been small, either a rowing skiff used by watermen to carry passengers or an easily manoeuvrable cut or spritsail barge used by lightermen, able to pass into the Regent's Canal and through its low bridges. Such barges would have a below-decks cabin and would carry a dinghy astern for relays to land. A boat, or a boatyard, might provide secure premises for him to murder and dismember his victims.

An analysis of the disposal sites, ignoring items that were found in the River Thames or washed up on its foreshore, proves helpful. Several limbs in the Rainham case were dumped at St Pancras Lock in the Regent's Canal, which is non-tidal, and the nearby Midland Railway Coal Dock. The perpetrator visited those sites in person, most likely by boat or by rail, but was it for work, delivering coal, or for another purpose? The most likely suspect is a bargeman, who could visit both the Midland Railway coal dock and the Regent's Canal in an expedition from Limehouse Docks.

For the body parts left in the New Scotland Yard foundations, he had to enter the site on foot from either the south (riverside from Victoria Embankment) or north (from Whitehall). The sack that contained the body parts would be best disguised if approaching from the Thames by boat, although they were individually wrapped and tied. In the Battersea case, the bundles that were found on opposite sides of the river in Battersea Park, and at the front of Shelley House, could have been thrown from the embankments or even the river. A man might push his boat away from the landing stairs by Albert Bridge, with the quick chuck of a parcel into the park's frame ground, row across the river and throw again. But such riverine deductions are challenged by the next case, in which a woman's torso was left under a railway arch in Whitechapel, over half a mile inland and firmly inside Jack the Ripper's territory.

# 5

# The Pinchin Street murder, Whitechapel, where a woman's torso was discovered at 5.25 a.m. on Tuesday, 10 September 1889

The game is afoot.

> Sherlock Holmes, from 'The Adventure of the
> Abbey Grange' by Sir Arthur Conan Doyle

Approximately three months after the murder of Elizabeth Jackson, a woman's headless and legless torso, although with its arms intact, was discovered in a railway arch in Whitechapel. The arch was located at the western end of Pinchin Street, and was the first opening on the right from Backchurch Lane. It could also be accessed via a cart track running from Backchurch Lane into a yard at its rear. The press described the arch as 'A passage up under the coal depot of the Great Eastern Railway, a long, dark avenue grimy with coal dust.'[1]

That location was three minutes' walk away from Leman Street police station, the headquarters of the Ripper investigation. It was a comparable distance from Berner Street, where Ripper victim Elisabeth Stride was killed. Speculation began that this was another Ripper murder, or possibly a copycat crime, while similarities with the Battersea case were immediately noted. Detective Inspector Tunbridge was called in and, with Chief Constable Colonel Monsell, viewed the remains at the mortuary in the grounds of St George-in-the-East Church, where Elisabeth Stride's body had been kept and her post-mortem examination carried out.

H Division was still preoccupied with the Ripper investigation following the recent murder of Alice Kinsey, whose body was found in Castle Alley on 17 July 1889. That murder, like this, was compared to those of other women generally considered to be killed by the Ripper between August and November 1888. The main investigators from the Ripper case came into play, headed by Detective Inspector Henry Moore, who had taken over from Abberline, and worked under Chief Inspector John West. The latter, a long-term resident of Cartwright Street,[2] a few blocks west of Wellclose Square, lived extremely near to the route posited by the author as taken by the Torso Killer to dispose of the remains and escape. The Ripper veterans also included Superintendent Thomas Arnold, Chief Inspector Donald Swanson, and Inspectors Charles Pinhorn and Edmund Reid. Thames Division's Inspector John Regan was again in charge of the searches of craft and personnel on the river, assisted by Sergeants Moore, Francis, Howard, Davis and Scott. Police surgeons involved in the Ripper case both conducted and observed the post-mortem examination, and Wynne Baxter was the coroner.

On the same day that the body was discovered, the police issued two public statements, firstly a notice with a timing disrepancy:

> At 5.40 A.M. trunk of a woman found under the arches in Pinchin-street, E [East]. Age about forty. Height 5 ft. 3 in. Hair dark brown. No clothing except chemise very much torn and bloodstained. Both elbows discoloured as if from habitually leaning on them. Post-mortem marks around waist apparently caused by a rope.[3]

That notice was followed by a more detailed description of the dead woman, reporting a younger age:

> Aged about thirty-five years; height 5 ft. 3in; hair dark brown; skin fair; hands soft and shapely; nails well kept; small circular hardening,

but no corn, on right little finger; arms small but well shaped; body plump and well formed, with full breasts. No marks of rings on fingers, and no evidence of maternity.[4]

CID Central Office tasked all divisions of the Metropolitan Police to investigate 'as to whether any woman of the unfortunate class or otherwise, answering the description has been reported, or can be ascertained to [be] missing'.[5] The general public was permitted to view the body for the purposes of identification. The press stated:

> Many unfortunates called to see the trunk, but none could identify it. In fact, there are no marks whatever on the remains which would enable any one to conclusively identify the body, and unless some other portions are discovered, it is quite possible that the matter will for ever remain a mystery ... [6]

Fingerprint identification was not yet in use.

On Wednesday, 11 September, Commissioner Monro, who had replaced Warren in Autumn 1888, applied to the Home Office for an increase of 100 men.[7] An extensive search was under way on land and river for any other parts of the woman's body, and the streets were flooded with policemen both in and out of uniform. On the same day, Baxter opened an inquest into the unknown woman's death at St George's Vestry Hall on Cable Street, where he had held Elisabeth Stride's inquest eleven months previously. The jury viewed the torso in the mortuary before the hearing began.

Constable William Pennett, who had discovered the remains, was the first witness. Unluckily for him, it was his first night on that shift, although he was not inexperienced, having joined up in April 1884.[8] He testified as follows:

> I went on duty at 10 o'clock on Monday night, when nothing attracted my attention as unusual. My beat took me through Pinchin-street every half-hour or a little more. I always entered it from Christian-street, occasionally turned down Frederick-street, under the railway arches, and usually returned to the starting-point in Pinchin Street, but sometimes went into Backchurch-lane.

[At] about 25 minutes past five I came from the direction of Christian-street to Backchurch-lane. I was on the northern side of the road (that further from the railway), and when opposite one of the arches saw an object under one of them which looked like a bundle. I thought at first it was such as Jews throw away in the night time. The arch is used by the Board of Works as a stone-yard, and is protected by the uprights and cross-bars of a wooden fence, the boards having been taken away. There is also a cart entrance (which was closed) from Backchurch-lane.

I found the object four and a half to five yards inside the archway, measured from the pavement, and was near the wall of the western end. On going close I found it to be part of a human body, with two or three pieces of rag on it. Otherwise it was naked. The head and legs were missing. The trunk lay with the shoulders towards the west. I noticed no wounds nor drops of blood about.

I waited a minute or two till a man came along with a broom, and I asked him to go and fetch my mate at the corner. He asked, 'What's on, guv'nor?' I said, 'Tell him I have got a job. Make haste.' He went up Backchurch-lane towards the adjoining beat, and two constables afterwards ran towards me. Inspector Pinhorn afterwards came, and we searched the arches. Up to this time I had seen no one pass.

Two men, who had the appearance of sailors, were lying under the further of the arches from Backchurch-lane, and under the middle arch (the next to that under which the body lay) there was a shoe-black. The latter was asleep, so was one of the sailors, but I am not certain as to the other. He had a pipe in his mouth. The three were taken to the station.

I had last passed the place prior to the discovery just before five o'clock, and was then on the north side of the road. It was then just before day-break. [I] looked into the arch, but did not see the trunk. I should have seen it had it been there. I then went up Backchurch-lane, and, it being five o'clock, called a man who had asked me to do so at that time.

I saw no one with any bundle, nor any costermonger's cart. [A costermonger sold fruit and vegetables from a handcart in the street.] I saw a barrow standing still, with a board on it; but it had been there all the time I had been on duty. I saw no cart except those in Christian-street, belonging to Mr Farclough [sic], which came out every morning. Neither of those came down Pinchin-street;

they would go into the main streets as quietly as possible. Dr Clark, assistant to the police surgeon, arrived about half an hour after the discovery, and the body was removed to the mortuary. It was the first time I had been on the beat.[9]

Messrs Fairclough and Sons were carriers and contractors occupying numbers 10 and 12 Christian Street, which was at the eastern end of Pinchin Street and perpendicular to it.

In response to questions from the jury, and penultimately Inspector Reid, Pennett provided the following additional information, paraphrased here:

> The torso had been simply laid there. There were no marks of a trail on the ground. There was no sign of the dust having been disturbed, and there was no dust on the body. There were a lot of loose stones and gravel, so that if there had been a struggle there would be no traces of it. If I had seen a person carrying a bundle at that time I should have stopped and searched him. So would any other constable.[10]

Inspector Charles Pinhorn was the next witness. Like Pennett, he was based at Leman Street police station. Pinhorn was also involved in the investigations into the murders of Elisabeth Stride and Alice Kinsey, who was also known as McKenzie. The latter investigation was ongoing as the Pinchin Street torso was discovered. Pinhorn stated:

> On being summoned I searched the arches and had the street cleared, except as regards men passing through to go to their work. The men found under the arches were taken to the station, and made statements. Two of them said they had entered at about four a.m., and the other at about two. All said they had heard nothing. As far as possible we prevent people sleeping under the arches. No constable saw anyone with a bundle, such as to attract attention that morning. I see no reason why costermongers' barrows should be going that way at such an hour. The condition of the men found would hardly have warranted them saying more than that they did not hear anything [laughter in court].

The nearest lamp is a dozen or 20 yards [10–18 metres, or 36–60 feet] from where the body was found. The arms were close to the body, and the hands in front, as they would have been if the remains had been carried in a sack. The trunk lay breast downwards, and there was no dust on the back. Some pieces of a dirty old chemise lay round the arms and neck, with bloodstains upon them. There was a little oozing of blood at the neck, but there was no blood on the body. I cannot say whether it had been washed. The chemise had been cut open from top to bottom, and had also been ripped at the armholes. There was some blood on every part of it. No name nor other ink mark was upon it.[11]

Unlike the clothing of Elizabeth Jackson or Ripper victim Polly Nichols, the victim's chemise was not marked with the name of any person or workhouse. In response to questions from the jury, Pinhorn added that people with barrows from Billingsgate Fish Market would not reach the railway arch so early in the morning. He emphasised that none of the men sleeping in the other arches could have seen the body being deposited on the spot where it was discovered. No speculation was made about whether any of them got up in the early hours to relieve themselves.

Inspector Reid briefly testified in support of his colleague's evidence, stating that he had questioned the three men found under the arches, and was satisfied that they had gone there drunk, and knew nothing of the affair. He assured the court that: 'Inquiry was being made among all the people in the neighbourhood who let out barrows.'[12] Reid was also overseeing a comprehensive search of the area for additional body parts, managing door-to-door enquiries, and tracing any missing women.

The coroner said that he would adjourn the inquest until Tuesday, 24 September, as Doctor Clark, who first examined the body, was engaged until then at the Old Bailey, and Doctor Phillips and other medical colleagues were still working on the post-mortem examination of the body. He concluded by saying that although the victim had not been identified, it was not a hopeless task, merely very difficult, and some little time would enable the police to see what they could do.

The second and final day of the inquest started with the medical evidence. Doctor Percy Clark, aged 24, who had only qualified as a surgeon in the previous year, testified as follows:

A little before six a.m. on the morning of Sept. 10 I was called by the police to Pinchin-street. Under the railway arch there, about eight feet from the road and about a foot from the right wall of the arch, I saw the trunk of a woman minus the head and legs. It was lying on its chest, with the right arm doubled under the abdomen, the left arm lying at the side. The arms were not severed from the body. There was no pool of blood, and no sign of any struggle having taken place there.

Covering the cut surface of the neck and right shoulder were the remnants of what had been a chemise, of common make, and of such a size as would be worn by a woman of similar build to the trunk found. It had been torn down the front, and had been cut out from the front of the armholes on each side. The cuts appeared to have been made by a knife. The chemise was blood-stained nearly all over, I think from being wrapped over the cut surface of the neck. There was no clotted blood on it, and no sign of arterial spurting. I could find no distinguishing mark on the chemise.

*Rigor mortis* was not present, and decomposition had set in … I should think the woman had been dead about 24 hours. Besides the wounds caused by the severance of the head and legs there was a wound 15in. long through the external coats of the abdomen. The body was not blood-stained, except where the chemise had rested. The body seemed to have been recently washed.

On the back were four bruises, caused before death. None of the bruises were of old standing. Round the waist was a pale mark and an indentation such as would be caused by clothing during life. On the right arm there were eight distinct bruises, and seven on the left, all caused before death and of recent date. The backs of both forearms and hands were much bruised. On the outer side of the left forearm, about three inches above the wrist, was a cut about two inches in length, and half an inch lower down was another cut, both caused after death. The bruises on the right arm were such as would have been caused by the arms having been tightly grasped. There was an old injury on the index-finger of the right hand over the last joint.

The arms were well formed. Both elbows were hardened and discoloured, as if they had been leant upon. The hands and nails were pallid, and the former were not indicative of any particular kind of work. The breasts were well formed, and there were no signs of maternity about them.[13]

Clark contradicted the police notice which had stated that the so-called rope mark around the victim's waist was made after death. Although observing the old injury to her right index finger, and her discoloured elbows as if from habitually leaning on them, he made no assumption about the woman's occupation. Although not stated in court, the extensive bruising seemed to indicate a violent struggle with her killer before her death.

Doctor Phillips corroborated his colleague's evidence, adding:

The marks upon the fingers had fairly healed, and had evidently been in the process of healing for some time previous to death. I think the pallor of the hands and the nails is an important element in enabling me to draw a conclusion as to the cause of death. There was throughout the body an absence of blood in the vessels. The heart was empty; it was fatty, and the vessels coated with fat, but the bowels were healthy. The right lung was adherent, except at the base, the left lung free, and taking them both together, fairly competent, and especially considering the decomposition of the remains. The stomach was the seat of considerable post-mortem change, and contained only a small quantity of fruit, like a plum. In my opinion the woman had never been pregnant. I believe her to have been under 40 years old. There was an absence of any particular disease or poison. I believe that death arose from loss of blood.

I am of opinion that all the mutilations were subsequent to death; that the mutilations were affected [sic] by someone accustomed to cut up animals or see them cut up; and that the incisions were effected by a strong knife, eight inches or more long. The supposition – and it is only a supposition – which presents itself to my mind is that there had been a former incision of the neck, the signs of which had disappeared on the subsequent separation of the head [from the trunk]. The loss of blood could not have come from the stomach, and I could not trace it coming from the lungs. I have a strong opinion that it did not.[14]

In response to a question from the jury, he added:

I cannot say whether the person who severed the head from the body was a butcher or not. I merely wish to say it was someone accustomed to use either a knife or some sharp instrument in cutting up animals. I have no reason for believing that he had human anatomical knowledge. In fact, it is probably known to you, and to most people, that the spine is not the part which would be disarticulated by a medical man.[15]

Of the cuts on her forearms, Doctor Phillips said they 'had apparently been caused by a sweep of the knife whilst the thighs were being separated from the body'.[16] The medical evidence provided by the two doctors suggested that the victim had strongly defended herself against an extremely violent attacker. His post-mortem report contained further information that is summarised here:

There is a long division of external wall of abdomen, not penetrating the cavity ... Commencing 2 inches below cartilage of chest and slightly penetrating the vagina below, being about 15 in. long, rather to left side ...
Weight of whole remains: 67 lbs. [4 stone 11 pounds or 30 kilograms] ...
Marked absence of blood in Vessels, but not so complete as in some cases of death from bleeding ...
Death ... chiefly indicated as arising from loss of blood ... especially indicated by empty Heart & blood vessels ...
Womb ... congested at cervix ...
Vagina rather dilated, no sign of recent coitus ...
No evidence of child bearing but strong evidence of prostitution.[17]

The long cut to the abdomen, probably preparatory to intended organ removal, was reminiscent of the mutilations carried out by Jack the

Ripper. Regarding the cause of death, a cut throat seemed the obvious method of killing, again the modus operandi of the Ripper. And, although she did not appear to have had recent sexual intercourse, Phillips observed signs of prostitution, presumably referencing her congested cervix. Hebbert also observed some uterine discharges, without stating specifically whether they indicated a sexually transmitted disease or menstruation: 'There is a little whitish thick mucous [sic] oozing from the *os uteri* [opening of the cervix into the vagina]. The mucous membrane [endometrium] is rather thick, and covered with a reddish mucus.'[18] Hebbert stated: '*She was apparently not a virgin*, and the vagina had been distended, though not so patent as after childbearing.'[19] His report noted that there was no hymen.[20]

The next witnesses at the inquest were two of the three men who had camped out in the arches and the local tradesman who was knocked up by Constable Pennett. Michael Keating, of 1 Osborne Street, Brick Lane, who was described in court as a licensed shoeblack, received a more colourful portrayal in the press, who called him 'an old Irishman with a wooden leg, who knocks about Commercial Road with his box of brushes'.[21] He testified as follows:

> He passed up Pinchin Street on the night of the 9th, between 11 and 12 o'clock. He saw no one about, and observed nothing under the arch, but he was not very sober at the time. He went to sleep under the arch, and was not awakened during the night. The police roused him in the morning, and as he was leaving he noticed the body, which the inspector was covering up. He lent the police the sack in which he carried his blacking-box.
>
> If the body had been there when he went in he was not certain he was sober enough to have seen it. As far as he remembered, however, he went in on the other side of the arch. He did not hear anyone else coming in during the night. [He] had never slept there before, but he knew it was a quiet and convenient place.[22]

Richard Hawk, a seaman from St Ives in Cornwall, stated that he had been paid off his ship about seven or eight weeks previously, and was in hospital until 9 September. He continued by stating that:

> He walked about the streets until about 20 minutes past four a.m. on the 10th, when, happening to be in Pinchin-street, he went under a railway arch to lie down. It was dark, and he was not exactly sober.
>
> [He knew the time because] he asked a policeman he saw close to the arch. He did not see anyone or anything in the arch when he went in. There was another man with him. His companion was in about the same condition as himself. They met in a public-house. He neither heard nor saw anything, and went to sleep very soon.[23]

Hawk drew laughter with his reference to a line from a comic music-hall song first performed in 1888, 'If you want to know the time ask a p'liceman'.[24] Anything but complimentary about the police, that popular song was usually performed by a humbug in uniform. In uncomfortable proximity to that quotation, Constable Pennett was recalled to ask if he had told Hawk the time, which he had not. The coroner then read out a statement from Hawk's companion, which corroborated his testimony.

Jeremiah Hurley, a 31-year-old general labourer, was the next witness to give evidence:

> He lived near Pinchin-street, and was called by a policeman as usual at five a.m. on the 10th [as a scheduled wake-up call] ... Work commenced with him occasionally at half-past five, but he left the house on the morning in question at 25 minutes to six. He went by way of Phillip-street, where he saw a man standing at the corner, having the appearance of a tailor waiting to go to work. [He] observed no one else until he got into Pinchin-street, where he saw an inspector and other police standing by the arch under which the body had been found.[25]

Hurley lived in Anthony Street, Stepney, ten minutes' walk away from Pennett's beat. The duty of knocking him up, commonly done by police in the Victorian era, took Pennett away from the Pinchin Street area at the critical time. Hurley's sighting of someone he called 'a Jewish tailor' was too late in the morning to be significant.

Inspector Moore took the stand and confirmed that he was the policeman in charge of the case. He produced a plan of Pinchin Street and its surrounding neighbourhood and then advised the coroner that the police did not request a delay in concluding the inquest:

> There was nothing at present to show how the body was placed in the position in which it was found. He saw no reason for adjourning the inquiry. The chemise he produced had been torn and cut. It was of common material, hand-stitched, and was certainly not made by an experienced needlewoman. It looked like a garment made at home by some poor person.[26]

He added that he had had the chemise found on the body cleaned, but no marks were discovered that would give them any clue as to the owner or maker.

The coroner briefly summed up, commenting that it was a matter of congratulation that the present case did not appear to have any connection with the previous murders in the immediate neighbourhood, meaning Whitechapel. There was no evidence as to the identity of the deceased, but the medical statements clearly demonstrated that she had met with a violent and criminal death caused by loss of blood. The jury immediately returned the same verdict as that given in the Battersea case: 'Wilful murder by some person or persons unknown.'[27]

The police files include several fascinating reports containing early analysis of the case by senior officers. Donald Swanson, who was placed in charge of the Ripper investigation after the murder of Annie Chapman, picked out key facts, as did Commissioner Monro. An extract from Swanson's well-considered report dated 10 September 1889 itemised several of his deductions about the killer's modus operandi:

> 1st. Upon the spot where the trunk was found, there was no evidence of any blood, and a footmark from the nature of the ground was an impossibility; nor was there left anything in the shape of a cloth or sack to carry the trunk in.
>
> 2nd. The place of disposal must have been a selected spot; i.e. it must have been decided upon by viewing, for on all sides of it not

a single inhabitant resides but it is faced by a pailing [sic] or wooden fence, and flanked by a dead wall …

3rd. The appearance of the trunk minus head and legs, was as follows:- the head which had been cut off by clean <u>right</u> handed cuts, the vertebra being 'jointed' left the neck with blood oozing from it, while both legs had also been 'jointed', by right handed cuts, but the dismemberment had taken place at an earlier period than the head for the raw flesh had from continued exposure dried on the surface which presented a blackened appearance in consequence. The wound beginning at the lower part of the sternum, cutting through the skin, fatty substance, and penetrating the bowels, and uterus slightly, extended to the left side of the <u>labia major</u> [meaning the outer folds of the vulva].

The trunk presented the undoubted appearance of having decomposition begun. Upon the chemise which was cut at the arms and down the front, I understand from Inspr Reid who examined it, there was not a single mark of any kind and the article itself of common manufacture and fabric. Beyond a small semicircular cut on the index finger of the right hand, and bruises on both arms … there is absolutely nothing by which the trunk could be identified.

From Nos. 1 & 3 it becomes evident that death by whatever means foul or otherwise, took place, not at the spot where the trunk was found, but at some house or place, near or distant, according to Dr. Hibbert [sic] twenty four hours prior to the finding, and according to Mr. Clark, Dr. Phillips' assistant, two days, so that under any circumstances the body must have lain twenty four hours in some house or place, before removal, and disposal, so that the place of disposal (no. 2) could be decided upon in the meantime.

Now from the surgeons it was ascertained, firstly that as the trunk was so full of blood death did not take place from hemorrhage, therefore death could not have taken place by cutting the throat, and the absence of the head prevents them saying that it was from violence to it (which appears to me most probable as the trunk contains no stabs to cause death).

What becomes most apparent is the absence of the attack upon the genitals as in the series of Whitechapel murders beginning at Bucks

Row and ending in Miller's Court. Certainly if it ... be a murder there was time enough for the murderer to cut off the head and limbs [and] there was time to mutilate as in the series mentioned. It appears rather to go side by side with the Rainham, Whitehall and Chelsea murders.

The question of how [it was] conveyed is in the region of theory, for if conveyed by cart, then no limit can be fixed, but if by hand about 250 yards [approximately 229 metres] would be the limit; consequently enquiry has been made to find any shed house or place within that limit, so as to ascertain who what, and how the occupier was engaged, but more especially to find the missing parts.

The enquiry is being continued so far as barrows, houses[,] sheds or places are concerned.[28]

Swanson established a defined search area in an attempt to find any type of premises where the perpetrator could kill and dismember a body, and his means of transporting the torso to an obscure site of which he had prior knowledge. It was a similar scenario to the depositing of the Whitehall torso and leg and implied that he did not have access to private outside space, otherwise he might have buried the body parts in his yard. Swanson's report was also significant in establishing that the killer removed the legs before the head, and providing, in an apparent contradiction to Bond's testimony, the medical opinion that the victim's throat was not cut. He confirmed the series of four Torso Murders as: Rainham, Whitehall, Battersea, and now Pinchin Street. In this case, no other body parts were found, and the torso was unusual in having its arms intact.

On the day after the murder, Commissioner Monro provided a thorough report to the Home Secretary Henry Matthews via his Private Secretary, John Satterfield Sandars. Like Swanson, he made a number of fact-based assumptions about the murder:

The constable discovered the body some what after 20 minutes past five on the morning of Tuesday ... He is positive that when he passed the spot about five the body was not there ... It may therefore be assumed that the body was placed where it was found some time between 5 & 5.30 a.m. of Tuesday the 11th.

Although the body was placed in the arch on Tuesday morning, the murder ... was not committed there nor then. There was almost no blood in the arch, and the state of the body itself showed that death took place abt. [about] 36 hours or more previously. This, then enables me to say that the woman was made away with probably on Sunday night, the 8th September. This was the date on which one of the previous Whitechapel murders was committed.

The body then must have been concealed, where the murder was committed during Sunday night, Monday, & Tuesday up till dawn. This leads to the inference that it was so concealed in some place to which the murderer had access, over which he had control, and from which he was anxious to remove the corpse. We may say then that the murder was committed probably in the house or lodging of the murderer, and that he conveyed the portion found to Pinchin Street to get rid of it from his lodging where the odour of decomposition would soon betray him.

Why did he take the trunk to Whitechapel and what does the finding of the body there show? If this is a fresh outrage by the Whitechapel murderer known by the horribly familiar nickname of Jack the Ripper the answer would not be difficult, altho' this murder, committed in the murderer's house would be a new departure from the system hitherto pursued by this ruffian. I am however inclined to believe that this case is not the work of the 'Ripper', [that] which has characterized the previous cases has been

a)   Death caused by cutting the throat,
b)   Mutilation
c)   Evisceration
d)   Removal of certain parts of the body
e)   Murder committed in the street, except in one instance in Dorset Street [the murder of Mary Jane Kelly].

In this last case there were distinct traces of furious mania, the murderer having plenty of time at his disposal slashed and cut the body in all directions, evidently under the influence of frenzy.

In the present case, as far as the medical evidence goes there is

a) Nothing to show that death was caused by cutting the throat.
b) There is no mutilation as in previous cases, altho' there is dismemberment.
c) There is no evisceration.
d) There is no removal of any portion of the organs of generation or intestines.
e) The murder was indubitably committed neither in the street, nor in the victim's house, but probably in the lodging of the murderer. Here where there was as in the previous case of murder in a house, plenty of time at the disposal of the murderer, there is no sign of frenzied mutilation of the body, but of deliberate & skilful dismemberment with a view to removal.

These are all very striking departures from the practice of the Whitechapel murderer, and if the body had been found elsewhere than in <u>Whitechapel</u> the supposition that death had been caused by the Ripper would probably not have been entertained.

But the body has been found in Whitechapel and there is a gash on the front part extending downwards to the organs of generation – and we have to account for these facts. I place little importance on the gash; it seems to me not to have been inflicted as in the previous cases. The inner coating of the bowel is hardly touched, and the termination of the cut towards the vagina looks almost as if the knife had slipped, and as if this portion of the wound had been accidental. The whole of the wound looks as if the murderer had intended to make a cut preparatory to removing the intestines in the process of dismemberment, & had then changed his mind ... It may also be that the gash was inflicted to give rise to the impression that this case was the work of the Whitechapel murderer & so divert attention from the real assassin.

As to how the body got to Whitechapel this is a great difficulty unless it be supposed that it was removed in some conveyance & placed where it was found, & unless it be supposed that the murderer, being other than the 'Ripper', had good knowledge of the locality ...

I am inclined to the belief that ... this is not the work of the Whitechapel murderer but of the hand which was concerned in the murders which are known as the Rainham mystery, the new Police buildings case, and the recent case in which portions of a female body (afterwards identified) were found in the Thames.[29]

The report was annotated by Henry Matthews: '*Thank Mr Monro for this report.*' Monro raised the intriguing possibility that the killer made a copycat slash on his victim's abdomen to incriminate Jack the Ripper. His musings about the discovery taking place in Whitechapel might indicate a suspicion that the body was deliberately placed in that suggestive location. Like Swanson, he named the same four murders as being in the Torso series.

Monro's opinions were verified by CID Chief Constable Sir Melville Macnaghten, who commented about the case and its place in the Thames Torso Murders series in his often-quoted *Memoranda*:

> On 10th Sept. '89 the naked body, with arms, of a woman was found wrapped in some sacking under a Railway arch in Pinchin St: the head & legs were never found nor was the woman ever identified. She had been killed at least 24 hours before the remains, (which had seemingly been brought from a distance,) were discovered.
>
> The stomach was split up by a cut, and the head and legs had been severed in a manner identical with that of the woman whose remains were discovered in the Thames, in Battersea Park, & on the Chelsea Embankment on 4th June of the same year; and these murders had no connection whatever with the Whitechapel horrors. The Rainham mystery in 1887, & the Whitehall mystery (when portions of a woman's body were found under what is now New Scotland Yard) in 1888 were of a similar type to the Thames and Pinchin St crimes.[30]

In the early stages of the police investigation, the London edition of the *New York Herald* reported that a man called John Cleary had visited their offices at five past one on the morning of Sunday, 8 September, with information about a murder in Backchurch Lane. Significantly, the police had already estimated that the murder took place on that day, although the body was deposited in the railway arch in the early morning of Tuesday, 10 September. The commissioner himself instructed Swanson to make a full inquiry, stating: 'We must try to get Cleary if feasible.'[31]

Police reports and press clippings about this apparently well-informed source take up several pages of the official Whitechapel Murders files. In truth, the story was a red herring and wasted days of police time. It was almost debunked on the same day it was reported, when Inspector Josiah Pattenden explained that:

> At 12.15 am 8th, P.C. 394H Millard found a woman ... in ... [Whitechapel] High Street, and conveyed her on an ambulance to the Whitechapel Infirmary, this may have been observed by the person who gave the information to Newspaper Office, and who for the purpose of reward exaggerated the case.[32]

But this account proved to be incorrect. On the hunt for a John Cleary, Swanson went on a wild goose chase around Drury Lane and the Strand looking for a Cleary whose name mutated into Leary and Lynch. 'Cleary' himself read the newspaper article, and realised that the police were looking for him under a false name and address, which he had given to the newspaper to avoid difficulties with his ex-wife. At 4.30 p.m. on Thursday, 12 September, he approached Sergeant Frank Froest at Charing Cross station, who took him to Scotland Yard, where he made a statement.

His real name was John Arnold. According to Arnold, on Saturday night, on his way home from the pub, 'a man dressed as a soldier in black uniform' came up behind him and said, 'Hurry up with your papers, another horrible murder.' When asked where, the man said, 'In Backchurch Lane.' As Arnold was a newspaper vendor for the Sunday edition of the *New York Herald*, he hurried to their office in the hope of a pay-out.[33]

On 12 September, the plot thickened with the unexpected arrival at Leman Street police station of Claude Mellor, the journalist who had found the right thigh of Elizabeth Jackson in Sir Percy Shelley's garden. Mellor too had read the article, and said that he 'attached suspicion upon an ex-compositor [typesetter]' called John Cleary, who formerly worked for *The Globe*.[34] Mellor risked being investigated as the perpetrator himself, fitting the profile of a suspect who repeatedly inserts himself into an ongoing investigation for the thrill of toying with the police and witnessing the trouble he is causing them.

His information was wired to Swanson at Scotland Yard, who was attempting to track down Arnold's so-called soldier, who he deduced might be a commissionaire, meaning a uniformed door attendant or messenger. An E Division (Holborn) officer was detailed to take Arnold to the headquarters of the commissionaires on the Strand to see if he recognised their uniform. No further information is recorded on the official files, and Arnold's information probably had no bearing on the case. Another red herring was a bloodstained petticoat found on a stretch of waste ground on Hooper Street. Doctor Clark was called to examine it, but concluded that it had been folded for use as a sanitary towel, and was stained with menstrual blood.[35]

The Pinchin Street victim's actual cause of death was never definitively stated. Doctor Phillips referred to loss of blood, and Clark to haemorrhage, meaning an escape of blood from a ruptured blood vessel. However, Swanson's report stated that there was insufficient blood loss for death to be caused by a cut throat, and that the cause of death was probably violence to the head.

The Hebbert report adds some further deductions to the medical evidence:

> The edges of the cuts showed that *a very sharp knife* had been used; all the cuts had been *made after death*.
>
> All the cuts were made from left to right except those separating the right thigh and right arm, which had been carried from right to left across the flexures of the joints, and so probably done by a right-handed man.
>
> The incisions were evidently made with design and were skilfully performed, as by a man who had some knowledge of the position of joints and the readiest means of separating limbs – such knowledge as a butcher or slaughterer would possess. They do not indicate a special anatomical knowledge of the human body.[36]

After the inquest verdict, Inspector Moore closed the case, noting that no further information had been obtained, nobody had been detained or liberated and that the missing portions of the remains had not been found. He advised that the unidentified body could go for burial, 'if it will not interfere with our being able to fit the head to the trunk, if we ever get it. Till all chance of recovery of the remaining parts of the body is gone it might be advisable to keep the trunk in spirits.'[37]

No further remains were found, and the victim was never identified. Only three named women were investigated by the police in connection with this case. The first, 19-year-old Emily Barker, had run away from Northampton after a row with her brother, and had appealed to a vicar in Bethnal Green for help. Her father travelled to Whitechapel to meet with H Division detectives. After a long interview, it was clear that his description of his daughter did not tally with the remains. Emily had 'a peculiar mark' which the torso was lacking. Her father returned home 'satisfied that the deceased was a stranger to him'.[38]

Rosina Lydia Smith was just 15 when her mother reported her missing from her home on the Old Kent Road. Her age and previous history of truanting ruled her out from further investigation by the police. Later records, such as her marriage certificate dated August 1893, demonstrate that she survived.[39]

A woman called Lydia Hart, who was 'well known as a dissipated creature', had been 'missing for three or four days'. Hart lived in a room in Ellen Street, one block north of Pinchin Street, and two minutes' walk away. The question of what happened to 'Lyddy', who liked to go 'on the drink', was answered when 'her two sons went in the company of a sympathetic little group to the local infirmary, and there to their intense relief found [her] ... She had gone on a bit of a spree, and thought it necessary to get medical treatment.'[40]

Having consulted Doctor Phillips, Inspector Moore commissioned a metal worker to make a tin vessel to store the remains in spirits. The vessel was placed in a black-painted wooden box with a metal plate stating:

> This case contains the
> body of a woman (unknown)
> found in Pinchin Street
> St. Georges-in-the-East
> 10th Septr./89 [41]

The burial, on Saturday, 5 October, at the East London Cemetery in Plaistow, was witnessed only by Moore.

It is possible that the Pinchin Street murder was avoidable. Approximately a month before the Pinchin Street murder, when remanded in custody for another crime, the author's prime suspect as the Torso Killer applied for bail from Thames Police Court at Stepney. A lenient magistrate granted it, and released him.

# 6

# Profiling the Thames Torso Killer

We grasp. And what is left in our hands at the end? A shadow.

Sherlock Holmes, from 'The Adventure
of the Retired Colourman' by Sir Arthur Conan Doyle

The Pinchin Street case introduces new evidence about the killer's method of killing and disposing of that body. It provides a reasonable level of detail about a woman who represented his preferred victim type, without answering the question: *Who was she?* According to Charles Hebbert, the Pinchin Street victim had distinguishing features on two fingers of her right hand:

> On the first joint of the dorsal surface of the right little finger is a small round hardening, not amounting to a corn, and a similar but smaller hardening on the inner side of the back of the first joint of the right ring finger ...
>
> There are no marks indicating any occupation, except that on the right little finger is a small circular hardening, but no corn. The mark is such as might be made by writing.[1]

Despite the observation that she might have used a pen, it is more likely that the woman was a manual labourer, and possibly illiterate. Given the marks on her fingers, and a similar type of rubbing on her elbows, she might have been a spinner or rope factory worker. Spitalfields, Whitechapel and the docks housed many such trades. Frost Brothers' rope factory at 340–342 Commercial Road was near Pinchin Street, employing women recorded as joining their male co-workers in the 1889 strike. That strike might put the victim at liberty in early September 1889.

Women workers tied themselves in sacking for safety reasons, to prevent their clothes from being pulled into a factory machine.[2] This might explain the mark around the torso's waist, if made before death. If made after death, it could have been made by a rope used to tie it into a sack for disposal. Another possible explanation for the 'rope mark' is the use of corsets or stays. In an inquest held in 1889, a female servant was found to have died 'from pressure round the waist' caused by a 'remorselessly buckled' belt worn beneath her stays.[3]

Despite her worn elbows and skin hardening that could have been caused by a finger-thimble, she cannot have been a dressmaker. According to Detective Inspector Moore, who by then had managed to find the source of its fabric, her chemise was 'made of Horrocks' calico ... hand-sewn, and stitched in an inferior manner'.[4] She is not identifiable as a purchaser of Horrockses, Crewdson and Company calico. In 1887, the company had offices in Preston, Manchester and London's Love Lane, meaning that the woman could easily have purchased her chemise fabric from multiple outlets in London. A final intriguing question is whether she might have been a book-folder, like Jessie Miller, the victim of a violent attack discussed in a later chapter.

Another piece of physical evidence was the partly digested plums in the victim's stomach. They might have been sourced from anywhere in London, and were probably scrumped, or pilfered. The Southwark Park area, where my prime suspect's family the Cricks lived, had plum trees. A more likely place to pick up some fruit for free was Charlton, 4 miles further east, the location of several orchards and market gardens. In the hours before her death, the Pinchin Street victim might have been a carefree young woman on the deck of a boat, reaching up to overhanging branches for their late summer fruit.

In the lack of available facts, we will never be able to identify any of the Torso Killer's unidentified victims. Their killer picked them up on the fly, and deliberately moved them away from their usual haunts to deflect suspicion. The Pinchin Street victim's profile is closer to that of Elizabeth Jackson than the Whitehall victim, who was differentiated by her dress and standard of grooming. The perpetrator was able to mix with a range of women, and not only as a possible client for sex. And he treated them roughly. This victim had extensive defence wounds on her arms, and, like Jessie Miller, massive bruising on her back.

In his summary of all four cases, Hebbert observed that the killer had learned from experience by the time of the Pinchin Street murder, and separated the bones more cleanly:

> In the first two cases the vertebrae had been sawn through, in the third the sixth cervical vertebra was sawn through, but the dorsal and lumbar vertebrae were separated by cutting through the intervertebral substance, and in the fourth the intervertebral substance in the neck was cut, showing that the man was aware of the projecting anterior lip on the under surface of the vertebra, and suggesting that he was becoming more expert in his work, at the same time indicating that he was not necessarily a good anatomist, but rather a man accustomed to cut up bodies quickly in somewhat large pieces.[5]

The Pinchin Street case indicates the sequence in which the killer dismembered the body. We know that the killer cut off the woman's legs before her head, suggesting that he was operating in a confined space. He must have run out of time in both that instance and in the Whitehall case, when the dismemberment was also incomplete, but the arms and pelvis were removed. If he had followed the sequence, his final cut would be across the bottom of the breastbone, dividing the torso into three parts as in the Rainham and Battersea cases. However, it is worth noting that his sequence of disposal was unlikely to mirror the dismemberment. He might have disposed of the head first, as the most incriminating item. Its weight would sink it to the bottom of the Thames.

This case again suggests that the killer was a local tradesman. In an echo of statements about the New Scotland Yard building site, no stranger would have found his way to the Pinchin Street railway arch.

The stoneyard at the back of the arch was used by C. Hinchcliffe and Company 'for dressing and storing granite blocks for road-making purposes, and also for preparing flagstones as pavement'.[6] It was customary that most manual trades began work at six o'clock in the morning. Any working man would have known that there was nobody on site when he dumped the torso.

Pinchin, Johnson and Company had a significant oil and colour works on Cable Street, backing onto Pinchin Street, which was named after its founder William Pinchin. A colourman, or paint dealer, appeals as a suspect, as does the company's geographical spread from the Albert Oil Mills in Hammersmith to Pinchin Wharf at Ratcliffe and its transport capability on land and water. Sherlock Holmes exposed a murderous colourman, who gassed his younger wife and her lover in his strongroom and used his own green paint on the woodwork to disguise the smell. Yet no credible suspect can be linked to that trade.

Next under consideration comes the 'coalie', a bogeyman covered with coal dust, whose face was as obscured and smudged as his identity. The coal docks on the Regent's Canal were used as dump sites for body parts belonging to the Rainham victim. The concept of a coal bargeman being the killer extends convincingly to the fuel requirements of Whitehall departments and mansion houses, and beyond to the industrial wharves of Battersea. The railway company that owned the Pinchin Street railway viaduct stored a significant supply of coal in that immediate area, in a depot occupying the space between numbers 32 and 8 Backchurch Lane, and extending into Frederick Street. Frederick Street originally ran in an L-shape southwards from roughly the middle of Pinchin Street and then west under the railway viaduct. Anyone in the coal trade would know where the main coal stores were held. Local people would be aware of the regular deliveries to and from that site, and make purchases from the coal shop based at 51 Cable Street.

Commissioner Monro's report offered the suggestion that the murder and storage of the body took place in the killer's house or lodgings, but he had 'great difficulty' in working out how it was conveyed to Whitechapel 'and placed where it was found'. Monro's questions can be addressed using Swanson's 'region of theory', referring to the maximum distance that the killer would choose to travel by cart, or on foot, possibly using a barrow. It must be convenient to him to deposit at that location. It must be close to where he is storing the body. It must not point to his own identity, home or premises, which might be on the opposite side of the river.

A contemporary press interview with an unnamed detective offers some solutions in suggesting that the murder took place elsewhere in London, and that, post-dismemberment, the killer moved the body to store it in local premises, before transporting it by cart to nearby Pinchin Street:

> I am convinced in my own mind that the actual murder did not take place in East London, but more probably in the west, the west central or the south districts. The body would of course in that case have had to be carried from there down to the East End; and of this I am pretty sure, too, that it was brought in some vehicle – probably in an innocent-looking box or bale, and deposited in some house or place in the East End on Saturday night or Sunday. Had it been brought on Monday, the finding of the body on Tuesday might possibly have resulted in the arrival of the box or bale being looked at with suspicion, and hence it is that I place its arrival here on Saturday or Sunday.
>
> There need have been nothing suspicious about the covering for the body, whatever it was, for the legs and head, I imagine, were removed prior to the body being brought here, while, as decomposition had scarcely set in even when the body was found, there need have been no suspicious smell. The trunk or bale couldn't have been carried away very well by a man; it must have been conveyed in some kind of a vehicle, and it is upon that clue that we intend to work first.[7]

Sightings were reported of a man carrying a sack, firstly at 8 p.m. on the Monday evening on Christian Street, and secondly just an hour before the torso was discovered:

> Then came the story of a man who said he had seen another man with a heavy bag of something on his back, about four o'clock. He was questioned, but his information was not important, the police feeling confident that the body was brought nearly to the spot in a vehicle of some kind.[8]

The suggestion is that the perpetrator used a barrow, if not a cart, to transport the torso. It is not possible to state where the murder location was, whether that was the same place as where the body was stored, and how and when the torso was moved into the railway arch.

Despite the challenge of the killer's mobility, the key to his identity lies in his movements and timings. Other researchers have focused on the drops in the tidal river, but the drops on land and in the Regent's Canal – spots that he needed to visit in person – can be plotted firmly onto a map. The defined area almost fits within today's London Transport Zone 1, pushing into Zone 2 at Whitechapel and Battersea on its eastern and southern sides. If the murders were contemporary, police would conclude that the perpetrator was a taxi driver. Owing to his mobility on water, he must have been a river worker, not a hackney cab driver. The cab stands were deliberately placed at a distance from the river to avoid direct competition with the watermen.

A waterman would ferry passengers up, down and across the river, offering a taxi service by boat. Such a person might also be a lighterman, operating on the busiest part of the river between Ratcliffe and Wapping. A summertime killer, he worked during the day and was free to pick up women in his evenings, when he might sleep on a barge overnight to guard its load. He had to dispose of their bodies before 5 a.m., when his working day started.

The weather and tide reports assist in estimating when the other women's deaths occurred. The date of the Whitehall murder must be around the date of the scrap of newspaper found with the torso: Friday, 24 August 1888, four nights after full moon. In a year of 'very little summer', the end of August was warmer with a southerly wind, although it continued to be showery. On Friday, 24 August, high water at London Bridge was early, at 3.32 a.m. and 3.50 p.m. The killer must have run out of time and missed the tide, failing to cut the torso into three parts and being left with body parts that were too buoyant to be put in the river at low tide.

Elizabeth Jackson was killed and dismembered overnight on Monday, 3 June 1889. The weather was changeable, with thunderstorms and heavy rain. The morning high tide was at 4.31 a.m., perfect timing for a morning shift-worker to dispose of her remains in the river.

The date favoured by the police for the Pinchin Street murder was Sunday, 8 September 1889. The weather was fine with moderate easterly and north-easterly breezes. The morning tide was unusually early, at 1.28 a.m. It was also extraordinarily low. On Wednesday, 11 September, it was so low that the saloon steamer *Alexandra* ran aground and sank just off Old Swan Pier, London Bridge.[9] The Pinchin Street killer must have missed the early tide and dumped the torso, as the most buoyant body part, on land.

It is apparent that, although the killer did not plan around the tides, he used them to best effect after the event. He killed impulsively and then had to work out a plan based on his knowledge of the local terrain, and the river. He must have been a bargeman, lighterman or waterman who used vessels that he did not own to kill, dismember and store body parts. In those trades, Sunday nights were almost never worked.[10]

The Thames Torso Killer was a man who operated on the water and who had a criminal record of violence against women. A man who fits that profile as the author's prime suspect was active in the 1880s, when he was accused of attempted murder and rape, and convicted of the latter. He was quoted by one of his victims as saying: '*I intend to settle you, as I have done other women that have been found in the Thames if you make a noise. If you keep quiet you will be perfectly safe.*'[11]

His name was James Crick, but was his threat of actual murder?

Working on the hypothesis that Crick was the Thames Torso Killer, the epicentre of this investigation moves east from Battersea to Horsleydown, today's Butler's Wharf. On 23 September 1862, James Crick was born at 1 Herold Place,[12] an alley that no longer exists in the vicinity of Jacob's Island, a Thames-side creek immortalised by Charles Dickens in *Oliver Twist* as the place where the murderous criminal Bill Sikes died, and featuring 'every repulsive lineament of poverty, every loathsome indication of filth, rot and garbage'.[13] James was the youngest of five children, the oldest two being half-brothers from his mother's first marriage.

James Crick's same-named father was a stevedore, a dockworker who loaded and unloaded ships. He was born and raised in Thame, Oxfordshire, where his first recorded job was as a cowman for the publican and bricklayer Robert Battin at the Nag's Head on the High Street. By 1857, aged 25, he had moved to Horsleydown and changed occupation. On 8 June 1857, he married an Irish widow named Ellen Coghlen née Donovan at St John's Church, Tooley Street. Ellen and her first husband John came from County Cork, where Arthur, the elder of their two sons, was born. Their second son, John, was born in Horsleydown. Five years later, John Coghlen Senior died.

By 1871, Arthur and John had left home, and James and Ellen Crick had two surviving children, Charlotte and James Junior. Another son had died aged 6. The Cricks relocated to the insalubrious location of 20 Clink Street,[14] near the former site of an infamous bone-rotting prison, hence the expression for a gaolbird, 'he's in the clink'. Another house move took them back towards Jacob's Island, and on 14 November 1878, aged 53, James Crick Senior died of bronchitis at 12 Horsleydown Lane.[15] His widow Ellen made the mark of a cross to represent her signature on his death certificate, demonstrating that she was illiterate.

In 1880, Charlotte Crick married Charles Sumner, who like her brother James was an apprentice waterman and lighterman to her older half-brother Arthur. Arthur, who had taken on the surname Crick, became a substitute father figure and witnessed the Sumners' marriage. By 1881, the young couple were living with her mother Ellen and brother James at 6 Barnham Street,[16] which ran south from Tooley Street behind today's City Hall. The men operated from Horsleydown Old Stairs, adjacent to the southern end of the yet-to-be-constructed Tower Bridge. The vantage point of their pitch at those stairs next to the Anchor Brewery building overlooked Shad Thames and any passing female.

Aged 17, James Crick was starting to make his reputation as a strong competitive rower. In August 1881, he won the Metropolitan and South-Eastern Thames (Bermondsey) Regatta's prize of a coat and badge,[17] and in August 1884, at the end of his apprenticeship, competed in the prestigious race for Doggett's Coat and Badge. In his Will, dated 1721, the comedian and author Thomas Doggett made provision for an annual race on the Thames to be rowed by six young watermen for the prize of a fine red coat with a silver badge weighing about 12oz and depicting the white horse of the House of Hanover, representing Liberty.[18]

The course of the race covered most of the terrain of the Torso Murders. It was originally rowed against the tide from the Old Swan pub at London Bridge to the White Swan at Chelsea. By the date of Crick's participation in the race, it was rowed with the incoming tide and, the White Swan having been demolished, its finish was marked by a flag boat at the Albert Suspension Bridge. The starting point was ½ mile west of Horsleydown.

James Crick was noted to weigh 10 stone, a considerable gain since he won the Bermondsey Coat and Badge in August 1881, when he was only 6 stone 7lb. Each man wore a different coloured vest to distinguish them; Crick wore yellow, the coward's colour. The six scullers were 'fractious' at the starting post. It took almost thirty minutes, and 'innumerable threats of disqualification' to get them off. James Crick finished fifth, coming in seven minutes after the winner, at 42 minutes and 42 seconds. His cash prize was £1 11s 6d.[19]

Over the next few years, Crick continued to profit from his sporting endeavours. He won second prize in the 1882 Tower of London, St Botolph and Wapping Regatta.[20] In August 1887, he won the prize boat *Ally Sloper* at the Horsleydown Regatta, afterwards challenging 'any below-bridge man [operating below London Bridge] at 8 st. 4 lb. [approximately 53 kilograms], for £25 or £50, a-side, in best boats, from Putney to Mortlake. An answer, with a deposit at the office of The Sportsman, will ensure a match. First come first served.'[21] The extortionate stake was put up by a group of subscribers.

Crick's boat was named *Ally Sloper* after the popular cartoon character, a working-class rogue who was enormously popular at that time, whose antics were serialised in a weekly comic paper. The annual Bankside Regatta had its own Ally Sloper impersonator mingling with the crowds:

> He would have a bottle labelled 'Unsweetened' [gin] protruding from the coat pocket, an umbrella of the gamp variety [meaning large and awkwardly wrapped], and a vermillion coloured nose. He would do some clowning along Bankside being followed by hundreds of kiddies, then on to ... blow kisses to the girls and encourage the rowers by offering the 'Unsweetened'.[22]

A later incident demonstrates that Crick was himself a fan of the cartoon character. Sloper had a pretty daughter, Tootsie Sloper, featured as a pin-up modelling a new outfit each week; Crick called one of his rape victims 'Tootsie Sloper' and made her laugh.

A year later, the following advertisement was placed in response to one of Crick's challenges:

> Hearing so much of the rowing abilities of James Crick (of Horselydown), a gentleman will match Robert Tizzard ... to row him in skiffs from London Bridge to Surrey Canal Dock Buoy, for from £2 to £5 a-side.[23]

The outcome of the race was not published. Crick clearly had a competitive streak as an opportunistic risk-taker hungry to prove himself. As a waterman, he would also have competed with other watermen at their plying places on the river stairs, to persuade would-be passengers to take his boat instead of another.

The following is an evocative account of how the lightermen's trade created their own world:

> We young lightermen were rather clannish and somewhat despised the 'landsman' or 'linen draper'. The chief topic was the river or work on the river. This had a language of its own so I presume that our shore friends were often fed up by attempting to listen to an account of an incident in the day's work given in the vernacular.
>
> You either ...'saved tide' or 'lost tide'; 'went clear [when passing another vessel]' or 'athwart hawse' [across its stem]. Arches were called 'bridge holes' or 'working locks'. A Brentford man if bound to Brentford would be going 'right out'. A Battersea man would be bound 'up home'. A coal lighterman would be going 'down the Derrick' [back to the cargo lifter] ... Back-slang was often used, cabin becoming *nibac* and so on.
>
> A large number of lightermen went by nicknames, all very apt, either featuring physical or psychological defects or assets, such as Tubby, Podge, Narrow, Rasher, Dabtoe, Winkle-eye, Hoppy, Humpy and Wiggie ...
>
> 'A full roadun' was a week's work including Sunday and nights. A 'thgin' (tidgeon) was an easy night; Carman's night or Early Turn Out was to be ordered for 2/- [shillings] at 5 a.m. between the radius

of Victoria dock and Nine Elms. Tarpaulins were cloths, extra rope a warp, oars paddles and a pump was the organ ...

'Stand hard' is a caution to look out and stand firm, or crouch, holding on tight if the blow is going to be heavy. The 'ditch' is the river, 'fell in the ditch' is falling overboard. 'Gutsers', 'sidewinders', 'chimers', 'stern butt' (always a more vulgar term is used) and 'glancing blow' were terms describing blows to craft either by collision with another craft, or themselves colliding with a fixed object.[24]

This account confirms that early shifts began at 5 a.m., which synchronises with the early dumping times of the Battersea and Pinchin Street remains.

Young lightermen, flush when they were paid at the end of the week, would 'hit the town'. Apart from the pubs, the music halls were popular, and Crick might have frequented 'the Old Vic Thursday night, Gattis Music Hall Friday night'[25] and others, including his local, Wilton's Music Hall off Cable Street, for a big night out on a Saturday. Wherever he went, he would have treated a pretty girl to a drink and maybe a sixpenny entrance ticket, which was worth tuppence at the bar.

On 1 May 1886, James Crick married local girl Rosina Caroline Gorsuch, a bricklayer's daughter, at St James's Church, Bermondsey.[26] A lighterman aged 24, he signed the certificate neatly and confidently, as did Rosina. At 25, Rosina was a year older than her new husband. They were both living at 67 Layard Road, off Southwark Park Road, due south of Cherry Garden Street from the Thames. Their elder daughter, named Rosina after her mother, was born on 27 February 1887 at 35 Horsleydown Lane.[27] A younger daughter, Daisy Sarah Annie, arrived just over a year later, on 25 April 1888, when the family were living at 8 Gainsford Street,[28] two blocks north of Tooley Street.

Seven weeks after Crick's wedding, the construction of Tower Bridge began. The Watermen's Company had opposed the project run by the Tower Bridge Company as a threat to their livelihood, and received financial compensation.[29] Taking eight years to complete, the ongoing works were supplied by watermen and lightermen, while causing some obstruction to river traffic. The lightermen were employed by lighterage companies, who typically owned a fleet of steam tugs, lighters and canal barges.

Lightermen had a reputation for supplementing their earnings by being light-fingered, operating in the hazy divide between theft and taking stuff home that nobody wanted, or would miss. Examples included taking home spoiled goods such as overripe fruit and vegetables, and pilfering from their cargoes:

> The majority of men carried 'screws' [gimlets], and as cargoes were often wine, rum and gin, the drink was cheap. Tapping a cask could be done without showing any evidence from the outside.[30]

For a minority, their trade enabled more serious theft and smuggling. In James Crick's case, any minor criminal activities extended to rape and possibly murder.

Crick's physical and sexual aggression might have started with his adolescent growth spurt. Like Ripper suspect Hyam Hyams, the first victim of his violence was his wife. The Ripper also attacked his own mother, albeit accidentally, while by contrast Ellen Crick would reveal herself in an 1889 court case to be more of a bruiser than abused. The Criminal Registers contain the following physical description of James Crick:

**Height:** 5′ 7″.
**Complexion:** Fresh.
**Hair:** Brown (thin).
**Eyes:** Blue.
**Distinguishing marks:**
  Tattoos: Initials J.C. on left forearm.
  Scars on third left finger, on left thumb, back of right hand, on right forearm, bridge of nose, and each side forehead.
  Mole on right of face and two right of back.[31]

From his rowing exploits, we know that Crick weighed 10 stone, rendering him of average height and build. His sporting prowess proved that he was of above average strength. His tattoos, scars and moles, in addition to his visibility as a regular waterman and lighterman, made him recognisable. His tattoo was probably self-inked. He was listed in criminal records as being of the Roman Catholic faith.[32] Crick's level of literacy was noted as 'imperfect', meaning that he could read and write at a basic level.[33]

James's older half-brother, Arthur Crick, had a notable criminal record and was aged 18 on his first offence in June 1863. With an accomplice, Henry Fowler, he was convicted at Southwark police court of stealing five bags of coffee worth £20 from a warehouse on Butler's Wharf. Local grocer George Long was convicted of receiving the stolen goods, and all three men were sentenced to twelve calendar months' hard labour at Wandsworth Prison. Like his brother James, Arthur Crick could read and write imperfectly.[34]

Crick's next detected crime delivered a more severe sentence. On the afternoon of Saturday, 9 September 1865, he and a 16-year-old accomplice, James Sullivan, broke into the Nash and Hicks warehouse off Tooley Street and stole a large quantity of hops. After a tip-off from the proprietor of the Telegraph beerhouse in Free School Street, who was also landlord to Sullivan, Crick and his wife, police found several bags of hops in their room, marked 'Nash and Hicks'. The case went before a magistrate at Southwark police court, and then to trial before Mr Thomas Tilson at the Surrey Sessions.

Crick's defence was that he knew nothing of the theft, as he was at work from 6 p.m. on the Saturday until 9 a.m. on the Sunday, and that what his landlord and fellow lodger had testified about seeing him and Sullivan carrying the bags into their room was 'all false'. Sullivan had said that a man had asked him to mind a horse and cart, and he had taken the bags upstairs to his own room 'for safety'. Their lawyer urged that the bags of hops had not been fully identified as stolen, but the jury returned a guilty verdict. Crick, then using the name of Patrick Coghlan, was sentenced to seven years' penal servitude at Wandsworth Prison, and Sullivan who had no previous convictions, to twelve months' imprisonment with hard labour.[35]

Crick either went straight or was more careful on his release from jail, as his next appearance before the law involved a civil case in the summer of 1880. The case of *Crick versus Watts* went before Lord Chief Justice Cockburn at the Nisi Prius Court of the King's Bench Division. Barrister Francis John Sims represented Crick. Although the facts of the case are not well recorded in the press, it is clear that the Crick family knew the law sufficiently to protect themselves, or even to exploit a loophole in it. On several occasions, they were reliant on the Watermen's Company to bolster their credibility and support their version of events. And yet again, Crick had someone to back him up, whether a family member or an accomplice.

In lieu of debts, Rotherhithe boat-builder Walter Watts had seized several boats belonging to Arthur Crick. Crick argued that the ownership of the boats was entirely vested in his mother Ellen Crick. Noticing some laughter as his manner of giving evidence was causing amusement in court, he said, 'You must excuse my roughness, I was rather roughly brought up.' This elicited more laughter, which turned sour with the Judge's reprimand: 'If you give me so insolent an answer again you will go somewhere you won't like.' Crick was quick to apologise: 'I beg your pardon, sir, I hope I am not insolent. I did not mean to be …'[36] For once, Crick won his case. Although Watts was considered to have acted in good faith, the evidence of the Watermen's Company licences was against him.

In early 1881, Crick went before Mr Franklin Lushington at Stepney's Thames Police Court on a charge of carrying more passengers than his boat was licensed for. Lushington was the magistrate who, in December 1888, charged Ripper suspect Hyam Hyams with being a 'wandering lunatic' in a sequence of events that led to his permanent admission to an asylum. Crick was in his usual combative form, as reported in a press article entitled 'The River Lawyer'. Inspector Charles King of the river police had witnessed Crick carrying ten passengers, when he was licensed for eight. After cross-examining the police officer 'with considerable skill', Crick concluded that:

> he considered the summons was bad, as the police really had no *locus standi* [right to bring the action] … [as] … the nominal prosecutor, Inspector King was not a member or constable of the Watermen's Company, and he was not really the party aggrieved; secondly he was not plying 'for gain or hire' within the meaning of the words of the statute.

Crick's points were cleverly made, implying that it was for the Watermen's Company, not the police, to enforce the terms of his licence, and presumably arguing that these were not paying passengers, but people to whom he had given a ride. Lushington was not swayed by his arguments, fining Crick 30s and costs.[37]

In August 1882, a 'Patrick Coghlan', described as a 'powerful-looking' young man, was convicted at Southwark police court of assaulting three M Division police constables while helping a companion to resist arrest, and, earlier on the same day, of assaulting a policeman at London Bridge railway station. Coghlan (who was probably Arthur Crick using that name) and another man were each sentenced to two months' hard labour.[38]

A case of tobacco smuggling was brought against Crick in January 1883, again at Southwark police court, this time before Magistrate Wyndham Slade, in his own name with his alias stated as Thompson, possibly a mishearing of the name Coghlan. Detective Sergeant Samuel Howard testified that he was passing along Cherry Garden Street on the evening of Thursday, 25 January, when he saw Arthur Crick 'coming from the waterside with his coat hanging on his left arm. Perceiving that it looked rather bulky, he stopped him and asked him what he had in the coat, when he replied, "Only a little tobacco."' Howard took him to Bermondsey police station and 'found concealed in different parts of the coat 22 packets of tobacco, each weighing 1 lb [pound], and in his pockets 2 lbs more'.

Inspector George Read stated that he was also an officer of the Customs and Excise, and was on duty when Arthur Crick was brought in. He 'saw the tobacco in 1 lb packages similar to those brought from Germany and Hamburg by smugglers. He found it to weigh 24 lbs, and it was of foreign manufacture.'

In order to calculate the fine, Slade asked what the treble value and duty of the tobacco amounted to. The answer was £19 14s. In his defence, Crick said he found the tobacco on his boat, and thought he might as well have it as anybody else. The magistrate applied the fine, or one month's imprisonment in lieu.[39]

On Friday, 23 September 1892, at the City of London Court, Crick and his fellow plaintiff Burgess failed to be recompensed for damage done to their boats by the steamer *Asia* 'causing a swell on the river by going at an improper speed, and dashing the boats on to the beach, damaging their sides very seriously and breaking the stern posts'. The judge, Mr Julian Robins, found that the evidence was not sufficient to show that the damage was caused by the *Asia*, and he gave judgment for its owner, the Hull Steam Fishing and Ice Company, with costs.[40] In a later test case, Crick won 3s 6d plus costs for damage caused to his skiff by the swell from a passing steamer.[41]

The earliest mention of any unlawful activity by the author's prime suspect as the Thames Torso Killer, Arthur's brother James Crick, was an allegation by his wife of assault. It was reported in a local newspaper article under the heading: 'And only married a year!' The case went before Mr James Sheil at Southwark police court on Thursday, 12 May 1887. Rosina Crick, who was described as a respectable-looking woman, testified as follows:

> On Wednesday night she came home, after twelve o'clock, having been out to look for her husband, there being at the time no food in the house. It was no uncommon occurrence for her to have to do this, as he stayed out night after night. When she came home she asked him for some money, but he refused to give her any, and commenced throwing her work [assumed to be needlework] – which she had to do to procure the common necessaries of life – about the room. He then stamped on it, and did other acts which tended to destroy it.
>
> She caught hold of him to restrain him, when he kicked her twice. Her screams brought the police. They had only been married a twelvemonth on the 1st of this month, and they had one child. She had been subjected throughout the whole of the year to his brutality.
>
> She had not the least idea how much he earned, as he never gave her any money. He frequently left her without food for days and days, and her life was a perfect misery.[42]

The article concluded: 'The prisoner brought a counter charge of violence against his wife; and Mr Sheil remanded him for a week for inquiries.' The application of pressure using classic bullying tactics worked. Rosina did not appear at the next hearing, and the charges were dropped. Crick was released from custody to continue his usual activities.

Crick's behaviour cannot be excused, but his being out all night can. Night work was freely available for a lighterman. As one man explained to a newspaper reporter, 'The pay for a day was 5s [shillings] 4d [pence] and the pay for a night was 4s. Many jobs that could have been, and ought to have been done by day have been relegated to the night-time because they come a little cheaper.'[43] Goods were transported along the river by night, catching any late tides, with barges mooring up outside the docks until opening time. The lighterman would make himself as comfortable as he could: 'He lights a bit of fire in the cabin, tries to dry himself ... he stretches himself on the boards, perhaps with a lump of coal under a bit of paper for a pillow, and gets a bit of sleep with one ear open and on the alert should anybody set foot on the lighter.'[44]

An overnight shift on a barge fits neatly with a pattern of nocturnal criminal activities. The same bargeman observed: 'I have often come down with a barge by myself at one or two o'clock in the morning, and for miles I haven't seen a soul under way.'[45] It was not reported in any of the Torso cases whether any of the newspapers, sacking or clothes remnants found with the body parts were stained with any indication of a barge's load, such as coal dust. Nor can the deduction be made that a killer who used a newspaper to wrap remains was literate. An article immediately below the account of Rosina's assault by her husband, dating from the previous day, reads: 'On Wednesday morning the lower portion of the trunk of a female was washed ashore on the bank of the Thames at Rainham, Essex.'[46] Had Crick's history of violence escalated to murder?

# 7

# The non-fatal attack on Jessie Miller, Monday, 1 July 1889

Who, or why, or which, or what,
Is the Akond of Swat?

> From 'The Akond of Swat' by Edward Lear
> [An Akond or Akhond was a religious potentate]

In the summer of 1889, James Crick's luck began to run dry, or at least trickle through his fingers. The hypothesis that Crick could have been the Thames Torso Killer relies on charges brought against him in two documented criminal cases. The first case featured the improbable appearance of the Shah of Persia, Naser al-Din, who arrived in London on an official visit on Monday, 1 July 1889 – the same date as one of the inquest hearings into the death of Elizabeth Jackson and nine weeks before the Pinchin Street murder. Apart from his wife, the first known victim of Crick's violent behaviour was 31-year-old Jessie Miller, a young woman who had separated from her husband and was down on her luck. What better way to spend a summer's day than to witness the spectacular arrival of a foreign potentate on the River Thames?

The Shah's first visit to England was in 1873, when Queen Victoria had appointed him a Knight of the Order of the Garter. A representative of a friendly power, the purpose of his missions was not only diplomatic, but to collect 'all information and gathering experiences, which can be valuable for the Persian government and nation'.[1] A moderniser, he was keen to acquire Western technology and secure inward investment through the sale of industrial concessions.

Aged 57, and sporting a magnificent moustache, the Shah was a sight to behold, in a gorgeously decorated uniform frock coat, fez, and an extremely long ceremonial sword that must have hampered his movements.[2] His visit was one of the chief events on the river in the 1880s, other than the Oxford and Cambridge Boat Race, then called the Varsity Race, and Doggett's Coat and Badge, in which Crick had come fifth in 1884.

The Shah's entry into London involved two royal yachts. He travelled from Antwerp to Gravesend on *Victoria and Albert*, while the British royal party headed by the Prince of Wales, the future King Edward VII, sailed on *Duke of Edinburgh* from Westminster Bridge towards Gravesend to meet him. The timings lacked the military precision of today's royal events, as the Shah's vessel arrived early, and had to moor off Tilbury Fort for over an hour until the other yacht arrived. He then joined the royal party on *Duke of Edinburgh*, which departed for Westminster Bridge to a cannon salute 'surrounded by a crowd of pleasure steamers, tugs, &c., all gaily dressed with bunting ... All the bridges were crowded with people, and the embankment was lined by a crowd about seven deep all the way from Blackfriars to Westminster.'[3]

The remainder of the journey was not without incident, as the royal yacht was escorted to Westminster by fast torpedo boats, 'whose Commanders got in rather a pickle in their navigation of this part of the river'.[4] Westminster itself was packed with onlookers; as the Shah disembarked, he was welcomed by the Duke of Cambridge and other dignitaries in a marquee before transferring to the state carriage to Buckingham Palace:

> The Shah reached Westminster Pier at ten minutes to six ... the scene was an exciting one. The bridge itself and all the approaches were densely crowded. Troops lined the whole route, and cordons of police cut off all the approaches. All traffic was suspended. Near the marquee which had been erected on the Embankment the crowding was serious. Several slight conflicts occurred between the police

and the onlookers, and one or two cases of pocket-picking created momentary distraction ...

The Shah appeared to be deeply impressed with all he saw. On the steamer he carried on an animated conversation, and continued it until after he had landed, every now and again acknowledging with profound salaams [bows] the salutations of the crowd ...

The Royal carriages [were] in waiting close by ... Along the Mall dense crowds had assembled, and at the gates of the Palace a considerable force of police was employed to maintain order. In the Palace itself the Shah was received by the Princess of Wales and her three daughters.[5]

He was later received by Queen Victoria at Windsor Castle as part of a comprehensive programme of visits to the great and the good.

Joining the crowds of sightseers at Westminster on that summer afternoon, Jessie Miller must have been pleased to be plucked from the throng and invited to join two men and other passengers in their boat. Their plan was to row downriver to meet the royal yacht as it passed, and the boat provided a good vantage point. What actually happened was a rape and attempted murder, which, although a horrible experience for Miller, put Crick firmly in the sights of the river police as personified by Detective Inspector John Regan.

On that Monday, the Shah was due to arrive at 5 p.m. on the royal yacht at Westminster Pier, but in fact landed shortly before 6 p.m. He spent a short time in the marquee on the embankment before proceeding by carriage to Buckingham Palace. It must have been at around 7 p.m. when the boat containing Crick, his friend Thomas Ruffeitt, Jessie Miller and the other passengers returned to Horsleydown and everyone got off.

In an interval on land, after drinks at several public houses, possibly including the Anchor Tap on Horsleydown Lane, Miller and Rosina Crick, who had joined her husband, had an argument. James Crick left with his wife, after agreeing a pick-up time with Ruffeitt, who was still drinking with Miller. At the agreed time, Ruffeitt and Miller returned to the boat and Ruffeitt rowed less than 200m down to George's Stairs to pick up Crick. It must have between 9 and 10 p.m., starting to get dark before sunset at 10.30 p.m. Luckily for Miller, it was low tide.

Ruffeitt was rowing northbound across the river as Crick raped Miller in the bottom of the boat. They were off Tunnel Stairs by the Tower of London when watermen Webb and Edward Jones heard Miller's screams, saw her go into the river, and rescued her. She was a short distance from the side, where the water was about 5ft deep. After an unsuccessful pursuit of Crick and Ruffeitt, the watermen landed Miller on the north side of the river. She was taken by an H Division police constable to St George-in-the-East Workhouse Infirmary. Her name was the last in the admission register on that date, although no time was recorded. The reason for her admission by the master was the same as that given for the other women listed: she was destitute. She was discharged on the following day.[6]

There is no record of how the police identified Crick and Ruffeitt as the culprits. The most likely answer is that the watermen Webb and Jones knew Crick. Alternatively, as Crick and Ruffeitt had visited several local pubs with Jessie Miller in tow, presumably eyewitnesses could name them. On the afternoon of Sunday, 7 July 1889, Inspector Regan and Detective Sergeant Howard arrested James Crick at his plying place on the foreshore at Horsleydown.

Suffolk-born Samuel Howard, aged 48, was an experienced partner and foil to Regan. Already twenty-four years in Thames Division, he had investigated Arthur Crick's tobacco larceny case. A man of medium height, he had a tanned complexion and dark brown hair set off by hazel eyes.[7] He had started his working life as an apprentice seaman,[8] and his uniform hid his tattoos and the more recent scars on his left shin from slipping in a police boat.[9]

A week after the assault, Ruffeitt and James Crick were charged before Mr Thomas Saunders at Thames Police Court with two counts: 'Attempting to kill and murder Jessie Miller' and 'Violently assaulting the said Jessie Miller, and against her will did ravish and carnally know her'.[10] Inspector Regan watched the case on behalf of the Criminal Investigation Department. In 1889, Magistrate Saunders was 75 and would retire the next year, dying within days of resigning his post. After his death, his colleague Franklin Lushington, who had fined Arthur Crick for carrying too many passengers, described Saunders as 'always most anxious to do his duty, and to temper justice with mercy, under the most trying circumstances of ill health'.[11]

The case returned to a magistrate at Thames Police Court on a weekly basis, to take any further evidence and to determine whether or not the defendant or defendants should be remanded in custody, or, if bailed, continue to have it enlarged, meaning extended. The Treasury Solicitor had appointed a prosecutor, Francis John Sims, who by coincidence had represented Arthur Crick in the case when he claimed his boats were owned by his mother. For the defence was George Hay Young, who in 1888 defended a man who may have been Jack the Ripper's uncle, Abraham Mordecai, in a case heard by Saunders.[12]

At the second hearing, Sims opened the prosecution case by saying that, from what he could learn, it appeared that Ruffeitt took no part whatever in the affair, and he asked for him to be discharged. Saunders assented, and Ruffeitt left the dock. He would shortly appear on the witness stand on behalf of the prosecution. The first witness was Jessie Miller, widely described as 'a decent-looking woman' in her early 30s residing at 40 Commercial Road, Lambeth, who stated that she was a widow and worked in the book production trade as a book-folder. Her job was a low-skilled one, often done by women, to fold sheets of printed paper ready for a book-binder to sew.

Miller testified about what happened when she went to Westminster to see the Shah:

> ... Crick and Ruffeitt invited her into their boat, which was alongside the stairs [of Westminster Bridge]. She told Crick she had no money, and the accused said that did not matter. They offered witness a drink, and she took it.
>
> She went into the boat, and they picked up five or six passengers. They rowed down the river, and landed at Horselydown, where they had some drink. [She and Ruffeitt] then returned to the boat alone. He rowed the boat a little way, and they were then again joined by the other prisoner [Crick]. Witness thought they were going to take her back. It was then getting dark.
>
> Crick tried to take liberties with her, and she resisted. He then pulled her to the bottom of the boat, and outraged her. Ruffeitt was then rowing. Witness got very much excited. She could not say whether she jumped out of the boat, or whether the accused threw her out, but she found herself in the water, and the men rowed away ...

At that time the beer had taken considerable effect on her. She lost consciousness for a minute or two, and did not remember what else occurred until she found herself in the water ... She was very much bruised on the back.[13]

[She] cried for help, and two men in a boat rescued her and took her to the infirmary. She next saw Crick on Sunday at the police station, and she picked him out from among others [in an identity parade].[14]

The cross-examination by the defence focused on victim-blaming. Miller was asked if she knew the nature of an oath, implying that she was lying. The next questions put to Miller were not recorded, but her answers were. She said that when she met the men, she was excited on account of seeing the Shah. She did tell Crick she was miserable, and it would not take her long to commit suicide. However, she did not mean that. She was singing in the boat, but did not say she was 'Tootsie Sloper'. Crick said she was, and she laughed. She had been drinking before she came across them. She could not tell whether she used filthy language in the boat or not. She did not say she would go anywhere with Crick. He was sober. She drank freely in the public house, but was not very drunk. She did not throw the seats overboard. When she fell into the water she was near to the side.[15]

She admitted that she had claimed to be a widow, when in fact she was living apart from her husband. After the case was reported in the newspapers, she had gone back to live with him. On the day in question, she set out to enjoy herself. She admitted having drunk copiously at the public house on the date referred to. Crick was quick to state that she 'drank a gallon of beer'[16] – if taken literally, a quantity of eight pints. As part of her testimony, Miller said that 'Crick was advertising a paper'.[17] The prize skiffs often had decorated seat backs. Crick's *Ally Sloper* boat might have had a seat back painted with a scene including the Sloper himself, with decorative lettering about its award naming Crick as the winner. That might explain the banter between Crick and Miller about Tootsie Sloper, and how Crick was identified as her attacker.

The next witness, Thomas John Ruffeitt, took the stand. He stated that he was aged 22, single, and a packing-case maker living at 19 Camperdown, Snowsfields, Bermondsey. He testified as follows:

He knew Crick, and went with him to see the arrival of the Shah. On the Embankment near to Westminster they saw [Miller], and Crick invited her into the boat. On getting into the boat she said she had no money, and asked them to give her a drink of beer. She then said, 'I came out this morning with the intention of doing away with myself. I got drunk last night, and none of my friends would treat me this morning. I won't do away with myself now I have seen you. I mean to enjoy myself today.'

They picked up five passengers, and after the arrival of the Shah landed them all but two and [Miller]. They afterwards rowed to Horselydown, where the others left [to visit a pub]. On returning to the boat the prisoner committed the offence with which he was charged. The woman resisted, but did not scream. They then pulled to the shore, and in getting out she fell into the water. [He] heard someone call them a pair of scoundrels for leaving the woman, and as they rowed away a man followed them.[18]

Ruffeitt's testimony was incriminating as it included the rape. Although it exonerated both himself and Crick of any blame for Miller entering the water, it was clear that they made no attempt to rescue her.

Sub-Inspector Charles Lilley of Thames Division testified that:

On July 1st he saw the prosecutrix in a boat near Charing Cross Bridge with [Crick] and another man. [Crick] gave her something to drink, and rowed across the river. Ruffeitt, the man who was with the prisoner, had since surrendered, and was discharged.[19]

Doctor Michael McCoy, who had inspected part of Elizabeth Jackson's remains earlier that year, said that he examined Jessie Miller on the first of July:

He found both her shoulders and arms were bruised. She refused to be further examined [meaning an intimate examination]. The bruises on the back might have been caused by being dragged to the bottom of a boat.[20]

It is assumed that, if asked, Crick also declined to be medically examined. A prisoner like him, charged with rape, needed to provide his 'affirmative consent ... for, in the absence of consent, any examination would be an assault'.[21]

The next witness was Miller's landlady, Fanny Phillips, of 40 Commercial Road, Lambeth. She did not help Miller's reputation by saying that she had lodged at her house for four months with a man, whom she represented to be her husband. The witness had since ascertained that he was not her husband.[22] Mrs Phillips was followed by another unsisterly commentator, who had been one of Miller's fellow passengers on the boat. Mrs Scrivener, of 4 Queen's Road, Holloway, deposed as follows:

> On the 1st of July, she and her husband went to Westminster to see the Shah. They went into [Crick's] boat, in which were four other women, three of the women went away, and the remainder went down the river. On the way down, [Crick] and Ruffeitt acted indecently to [Miller], who used obscene language. They afterwards went to a public-house, where [Crick's] wife argued with [Miller]. [Scrivener] and her husband then went away.[23]

Joseph Webb, a waterman, said that on the date in question, between nine and ten o'clock, he was in his boat:

> He saw [Crick, Miller], and another man in a boat. Crick was splashing [Miller] very much, and she asked him to desist. Webb told him to desist, and he did so. Soon afterwards [he] heard a scream, and saw [Miller] in five feet of water. He rescued her. He saw [Crick] and the other man run away [meaning row away].[24]

Inspector Regan testified that, when he arrested Crick, he said, 'I admit being in the boat, but the woman jumped overboard herself.'[25] Crick said that he rowed away because he noticed two other men row to her. Regan added that those two men, Webb and Jones, pulled Miller out of the river. Having rescued her, they chased her assailants, but without success.

After the necessary weekly hearings, on 27 August, the case was committed for trial at the Central Criminal Court, or Old Bailey. On Monday, 16 September, the depositions in the Jessie Miller case were assessed there by a Grand Jury. A Grand Jury hearing took place before any criminal trial to ensure that the prosecution case was sound. That jury found that there was insufficient evidence to support a criminal prosecution, and the case was closed.[26]

It is difficult to track the extent that Crick was at liberty in the period prior to the Pinchin Street murder. The contemporary police estimated that the date of that murder was the evening of Sunday, 8 September 1889, and the torso was discovered on the Tuesday morning. In the case regarding Jessie Miller, from Tuesday, 8 July, if not earlier, Saunders offered both Crick and Ruffeitt bail, the former with two bonds of £20 each and the latter a single one of £10. At the next hearing, Ruffeitt was discharged and Crick's bail was halved to one bond of £20. That lesser amount still represented almost half of the average worker's annual wage.

On 30 July, Crick came before Franklin Lushington, who made a spidery handwritten note in the court register, 'Bail enlarged to August 6th.' On that date in early August, Saunders extended Crick's bail 'on his own recognisance', meaning that no surety was required. That state of affairs continued up to and including Tuesday, 27 August, when Crick was committed for trial at the Old Bailey.[27] He had been continuously at liberty since 6 August, when he was bailed without surety, if not earlier.[28] It was a month before the Pinchin Street murder.

The original indictments at the National Archives do not provide the details of the bill's rejection or why Miller's account of her rape and exit from the boat was not considered credible. The charges are starkly put, the first, of drowning, reading: '[Crick] feloniously did cast and throw Jessie Miller into the waters of the river Thames there with intent to drown suffocate kill and murder her and did thereby attempt feloniously wilfully and of his malice aforethought to kill and murder the said Jessie Miller.'[29] The second charge was that of rape.

On the back of each indictment was written 'Bill Not Found', together with the signature of the foreman. The names of thirteen prosecution witnesses were listed against each indictment, indicating that each charge was well supported.[30] No further documentation was held on file. To a modern observer, as a minimum Miller's rape allegation should have been pursued in court. The Grand Jury could have found a true bill as to that charge and ignored the charge of drowning.

She might have entered the water voluntarily, more likely seeking to escape than to kill herself.

The case against Crick may have failed on the question of consent and Miller's permissive behaviour and use of obscene language. Miller voluntarily went to the pub with them, drank approximately a gallon of beer, and reboarded the boat. During that final trip, Crick pushed her to the bottom of the boat and raped her. Her claim that she lost consciousness owing to the amount of alcohol she had consumed and her refusal of an intimate examination by the doctor might have counted against her. The jury might have been influenced by a minority of unsympathetic press headlines commenting on Miller's return to her husband as 'A curious reconciliation',[31] and another, perhaps referring to the quantity of beer she drank and its effect on her, which opined, 'Extraordinary evidence.'[32]

Comparisons can be made between the attack on Miller, the first of two taken to court, and the Torso Murders. The Torso Killer might have approached his victims in a similar way. Clearly at a loose end, and out of funds, the passing Miller was chatted up by Crick and Ruffeitt, and was persuaded to board Crick's boat. She was given something to drink, claiming to have temporarily lost consciousness, inspiring the headline, 'Drugged on the Thames'.[33] The Torso Killer might also have drugged his victims to ensure their compliance, and used accomplices such as Ruffeitt. Could Crick, as a prolific rapist who exerted physical control over his victims, have extended his violence to murder?

A parallel rape case came to Thames Police Court on the same day that Crick was there, 8 July, using the same defence counsel, and with Inspector Regan watching the case on behalf of the Metropolitan Police. Samuel Fiford, a 24-year-old waterman, was charged with carnally knowing a girl, 21-year-old Sarah Truett. The alleged crime having occurred the night before, Fiford was remanded in custody overnight. This case has some similarities to the sex attacks carried out by Crick, but demonstrates a less complex approach.

Truett was described as 'a smartly dressed young woman', who testified that she had known Fiford for two or three years. They both lived in the Poplar area of East London. On Sunday, 7 July, Fiford and Truett went out for the day with a party of two young men and two young women, whom the prosecuting counsel avoided calling couples.

Fiford took them in his boat from Blackwall to Gravesend and back. That evening, their four companions left at Blackwall, while Fiford and Truett crossed the Thames in his boat to visit a pub. On their return, Fiford stopped rowing in the middle of the river and raped Truett. She screamed, and in the struggle she almost fell into the water.

Constable Catlin of the river police stated that, at 11.55 that night, a man had made a report to him about the incident. He and others manned a galley and found a boat with Fiford and Truett in it. Truett made a complaint against Fiford, who was then arrested. Fiford was under the influence of drink and made no reply to the charge. Magistrate Saunders bailed Fiford to return a week later.

At the next hearing, Defence Counsel George Hay Young attempted to have his client discharged. He had already ascertained by cross-examining Truett that she had been out with Fiford before, but he had not molested her. Young argued that the testimony of two witnesses, a doctor and a police officer, demonstrated that the case had broken down, and that the accused could not be convicted. The evidence of assistant police surgeon Doctor Crane, who had examined Truett, was not explicitly stated in the press. According to Young, it somehow proved that Truett's statement was untrue. Her body and clothing may have showed no signs of violence. K Division's Inspector Burke's testimony that Fiford had said 'she commenced it' was taken by Young to show that 'she was a consenting party'. However, Saunders dismissed those arguments and committed Fiford to trial at the Old Bailey, while granting him bail.[34]

At trial, Fiford came before the Common Serjeant of London, Sir William Thomas Charley QC. He was found guilty of the second charge, not of rape but of indecent assault, and sentenced to nine months' imprisonment at Pentonville Prison.[35] If the same outcome had applied to Crick, he could not have committed his next sexual assault, in October 1889. Nor, if he were the Thames Torso Killer, could he have carried out the Pinchin Street murder in September. Crick's October assault differentiates him from men such as Fiford, demonstrating his capacity for extreme violence as a serial offender and a sophisticated modus operandi using multiple vessels that fits the Torso Murders.

Thanks to Jessie Miller and Crick's subsequent victim, Elizabeth Sarah Warburton, his crimes have been recorded and are open to analysis. The identification of Jessie Miller proves to be less than straightforward, as the official records list five potential Jessies who married a Mr Miller before 1889. Discounting the widows and the financially secure, one of the remaining Jessies was admitted and discharged from Holborn's Thavies Inn Workhouse in the period 1898–1900. Further details about her entry into its casual ward implied that she was destitute, and into its infirmary that she was unwell. She consistently told the authorities that she was married, and a book-folder. That positive identification reveals Jessie's full name to be Susannah Jessie Miller née Staff. Her mother Jane was a book-folder, like herself.

Susannah Jessie Staff was born on 24 August 1857, at 40 Parish Street, St Olave, Southwark, to Jane Eugenia née Cobb and Joseph Staff, a fancy box maker.[36] Her birthday of 24 August was by coincidence the same date as the *Echo* newspaper fragment in the Whitehall torso case. The house where she was born was close to St Olave's Workhouse, and a five-minute walk from Horsleydown Old Stairs. The Staff family had lived in Southwark for decades, but moved north of the river to Shoreditch before 1860, when their daughter was baptised at St Leonard's Church.[37] In November 1888, Ripper victim Mary Jane Kelly's body lay in its mortuary, and, immediately before her funeral, in the neighbouring Clerk's House.

Jessie Staff married George Oliver Miller on 31 October 1875 at Holy Trinity Church, Hoxton, and her signature on their marriage certificate proves that she was literate.[38] Miller was a printer's compositor or typesetter, who moonlighted as a comedian. Their only child was a daughter, Helena, born in 1876.[39] Jessie Miller cannot be located in the 1891 census, when her husband George was living with another woman. A Frances 'Miller' was listed as his wife, aged 35 and born in Bloomsbury.[40] Like the Ripper victims, Jessie Miller's split from her husband signalled a downturn in her fortunes. And also like them, she had few sources of support. Her widowed mother Jane had moved to Birmingham and remarried. Jane had a mention in the criminal records, once being acquitted of larceny, and was herself in and out of the workhouse after her husband's death, and after separating from her second husband.

Jessie Miller was a vulnerable woman attractive to sexual predators. She was alone and, more than that, lonely, just wanting a day out and some free fun. Crick flattered her as if she were a pin-up in the popular comic, *Ally Sloper's Half Holiday*. One edition of that paper, dated August 1888, features an unsettling cartoon entitled 'The man in possession'. The man in question is rowing a small boat from a semi-recumbent position, his oars askew, while his lady passenger asks, 'Why, what are you doing, Tom? You will upset us.' Tom's reply is brusque: 'And what's that to do with you, madam? If I like to drown you, am I not at liberty to do so? Are you master, or am I? Hold thy tongue, woman, or I will leave thee to thy fate!'[41] Its style of humour does not translate to a modern audience, and the parallels to Crick's attitude and actions are disquieting.

At the court hearings, Miller gave her address as 40 Commercial Road, in Lambeth.[42] It was fifteen minutes' walk away from where Crick picked her up at Westminster Stairs. However, by her own admission she did not walk directly there, having been drinking beforehand. She cannot be found in the 1891 census, and she may have spent many of her remaining years living in workhouses, lodging houses, or on the streets.

Miller spent part of December 1899 in Lambeth's Prince's Road Workhouse.[43] It is referenced in the life-story of Ripper victim Polly Nichols, who frequented it, and whose body was identified by the words marked on her dress: 'Lambeth Workhouse P.R. [Prince's Road].'[44] The workhouse's location is of possible interest regarding the Salamanca Place murder in 1902, covered in a later chapter. It was another case of dismemberment with the body parts dumped in a public place, which was compared at the time to the Torso series.

At a similar time to when Jessie was in Lambeth Workhouse, her mother Jane was in Stepney Workhouse Infirmary suffering from bronchitis. In the Admission Register she was listed as being the widow of John Breffett (or Breffitt), a carpenter, and usually resident at 88 Hanbury Street,[45] a road familiar in Ripper lore as Annie Chapman was killed in the backyard of number 29. Number 88 was occupied by a family, Jane might have worked for her keep as their servant and boarder. John Breffett was still alive in Birmingham, suggesting that Jane left him and used the old trope of widowhood to protect her from questions about her marital status. As Jessie was discharged from the Lambeth Workhouse on Christmas Day, and Jane was also at liberty in

London, mother and daughter may have spent the holiday together at Hanbury Street.

In 1900, both Jane and Jessie entered different workhouses. On 17 January, Jane Breffett died aged 61 at Holborn's Thavies Inn Workhouse, of phthisis (tuberculosis), and mitral valve disease of the heart.[46] In March of the same year, Jessie Miller was admitted to Lambeth's Mint Street Workhouse. She died aged 43 on 26 September 1900, but not at the workhouse, and not from any disease. The cause of her death was stated as: 'Severe injuries received caused by being run over by an omnibus at Ludgate Circus.'[47]

Samuel Langham, the City of London coroner who had refused to conduct an inquest on the Rainham thigh, and who was shortly to retire, presided over the inquest into Jessie Miller's death. That hearing was held where her body was taken, at St Bartholomew's Hospital. George Miller was called as a witness to testify that the deceased was his former wife, and he exceeded his brief. He claimed that she was 'a common woman', meaning a prostitute, whose pimp was his own brother.

> **[Miller]** stated that he had been separated from deceased for about 18 years [approximately since 1882]. Her character was known all over London as a common woman.
> **Coroner:** Is that all you have to say?
> **[Miller]:** No, I wish to God it was. When I first married her she was the best woman under God's sun, but the sole cause of our trouble was my own brother, and here in a public court I denounce his villainy. My brother is Charles Thomas Edwin Miller, who, dressed as a gentleman, masquerades under the false name of Herbert Cole, and is known as manager of Sadler's Wells Theatre.
>
> He – my own brother – first led my wife – his brother's wife, his own sister-in-law – from the paths of virtue, and for three years accepted money from her as the result of the life which he was pressing her to lead unknown to me.
>
> When, at the end of three years, he was told by my wife that she would give him no more money he came to me and told me she was leading a bad life. Yes, he told me what she had done, but he kept secret what he had done. I learned that afterwards; but that is my

brother, who robbed a good woman of her character, and I lay, before God and the world, her death as a drunkard and an unfortunate under the wheels of an omnibus, at the door of my own brother.[48]

After that dramatic speech, Miller 'became noisy', was stopped by the coroner and ejected from court.[49]

The rest of the hearing was covered briefly in a few stark facts:

Evidence was then given that deceased was crossing Ludgate Circus early on Wednesday morning intoxicated, and fell under the wheels of a passing 'bus. She was instantly killed, and the medical evidence showed that death was due to rupture of the liver and heart.[50]

The verdict was that of 'Accidental Death'.

George's brother Charles Miller sued *The People* for libel, stating that what was published about him and his sister-in-law 'was without foundation, as nothing of the kind occurred, and the statements … were utterly untrue'.[51] He was concerned about his professional reputation as the manager of Sadler's Wells theatre and a writer of music-hall songs, as that newspaper circulated among theatrical people. He testified that soon after the inquest, George had threatened to shoot him with a revolver. They had argued over payment for a wreath that was going to be placed on Jessie Miller's coffin. George had demanded money from Charles, whose refusal led to the threat. Charles stated that his brother had made these accusations on various occasions, and he had not seen his brother's wife since he was 13 years of age.[52] The case was settled with an apology and his expenses paid.[53]

Research into Charles Miller reveals that he was significantly better off financially than his brother, leaving £2,338 to his widow in his Will.[54] Using his stage name of Herbert Cole, he advertised himself in the press as a tutor preparing aspirants for a life in show business, urging anyone 'wishing to enter the Profession' to 'Beware of Cheap, Bogus and Self-Styled Tutors! They are *incapable* of Teaching!'[55] In that role, he might have trained Jessie and introduced her to disreputable characters who took advantage of her. It might also explain why she was singing in Crick's boat, to a captive audience.

One of Charles Miller's lyrics reads:

## THE NON-FATAL ATTACK ON JESSIE MILLER, MONDAY, 1 JULY 1889

I am a most unlucky chap
Of troubles I've had my share.[56]

Yet the most unlucky person was his former sister-in-law Jessie, with more than her fair share of troubles. Having turned to drink and prostitution, she was raped by James Crick, resorted to the workhouse, and was knocked down by a bus. In 1889, having spent seven years leading a dissolute life apart from her husband, her perceived lack of credibility meant that her attacker was not prosecuted. James Crick must have been laughing, as his risks were rewarded. He was virtually caught in the act, and still got away with it, leaving him at liberty on the day of the Pinchin Street murder.

# 8

# The non-fatal attack on Elizabeth Sarah Warburton, Wednesday, 23 October 1889

Come what come may,
Time and the hour runs through the roughest day

From *Macbeth* by William Shakespeare

Five weeks after the Grand Jury ignored the bill against him in the case of Jessie Miller, James Crick attacked another woman. Elizabeth Sarah Warburton's courage in testifying against him in court saved other women from rape, if not murder. On this occasion, with the victim's account strongly backed by the river police, Crick was convicted and sentenced to a long term of imprisonment. The Warburton case demonstrates that Crick was violent and dangerous, with access to vessels with enclosed cabins where he could attack his victims in seclusion, and possibly kill. It shows how easy it could be to accost a woman on the streets of London, as happened to Jessie Miller, and then move her to a private place. The modus operandi used by Crick potentially resolves many of the unanswered questions about how the Torso Killer moved his victims from vessel to vessel to suit his purposes.

Elizabeth Sarah Warburton was aged 39 at the time of the attack, and, like Jessie Miller, was estranged from her husband. She had reverted to using her maiden name and was lodging at 45 Blakesley Street, which approximates to today's Deancross Street, off Stepney's Commercial Road. By trade, she was a fur trimmer, skilled in sewing fashionable linings into coats, mantles or wraps, jackets and gloves.

Raised in Rotherhithe and Bermondsey, both of her parents and also both of her husbands were of local stock, who may well have known the Cricks. Born on 3 March 1850, she was baptised at St Mary's Church, Rotherhithe.[1] From her birth until her teens, her family lived in Rotherhithe, firstly at several addresses in Adams Gardens and then at Clarence Street. Her father was a shoemaker, who also worked as a labourer and warehouseman. George Warburton spent his entire life in Rotherhithe, placing him continuously within a half-hour walk of Horsleydown, and the same applied to his future wife. On 2 December 1855, he married Elizabeth Mary Winchester at St John's Church, Horsleydown, the church attended by the Cricks and where James Crick would be baptised in 1862.[2] The new Mrs Warburton worked as a tailoress, and passed her sewing skills on to her five daughters.

The Warburtons' second-oldest daughter, Elizabeth Sarah, married her first husband, porter and warehouseman Alfred Lester, on 12 March 1867 at Christ Church, St George-in-the-East. Her age was wrongly recorded as 18. Unlike Lester, Elizabeth signed her marriage certificate with a cross, indicating that she was illiterate.[3] The Lesters had four children together, their marriage coming into difficulty after the birth of their last, in 1876. In April 1881, Elizabeth was living with her sister's family in Camberwell, while Lester was living on the opposite side of the river in Shoreditch, with another so-called 'wife', Georgina.[4] On 1 May 1881, calling herself a widow, Elizabeth Lester entered into a bigamous marriage with plasterer Horatio Marshall, at Christ Church, Rotherhithe.[5] Bigamy was a criminal offence, and if discovered, punishable by up to seven years in prison, but it was often the resort of those unable to afford the necessary legal representation to arrange a divorce. By coincidence, the Marshalls' marriage date was exactly five years prior to that of James and Rosina Crick. It was an age when workers held such ceremonies on public holidays, in this instance May Day, instead of forfeiting a day's pay.

Like John Faircloth, Marshall was an ex-soldier and military deserter. A tall man at 5ft 11¼in, he joined the 2nd Dragoon Guards, the Queen's Bays, in 1871. Marshall deserted in April 1875, in Leeds, incurring a prison sentence.[6] He may have been trying to avoid service in Dublin, where his regiment spent most of the period 1875–85, assisting the local civil force during the First Irish Home Rule Bill. Other tours of duty included South Africa and St Vincent in the Caribbean. Marshall was medically discharged in 1880. The cause of his invalidity was specified as a painful and debilitating arthritis of the back, although his medical record also listed the venereal diseases gonorrhoea and syphilis.[7]

Marshall and Warburton had three sons together before they separated, the last born in autumn 1888. She was likely to have been breastfeeding her youngest, and lactating, at the time of the assault on her a year later. Whatever the cause of their estrangement was, it was brief, Warburton rejoining her husband and children after the attack. They had a baby daughter in the summer of 1891, and that October, Warburton died of apoplexy when only in her early forties.[8] Her ex-husband Alfred Lester had died of pleuropneumonia a year earlier.[9]

In October 1889, after an interval of two months, James Crick was back before Mr Saunders at Thames Police Court on two charges of assault against Elizabeth Sarah Warburton. The most serious was that of rape, with a lesser charge of assault occasioning actual bodily harm. The indictments were graphically phrased, in the first charge described as 'against her will violently and feloniously did ravish and carnally know [her]', and the second listing the actions carried out against her as 'assault, beat, wound and ill-treat'.[10] Those charges had a familiar ring to them, echoing those brought by Jessie Miller. And, as in Miller's case, the additional charge of 'Attempted Murder' was later included.

Saunders bailed Crick on his own recognisance when he came to court on Thursday, 24 October, the day after the assault. Bail was subsequently extended until, on Tuesday, 19 November, Saunders set a surety of £20 on each of the two charges against him. Reduced by Lushington at the following hearing to a single amount of £20,[11] it remained prohibitive. Crick was remanded in custody until he was sentenced at the Old Bailey.

In a series of hearings, Detective Inspector Regan watched the case on behalf of the police, and Francis Sims was again the prosecutor. Warburton, aged 39, testified as follows about what happened on the evening of Wednesday, 23 October:

On the day in question she had been drinking with several men and women in public-houses. She first met [Crick] in Tooley-street, and he first addressed her, saying his mother was in trouble. At that time a woman was with the accused, who said she was his mother, and this person told [her] she would be perfectly safe with him.

They afterwards got into a boat at Horsleydown Stairs, and Crick rowed them straight across the Thames. On reaching the other side, Crick's mother got out of the boat first, and when [she] got up to follow her, [Crick] pushed the boat off so that she could not land. She screamed out, when [he] said, 'I intend to settle you,' and then put his hand over her mouth while he criminally assaulted her. She afterwards picked up one of the oars to defend herself, but Crick got it out of her hand.

Crick again said, '*I intend to settle you, as I have done other women that have been found in the Thames if you make a noise. If you keep quiet you will be perfectly safe.*'

He then pushed her back into the boat, and knelt on her. When [he] rowed her to the barge a tall man was on it, and she told him she was afraid. The man helped her on to the barge, saying she was all right. [Crick] afterwards said he would row her ashore, but instead of doing so he rowed her to the steam launch. When in the cabin of the launch, Crick again threw her to the ground and outraged her. She went on her knees and said, 'For Heaven's sake, have mercy upon me!' He replied, 'No, you __ [expletive] cow, I will not.' She struggled and screamed.

[Crick] then picked up some puppy dogs and threw them on to her body. He then caught hold of a large dog, and said, 'Jacko, seize her,' and held her by the neck while the dog sprang at her and bit her behind the ear. Crick then tore off all her clothing ... [12]

During the struggle she picked up an iron bolt, struck [him] on the head with it, ran on deck, and screamed out.[13]

The iron bolt was variously described in court as an iron bar or, more likely, a poker. The press called the setting of dogs onto the victim 'medieval' in its cruelty, adding, 'It seems a pity that he should be sent into the obscurity of a prison. Failing the pillory, Mr Barnum [the American showman] ought to exhibit this interesting man.'[14] The *Alert* steam launch in which the final assault occurred was owned by the Tower Bridge Company,[15] which accounted for its mooring near the bridge works.

Crick appeared to have used threats and intimidation to transfer Warburton from one vessel to another. His use of the word 'settle' was a threat, yet it was unclear whether he threatened to kill Warburton, or to put her 'in the Thames', alive or dead. As in the Jessie Miller case, throwing someone overboard into the tidal currents of the Thames was extremely dangerous and tantamount to attempted murder. It is also possible that his threat was to kill her and dispose of her remains in the river, like the Torso victims.

Inspector Charles Ford of Thames Division, a handsome moustachioed man, testified about Warburton's rescue:

> On the night [of the 23rd of October] he was on duty on the Thames in a police galley. At about 8.30 he was passing Butler's Wharf, Horselydown, when he heard the barking of dogs from the direction of the Tower Bridge Works, and about midstream. There was a steam launch ... lying near the works, and the barking came from that direction. [He] directed his crew to row towards the launch, and then heard two screams from a woman. [He] then directed his crew to pull as hard as they could towards the launch.
>
> When about twenty or thirty yards from the vessel he saw a woman standing on the deck. She was nearly naked and only had on a bodice and part of a chemise. [He] then saw the prisoner come up out of the cabin of the launch. He hurriedly got into a boat that was lying alongside and rowed away.
>
> In consequence of what [the woman] said he rowed after the prisoner, and caught him off Irongate Stairs. On the way to the station [the woman] said the prisoner had thrown her down, and tried to take indecent liberties with her. She also said he tore off all her clothes and set the dogs on to her, and if she had not been as strong as he was he would have settled her.[16]

The use of the word 'settle', although providing the basis for the charge of attempted murder, was open to interpretation. Inspector Ford's colleagues Constable John Pascoe and Inspector Alfred Box corroborated his evidence.

The next witness was assistant police surgeon Doctor Michael McCoy, who had examined Jessie Miller after her assault by James Crick. He testified that, on the night of 23 October, he was called to Wapping police station to examine Warburton:

> On the left ear was a small cut, and it was swollen. On the back of the right hand were four small wounds, such as would be produced by dog bites. In consequence of what he was told he cauterised the wounds [in case of rabies]. At that time [she] made no complaint of any outrage.
>
> [Crick] was also there, and [McCoy] examined him. He had a contused wound [bruising caused by blows] on the top of the head, one on the forehead, and another on the left cheek. [McCoy] was shown the iron bar produced [in court], and that would have caused the wounds on the head and forehead.[17]

Warburton had vigorously defended herself, arguably saving her own life.

Inspector William Pullen testified that: 'On Oct. 24 he searched the cabin of the *Alert*, and found a man's brown felt hat, which he produced in court, and two portions of the panel of the door had been broken.'[18] Inspector Box stated that on showing Crick the hat, he said, 'Yes, that is mine.' Box had prepared the plan of the river produced in court, which Inspector Ford used to explain where he had run Crick down. Irongate Stairs was directly opposite Horsleydown Old Stairs, on the north side of the Thames. Upon his arrest, Crick remarked, 'I admit I took her on the barge [meaning the *Alert*]. Because I could not brass up, she hit me on the head with a poker.'[19] His clear implication was that Warburton was a prostitute who assaulted him because he did not pay for her services.

Crick said that he wished to give evidence on his own behalf and had three witnesses to call, and asked if the magistrate intended to commit him for trial. Mr Saunders said certainly; but as Crick had witnesses to call, he would remand him for a week. The hearing resumed on Tuesday, 3 December, when Crick took the stand to give his own account of the events of 23 October:

> On the day in question, he had been to Southwark police-court. Returning from there, and coming along Tooley-street, he was accosted by [Warburton], who said, 'Halloa! How are you getting on?' She then asked [him] to treat her, and they went into a public-house. [She] told him she had a fight on the previous day, and showed him how she struck out with her boot.
>
> While there, his mother told [Warburton] he was a married man. She replied, 'That does not matter. I am in good company.' He rowed [her] and his mother towards the other side. His mother got frightened, and he rowed back and she got ashore. [Warburton] would not leave the boat, and they then rowed to the Tower Bridge. [She] then went with another man, stayed with him some time, and then again got into [Crick's] boat. They then went on board the launch and into the cabin.
>
> After being there some time she demanded money of him, and because he had none to give her she struck him on the head with the poker. He caught hold of her hands, but she wrenched herself free, and made several other blows at him. He got out of the cabin, and got into his boat to bathe his head. [She] followed him with the poker.
>
> While he was bathing his head someone called out, 'Sculler!' and he rowed towards the spot. He heard someone shouting to him to return, and he at once stopped. The police then came up and arrested him.
>
> [In answer to questions from prosecuting counsel] He had worked on the river twelve years. On the day in question he was not well, but was able to work. He was a married man, and had two children. He had never lived apart from his wife. He had been charged with assaulting her, and was remanded for a week, and then discharged, as she did not appear against him.[20]

Crick's account was more involved than Warburton's, and implied that she had dealings with another man, with whom she 'stayed some time'. There was a suggestion from the manner in which she greeted him that they were already acquainted. He provided a plausible explanation for his own exit from the steamer, going to bathe his head before allegedly responding to a call for his rowing services. After three witnesses gave evidence on Crick's behalf, Saunders committed him for trial at the Central Criminal Court on the charges, not only of rape, but also of attempted murder.

On Monday, 16 December, at the Old Bailey, James Crick met his nemesis. He had the misfortune to come before Mr Justice John Day, a judge so severe that his soubriquet was 'Judgment Day'. And, more words to savour, he considered offences such as indecent assault 'breaches of the law of nature, to be loathed and detested by all right-minded human beings'.[21] An equally determined prosecution team supported this 'great, strong, and unselfish man'.[22] Barrister Charles 'Willie' Mathews was ably assisted by junior counsel Richard Muir, with Inspector Regan attending. Coming from an acting family, Mathews had the gift of creating in court an 'atmosphere ... as tense and emotional as that of a playhouse in which some moving drama was being staged'.[23]

On this occasion, Crick unwisely defended himself, introducing himself as a branch secretary of the Society of Thames Watermen. He thought he was clever enough to argue his own case and win. His confidence in his own abilities, and prospects, proved to be unwise. The official record of the trial[24] explains several points omitted from previous hearings. At the start of the incident, Crick and his mother Ellen were on their way home from Southwark police court on Borough High Street, where Mrs Crick had sought a maintenance order against another of her sons. Passing Warburton on Tooley Street, Crick invited her to sympathise with his mother and drink with them. Although the two pubs they visited were not named, strong candidates are the King of Prussia, Queen's Head, and Anchor Tap, all en route between the courthouse and the river.

Crick's later companions in crime were not only named, but appeared as witnesses. Joseph Babington, who lent Crick his skiff, had history with Crick dating from when they were both apprentice watermen. In December 1879, at the monthly court of the Watermen's Company, Babington accused Crick of taking his fare at Horsleydown Old Stairs. Although Crick argued his defence forcefully, he lost the case:

> There was some contradiction in the evidence given, and the Court having been cleared and the matter discussed, the Court eventually fined the defendant 2s. 6d [two shillings and sixpence].[25]

Crick's fine of 2s 6d was trivial compared to other fines awarded at the same hearing, of 40s or £2.

When with Elizabeth Sarah Warburton, Crick had asked Babington to lend him his skiff, and Babington reluctantly agreed on the second time of asking. Having transferred from the skiff, waterman Benjamin Turton made Warburton a cup of tea on a barge near the northern end of Tower Bridge, which was under construction. The skiff was then rowed to the steam launch *Alert* nearby, manned by Robert Still, which Crick used as the location of his second rape of Warburton. The distances travelled from London Bridge to Horsleydown Old Stairs, then back out to the barge, then the launch and finally Irongate Stairs, amounted to little more than a mile.

The description of the attack on the launch sheds light on Crick's modus operandi:

> [He] then took her to the cabin, and, having locked the door, threw her down with her head close under a stove where a fire was burning; she screamed and resisted, but prisoner again subjected her to outrage: that she struck prisoner over the head with a bar she caught up, and that prisoner set some dogs on to her, which bit her on one of her ears and one of her hands.
>
> She struggled and screamed against both man and beasts. Her clothes were torn off her in the course of the struggle. At length she managed to reach the door, which she burst open.[26]

It was a chilling account of calculated violence. If Warburton had not been strong enough to resist Crick, and break out of the locked cabin, she could have been killed.

Crick gave evidence, 'his line of defence being an admission of disgraceful conduct and an impeachment of the woman's moral character'.[27] In cross-examination, he answered as follows:

> [He] denied that in June, 1888, he had misconducted himself with a young woman in a boat, but admitted that in July last a woman named Hillar [sic: Miller] had made a charge against him of having been criminally assaulted by him, and thrown overboard by prisoner from a boat on the Thames on the occasion of the Shah's arrival at

London. It was, he said, not true that he threatened to throw overboard the prosecutrix in the present case.[28]

Crick then called four witnesses. The first was his mother Ellen, who claimed that her son had not accosted Warburton, but that Warburton had accosted her and her son. She also attempted to attribute Warburton's injuries to another cause:

> In the second public-house to which they went, [Warburton] said that she had had a quarrel on the day previous with a woman living in the same house with her, and that that woman assaulted her, cutting her ear and biting her hand.[29]

The next three witnesses were all watermen keen to avoid being implicated. However, it was only Robert Still who, at the application of the defence, was declared by the judge to be a hostile witness. Of the other two men, Turton's evidence was less helpful to Crick than Babington's:

> Joseph Babington said when [Crick] went to take his boat he refused sanction, but [Warburton] asked him to let [Crick] have the boat to take him over the water ...
>
> Benjamin Turton deposed to the woman's having a cup of tea on his barge. He swore that [Crick] asked him to commit perjury to save him ...
>
> Robert Still, whom prisoner had to treat as a hostile witness, denied that he saw prisoner with the female, or that he had carried her in his boat. He did not know whether or not he should lose his situation if the account given by the prisoner were true as to how he and the woman got on board the steam launch. He knew the dogs were in the cabin, and said he had never heard of their biting anyone.[30]

Whatever Robert Still's role in facilitating the assault, Crick was sufficiently familiar with the setup on the launch to call one of the dogs by name, 'Jacko'.

The jury deliberated for a mere half-hour before returning a verdict of 'Guilty' to the charge of rape. Referring to the Jessie Miller case,

Inspector Regan stated that Crick had been committed for trial in July for a felonious assault upon a female in a boat, but the bill was thrown out by the Grand Jury. He added that 'many complaints had been made about his conduct to young women'.[31]

Sentence was deferred until Wednesday, 18 December, when the judge delivered a well-deserved punishment, for which he gave full justification:

> Mr Justice Day observed that the assault had been committed under circumstances of the most brutal, cowardly, and unmanly character. No greater ruffianism, brutality, and unmanliness had ever been proved before him in connection with a case of this kind.
>
> Crick by his line of defence had done his best to aggravate his crime. He had endeavoured to escape justice by suborning perjury, and had induced his own mother to come and give evidence which was false upon the face of it. Society must be protected from ruffians of the type to which the prisoner belonged, and the sentence upon him therefore would be that he be kept in penal servitude for fifteen years.[32]

It was a severe tariff. Crick was transferred to Portland Prison in Dorset to begin serving out his time.[33]

Although the assaults against Elizabeth Sarah Warburton and Jessie Miller were rapes, not murders, those two cases have similarities to the Torso Murders. The two women fit the profile of the killer's ideal victim type in terms of their ages, social disconnect and poverty. If they had disappeared on the dates of the attacks on them, their landladies would have believed they had done moonlight flits, and simply left without paying their rent.

The four Torso victims ranged in age from 24 (Elizabeth Jackson), 24–25 (the Whitehall victim), about 26 (the Rainham victim), and about 35 for the Pinchin Street victim. They varied in height from 5ft 2in–5ft 4in (the Rainham victim) through to the extremely tall Whitehall victim at 5ft 8in or above, with the Pinchin Street victim's height estimated at 5ft 3in and Jackson's at 5ft 5in. With the exception of Jackson's sandy hair, all had hair described as dark, or dark brown. All were plump and 'well-formed', meaning full-figured, voluptuous or buxom, and Jackson was heavily pregnant. Little is known of the physiques of Miller and Warburton, and no photographs or drawings of them were published in the press. Her vigorous efforts at self-defence indicate that Warburton was physically strong. Miller was aged 31 and Warburton 40 when attacked. Crick's wife Rosina, whose physical description is also unknown, was aged 26 at the time of the Rainham murder and 28 on her husband's imprisonment. Those age ranges are consistent with those of the Torso victims.

Miller, Warburton and Rosina Crick had further commonality in their employment as manual workers. Miller was a book-folder and Warburton a fur-trimmer, while Rosina Crick is assumed to have done paid needlework, and was later a charwoman, or cleaner.[34]

The attacks on Miller and Warburton both took place in the evening. Crick was working in the late afternoon when he invited Miller into his skiff, on a summertime freebie with paying passengers. They viewed the Shah's arrival at around 6 p.m., moved the boat back to Horsleydown, went to the pub, and returned to the skiff when it was dusk. Miller's rape and entry into the river occurred between 9 and 10 p.m. Crick was walking along Tooley Street one evening when he hooked up with Warburton, and they first went to the pub. He somehow managed to get her onto his boat, and used threats and intimidation to move her onto the barge and then steam launch. Her rescue took place at around 8.30 p.m. Both women were raped on the river in the near-dark, and on both occasions it was low tide.

The manner in which Crick accosted his two known victims, in the presence of other people, was intrinsically reassuring. He offered free fun, exactly what the women were missing in the drudgery of their everyday lives. Jessie Miller was picked up at Westminster Stairs, having walked fifteen minutes riverside from her rented accommodation in Lambeth's Commercial Road. Elizabeth Warburton walked twice as far, from Stepney's Blakesley Street across the river to Tooley Street, where she bumped into Crick and his mother near London Bridge.

It is impossible to prove whether or not Crick knew his victims before assaulting them. He might well have known Elizabeth Sarah Warburton, as their families lived in some proximity to one another in Southwark and Bermondsey during their lifetimes, and her first husband was a Fellowship Porter and his brother was a lighterman.

He gambled that it might work in his favour to take both Miller and Warburton to pubs where he was a 'local'.

Crick's attacks were planned and repeatable, from the way he attracted the women's attention and convinced them to join him to the mechanics of isolating them mid-river and assaulting them. His possible use of drugs and actual use of both alcohol and accomplices offer an interesting angle on the Torso Murders, if he were their perpetrator. His mates and his mother were all willing to help; the only person who stood up to him, and argued with Jessie Miller, was his wife Rosina. No doubt she would have received her punishment afterwards.

Crick carried out his attacks with total confidence. Surely seen by members of the public with his victims in pubs and on his boat, he felt that his mates would aid and abet him. But in the Jessie Miller case, Thomas Ruffeitt was persuaded to give evidence in support of the prosecution, in exchange for the charges against him being dropped. And in the case of Elizabeth Sarah Warburton, neither Benjamin Turton nor Robert Still backed up Crick as he might have wished.

The mobility displayed in both of these cases, and the ease with which Crick moved the women from place to place, fits well with the Torso Killer's approach. He used a significant level of violence against them. He bruised Miller's back on the bottom of the boat as he twice raped her. He also twice raped Warburton, and imprisoned her in the steam launch's cabin, where he threw her to the floor before setting the dogs on her. He tore off her clothes down to her chemise and bodice. That chemise suggests a direct link to the Pinchin Street torso, as the body's only remaining item of clothing.

Desperate to escape, Miller jumped overboard, as Warburton might have done, if she had not been rescued from the deck of the steam launch. Were there other victims who were unable to escape, and did the ones who were compliant *live*, while those who fiercely resisted *die*? Testimony in the Warburton case referred to other alleged rapes by Crick, in addition to that on Jessie Miller. Crick responded to questions by the prosecution in some detail:

> [He] did not remember going in a boat on the river with a man named Crawley, and another man and three girls, in June, 1888. Those girls were not outraged by [him] and the other men.

He did not remember taking a girl of 15 on to a barge and outraging her. That was absolutely untrue.[35]

While searching without result for details about those two rape cases, the story surfaces of a fatal accident that took place while Crick was in the process of winning the 1887 Horsleydown Regatta. Although not significant in its own right, it serves as a useful reminder of the date when Crick won his rowing skiff *Ally Sloper*.

At around 7 p.m. on Monday, 22 August 1887, in the excitement of the final heat of the race, dozens of onlookers were standing on the top of a haystack, the cargo of the barge *Maria*, when the stack gave way and twenty-five people fell into the water. As many as thirty or forty boatmen went to the spot to try to rescue the people. Ezra Corpe, a 43-year-old waterman, found a man unconscious in the water, under a hay-bale. He got him onto his barge, and cut his clothes off, 'so as to be able to rub his body according to the rules of the Royal Humane Society'.[36] At half-past seven, Police Constable Ford fetched the local doctor, William Fitzrayne, who pronounced the man dead.

An inquest was held later that week, officiated by Coroner Samuel Langham, whose office covered both the City of London and Southwark. The dead man was identified as 31-year-old Jeremiah O'Brien, a labourer from Bermondsey. The jury returned a verdict of 'accidental death' and Corpe was commended for his efforts to save the man's life.[37]

The timing of James Crick's acquisition of the *Ally Sloper* prize boat occurred after the Rainham murder. If Crick were the Torso Killer, having his own skiff gave him greater mobility for his later attacks, when moving his victims, both living and dead. A barge must have been used as the location for the Rainham murder and subsequent dismemberment, as well as a platform for disposing of the body parts. The Rainham murder modus operandi could have been reused as a template for that of Elizabeth Jackson.

For the Whitehall murder, it is possible that the killer used several different vessels. If he were Crick, his own skiff would have been invaluable to transport body parts unsuspected. Mirroring the attack on Warburton, he could have moved his victim from a skiff to another vessel not only to rape, but for the kill and later dismemberment.

The Torso Killer's access to secure premises where he could kill, dismember and store body parts for a period of days, not hours, was confirmed by the final murder in the series, at Whitechapel's Pinchin Street. That murder was committed during the interval between the attacks on Miller and Warburton, both of whom were lucky to escape with their lives. And in another interval, four years after Crick's release from prison, a kill in Vauxhall's Salamanca Place might be the last in the Thames Torso series. Constitutionally violent, did Crick come back into circulation to claim another victim?

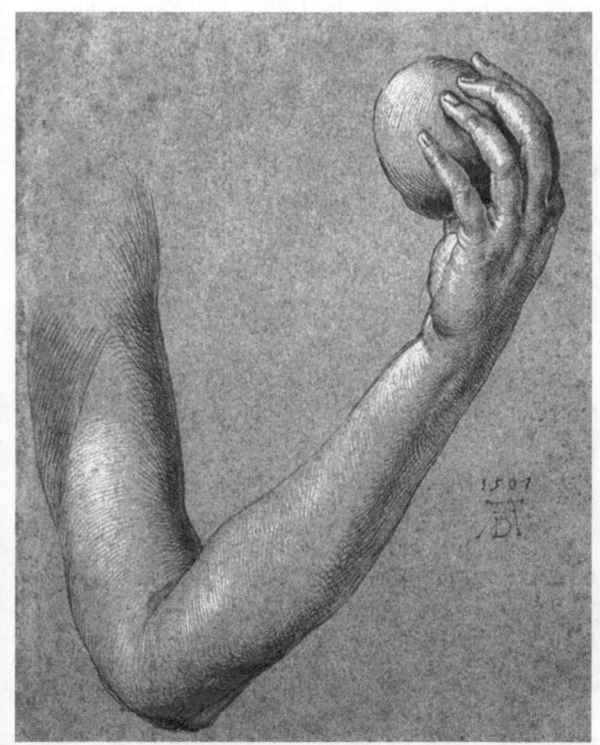

*Arm of Eve*, 1507. Albrecht Dürer (German, 1471–1528). Point of brush and grey and black wash, brush and grey and black wash, heightened with white gouache; sheet: 34.4 × 26.7cm (13.5 × 10.5in). (The Cleveland Museum of Art, gift of Alan Kennedy 1965.470. www.clevelandart.org/art/1965.470)

James Monro CB, Metropolitan Police Commissioner 1888–1890.

Detective Inspector John Regan of Thames Division, *Eastern Post*, Saturday, 23 June 1900. (© The British Library Board. All Rights Reserved)

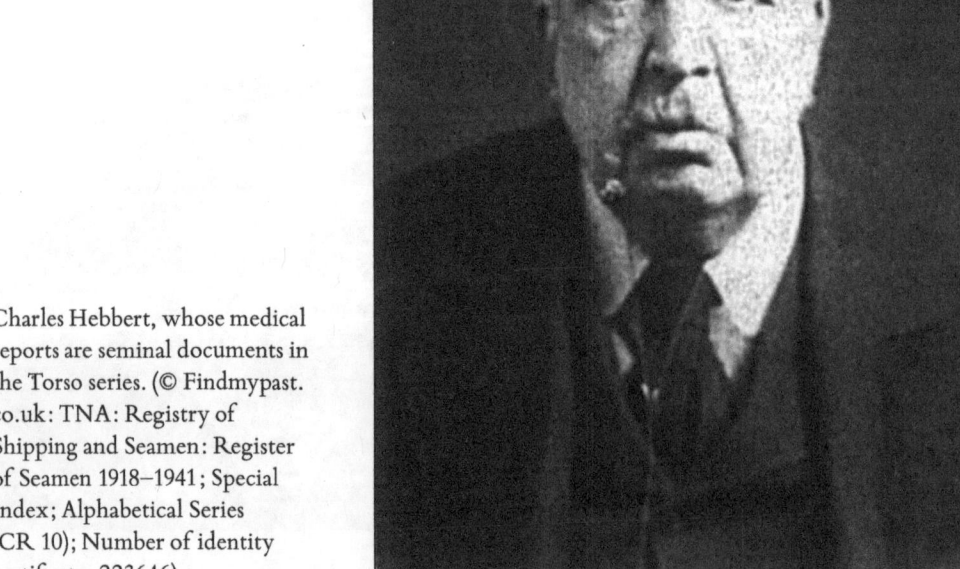

Charles Hebbert, whose medical reports are seminal documents in the Torso series. (© Findmypast.co.uk: TNA: Registry of Shipping and Seamen: Register of Seamen 1918–1941; Special Index; Alphabetical Series (CR 10); Number of identity certificate: 223646)

Thomas Bond, senior police surgeon and mentor to Charles Hebbert. (Obituary of Doctor Thomas Bond, *The Lancet*, 1901 Vol. I, p.1721)

The author's police ancestor H Division Sergeant Harry Garrett. (© The Garrett family)

The discovery of human remains at Rainham, Essex, from the *Illustrated Police News*, 28 May 1887. (© The British Library Board. All Rights Reserved)

Newspaper coverage of 'The Whitehall Mystery' from the *Illustrated Police News*, 13 and 20 October 1888. (© The British Library Board. All Rights Reserved)

The Whitehall torso was discovered in the foundations of New Scotland Yard in what is now known as the North building of the Norman Shaw buildings on London's Victoria Embankment, seen towards the right of this image. (Anthony O'Neil)

Newspaper reporting of the discoveries of the remains of Elizabeth Jackson, the third victim in the Torso series, *Illustrated Police News*, 15 June 1889. (© The British Library Board. All Rights Reserved)

Stonemason John 'Jack' Faircloth was the only named suspect as the killer of Elizabeth Jackson. This sketch was circulated in a police effort to locate him. Evening edition of *Star of the East*, 5 July 1889. (© The British Library Board. All Rights Reserved)

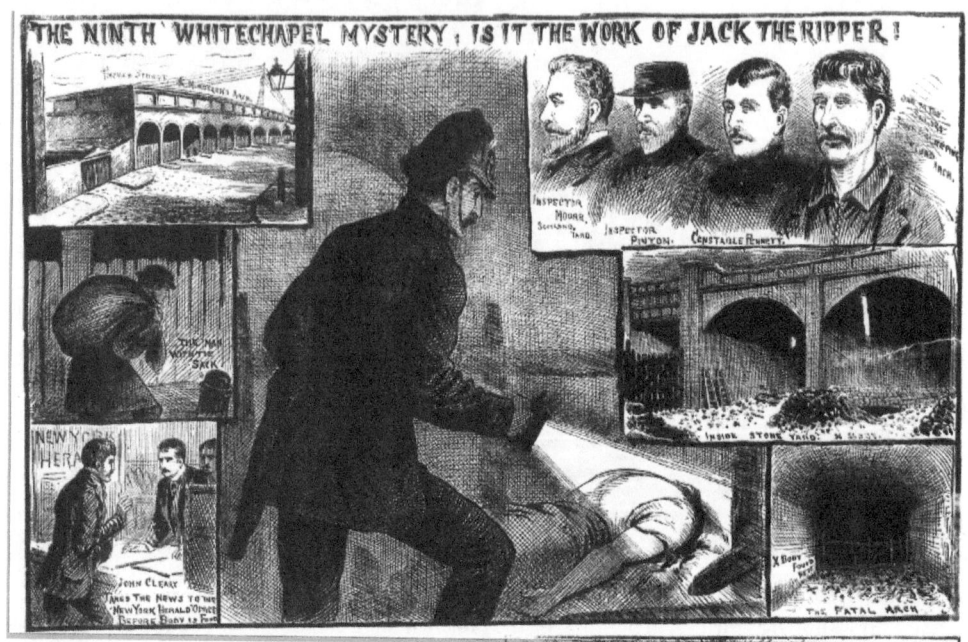

Press coverage of the discovery of the Pinchin Street torso, *Illustrated Police News*, 21 September 1889. (© The British Library Board. All Rights Reserved)

Lightermen on the Thames, 1877. (Courtesy of LSE Library)

Horsleydown Old Stairs. (Photograph by George Rinhart, 1900)

Sketch of the Shah of Persia, *Illustrated London News*, 6 July 1879. (© The British Library Board. All Rights Reserved)

Judge John Day, who passed a severe sentence on the author's prime suspect, James Crick. (© National Portrait Gallery, London)

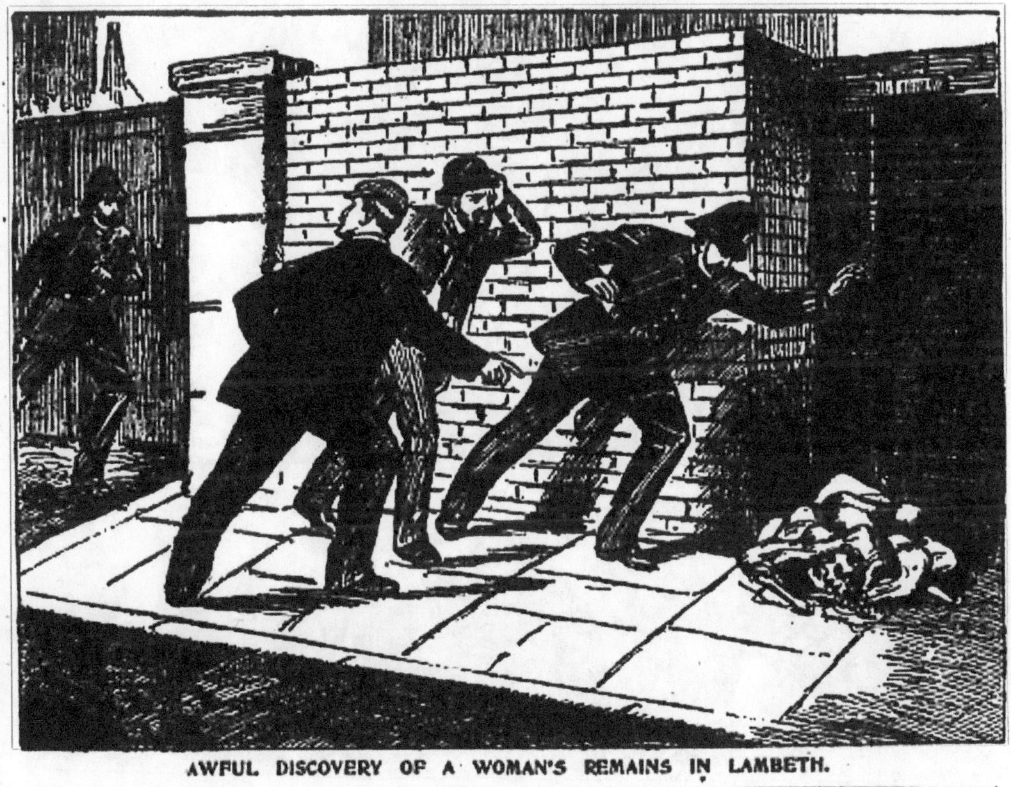

AWFUL DISCOVERY OF A WOMAN'S REMAINS IN LAMBETH.

Discovery of human remains at Salamanca Place, Lambeth, South London. *Illustrated Police News*, 14 July 1902. (© The British Library Board. All Rights Reserved)

Sketch of murderess Kate Webster and her victim Julia Martha Thomas, *Illustrated Police News*, 12 July 1879. (© The British Library Board. All Rights Reserved)

The trial and conviction of Kate Webster, *Illustrated Police News*, 19 July 1879. (© The British Library Board. All Rights Reserved)

# 9

# The Salamanca Place murder, Vauxhall, where a woman's dismembered body was discovered on Sunday 8 June 1902

Homo homini lupus
[Man is a wolf to his fellow man]

Latin proverb

In August 1898, two years before Inspector Regan's retirement, James Crick was granted early release for good conduct. He had spent the latter years of his term of imprisonment at Parkhurst Prison on the Isle of Wight, which also boasted Osborne House, Queen Victoria's favourite place of residence. In his final months in jail, he exchanged his coarse yellow breeches and jumper, patterned with the broad arrow that denoted his convict status, for a blue smock and trousers, and was permitted to grow out his cropped hair.[1]

Having served nine years of his fifteen-year sentence, Crick was discharged as a habitual criminal, meaning someone who had committed more than one offence. Assuming that the abandoned Jessie Miller charge did not count against him, a second offence might date to 19 July 1880 at Clerkenwell, when a James Crick was sentenced to four months' penal servitude for larceny and receiving stolen goods.[2]

Aged 34, Crick was a 'ticket-of-leave man' released on parole. If he committed any further offence, he could be sent back to prison to serve the rest of his term, which was due to expire on 15 December 1902.[3] In the Metropolitan Police Register of Habitual Criminals, his occupation was noted as a London lighterman.[4] The authorities cannot have thought too deeply about the connection between his trade and offences, nor how likely he was to conform to the stereotype of a 'ticket-of-leave man' reoffending. It was, however, a requirement of his release to report regularly to the police and give notice of any intention to leave the Metropolitan district.

Just four months before his release from prison, Crick's mother Ellen died of bronchitis and senile decay.[5] Her daughter Charlotte and son-in-law Charles Sumner lived with her at 50 Lucey Road and remained at that address after her death. Crick might have joined them there on his release, as it was an address he gave to the court in November 1889.[6] He is unlikely to have moved in with his wife. From 1901 onwards, if not earlier, Rosina Crick started co-habiting at Rotherhithe with the man whom she would eventually marry, bottle-washer Robert Marler.[7] James Crick cannot be located in the 1901 census, in which he was not listed as living with any of his family, including his half-brother Arthur. He might have been at work, or sleeping intermittently on boats, including in a lighter's cabin[8] when lying in the stream, or kipping at friends' lodgings, or in dosshouses. Maybe he exited the back door Ally Sloper-style, as the census enumerator walked in the front. Crick's omission from the census might indicate that he also slipped from the sight of the police.

On 22 January 1901, at the age of 81, Queen Victoria died at Osborne House on the Isle of Wight. Her state funeral was held on 2 February, at St George's Chapel, Windsor Castle. Having worn black since the death of her husband Albert in 1861, at her own wish she was buried wearing a white dress and her wedding veil. The Queen was succeeded by her eldest son, Albert Edward, known as Bertie, who took the regnal name of King Edward VII. His coronation was scheduled in the middle of the following year, 26 June 1902. The new king was within weeks of being crowned when, at 3.30 a.m. on Sunday, 8 June, a dismembered body was found in the corner of an alley close to the Albert Embankment at Vauxhall.

Two workmen on the night shift at Doulton Pottery Works were on their way to charge, or stoke, a kiln, when they saw a neat pile of human remains next to a gateway on Salamanca Place. They hailed the night watchman, 32-year-old John Cox, who went to fetch the local constable from his beat. The police took an immediate interest in Cox, who 'was taken from his cottage in another part of the Doulton yards, detained in the Kennington Lane Police Station until 3.30 on Sunday afternoon, subjected to all kinds of cross-examination, and then dismissed with compliments and apologies'.[9]

The discovery was reported in the press under the headline 'The Lambeth Mystery', accompanied by a sketch of the crime scene at Salamanca Place, a narrow cobbled street bending slightly at its southern end to meet Salamanca Street and a row of railway arches. Journalists posed unanswerable questions: why had the murderer not dropped the body parts in the Thames, or in one of the Doulton Works' kilns, where they would have been destroyed within five to six minutes? Theories that it was a medical students' prank or that the remains were thrown from a train on the South Western Railway were quickly ruled out.[10]

The day after the discovery of the remains, three medical experts examined the body at Lambeth mortuary, at the corner of the High Street and Old Paradise Street, one block north of where it was found. L Division's police surgeon Doctor George Nicol Henry, a 40-year-old Scot, consulted with Coroner Doctor Michael Taylor and Professor Augustus Pepper, a surgeon and lecturer in surgery at St Mary's Hospital often used as an expert witness by the authorities. Detective Inspector John McCarthy, aged 39, the lead police officer for the case, was also present. The press were disappointed in their hope of an early read-out, merely reporting: 'They remained at work, examining and consulting in private, for three hours and a half, and at the end of that time the statement was made that the authorities deemed it inadvisable to give the result of their inquiry until the inquest.'[11]

However, some new material was made available to the newspapers. Keen to have the body identified, the police issued the following description to the Press Association for circulation:

> The human remains which were found in Salamanca Place, Lambeth, on the morning of the 8th ... are those of a small woman, aged between twenty and thirty, height about five feet, complexion dark, hair straight and very dark, teeth in an excellent state of preservation,

prominent cheekbones and upper part of jaw, chin somewhat pointed, giving an angular appearance to face. Nose was probably somewhat turned up. Deceased, from the verminous condition of the little hair left on the back of the neck and temples, is supposed to be of the poorer and neglectful class.[12]

The inquest opened at 2.30 p.m. on Wednesday, 11 June, at Lambeth Coroner's Court, co-located with the mortuary off Old Paradise Street. Irish-born doctor Michael Taylor, the Deputy Coroner for Mid-Surrey, was middle-aged and experienced. He punctuated the inquiry with discerning questions and showed skill in dealing with erratic witnesses. The coroner opened by declaring that 'the case was of a very unusual character. The principal difficulty it … presented was the question of identification, but that matter was in very good hands, and if anything could be made out of it he was sure the police would do it.'[13]

The first witness, Charles Whiting, a 40-year-old potter's labourer, had been the first person to see something ahead of him on the cobblestones during the short walk southbound between the Broad Street Doulton works and its kilns on Salamanca Street. Salamanca Place, also referred to as Salamanca Alley, led between those two streets. Whiting's description of the remains explains his resulting state of shock:

> After working all night on the Broad-street premises, he went at 4 o'clock on Sunday morning in company with a fellow workman named Muntzer over to the Salamanca-street works for the purpose of charging a kiln. It was broad daylight at the time, and on turning into Salamanca-alley he saw a face turned towards him by the side of the gateway.
> **Coroner:** Was the face looking at you?
> **Whiting:** Yes, and the head was lying partly on its side.
> [Whiting] went on to say that, in addition to the head, he saw what appeared to be legs and arms all piled together, the head being on top. It looked as though the remains had been placed there carefully, and not as if they had been shot out of a sack. The body was really in three pieces. He drew his mate's attention to it by saying,

'Oh, what's that?' and Muntzer looked at the pile and remarked that it was a human being.

[Whiting] at once informed another workman named Cox, who attended to the kiln in Salamanca-street, and he came and opened the gate, telling witness to go and prepare his coke and coal for the fires, and saying that he would go and report the matter.

The remains were by the first gate on entering the alley from Broad-street, and Cox was inside the second gate. The first gate had not been opened since dinner-time on Saturday. [Whiting] had previously passed down the alley at 10 p.m., and he did not think the remains could have been there then, and some men told him that they passed there at 1 a.m., when there was nothing to be seen.

Cox returned with somebody, but [Whiting] was so upset that he did not know who it was. Very few people passed up and down Salamanca-street at night time. At 10 o'clock he had noticed two persons in the alley, but he saw nobody when he found the remains. While working inside they would not be able to hear anything that went on in the alley. He could not recognize the head as belonging to anybody he knew or had ever seen. He had seen the remains in the mortuary, and recognised them as being those he found.[14]

Whiting's colleague, 31-year-old Robert Muntzer, was the second witness:

[He] confirmed Whiting's statement as to discovering the remains. He did not share Whiting's opinion that the remains had been carefully deposited, but favoured the theory that they had been shot out of a sack, and that the skull had been placed on top.

[Muntzer] saw a man and woman in the alley at 10 o'clock on Saturday night, and they walked into Broad-street. He did not think he would know the man again, but the woman was wearing a white straw hat, with, he believed, a black band. He should say she was about 5 ft. high. He only saw the back of the man, who was wearing a cap. He looked like a working man in his best clothes, and was a trifle taller than the woman ... It was so dark that witness could not furnish any further particulars about the man and woman.[15]

The next witness was Constable James Birtle, an officer of fifteen years' experience. He had the misfortune to be called to the scene of the crime on his 38th birthday, and testified as follows:

> At 4.40 a.m. on Sunday he was on the Albert Embankment, when Charles Whiting came up and said, 'Come here, I want you.' He was very much agitated, and could not explain what he wanted him for until they reached the remains in Salamanca-alley. Whiting then, in the presence of Muntzer, told him how they found the remains.
>
> When they picked them up it struck him that they had been carefully placed there, and not thrown down. With assistance he conveyed them to the mortuary.[16]

Whiting was recalled and explained that it was not he but Cox who had fetched Constable Birtle from the embankment. On being pressed by the coroner, Birtle, presumably in some state of embarrassment, 'admitted that he did not know whether it was Whiting or Cox who called him, nor could he say who was present besides Muntzer in Salamanca-alley'.[17]

He then continued his testimony:

> He had patrolled Salamanca-alley half an hour before the discovery was made, and he was positive the bones were not there then, or he must have seen them. It was rather dark during the night. He was certainly under the impression that Whiting called him [to the scene of the crime], but it might have been somebody else.
>
> The Coroner said it was rather important, and he wanted the constable to make it clear if he could. He would not unduly press him, however, as he was not positive.[18]

Police surgeon Doctor George Nicol Henry testified about his examination of the remains:

> Shortly before 5 o'clock on Sunday morning he was called to the Lambeth Mortuary to examine the remains, which formed part of a female body. Three front teeth were missing from the lower jaw — two having been wrenched or knocked off, and one broken

off level with the jaw. The skin on the face had the appearance of having been subjected to moist heat; in fact, that applied to the whole skull.

The other parts were the left arm and left shoulder blade, the right forearm, the left collar bone, the left tibia [shinbone], the left fibula [calf bone], the right fibula, the whole of the pelvis, with the lower part of the spine, the middle part of the backbone, seven lower ribs in one piece, and the upper part of the backbone, with the first rib on either side attached ... They form[ed] part of one and the same body – that of a female. A good many of the bones [were] missing.[19]

The press reported that: 'The dismemberment had been done cleanly with some sharp instrument. Only a little hair remained on the head, around the base of the skull. Another noticeable feature was that, while the right ear was small and well shaped, the left was black and swollen.'[20] An intact right ear would have been regarded as a useful aid in the victim's possible identification.

After Henry's testimony, the inquest was adjourned for a week. The police worked hard to identify the victim, which might lead them to her killer. They made good progress, as:

Several people visited the mortuary to try to identify the remains as a missing friend or relative. One young man, a workman in the neighbourhood, says he is almost certain, in spite of the disfiguration and mutilation of the body, that the woman was his wife. She left him six months ago, he said, deserting her four children. He had not seen her since.[21]

The woman certainly appeared to be identifiable, with the press reporting that: 'The black hair, small head, white teeth, and dark olive skin give one the idea immediately that the woman was a foreigner – possibly an Italian.'[22] She was of distinctly small stature and poorly groomed, suggesting that she lived rough or in poverty. Yet her excellent teeth would have differentiated her from her peers. A further distinguishing feature were her 'strongly-defined eyebrows'.[23]

Although there is no mention of it in the official records, the newspapers claimed that the woman might have walked with a limp:

> Casual examination of the remains has revealed signs which are believed to be causable only by a severe fracture of the leg bones above the knee. If the diagnosis of this injury is correct, the woman would have been under surgical and medical treatment for months, and would in all probability have walked with a very slightly shortened limb, in which case there would be a slight, scarcely perceptible limp, known to the intimates of the injured person, but unlikely to obtrude itself on the notice of casual acquaintances.[24]

This amateur post-mortem diagnosis was probably spurious, not least because Doctor Henry's list of surviving bones did not include either femur (thigh bone).

The inquest resumed on Wednesday, 18 June. The first witness was John Cox, described as a stoker and night watchman at Doulton's, who had been an early police suspect, although quickly discarded. He testified as follows:

> He was on duty all the night before the discovery. At three o'clock on the Sunday morning he left the place to go on the embankment for 'a breath of fresh air'. He went into Salamanca Alley, but was convinced that the remains were not there then, or he would assuredly have seen them. He went back soon to his lobby [station], 70 yards [64 metres] from the spot where the remains had been deposited, and remained there till Whiting, who first made the discovery, called him. He heard no sounds to attract his attention at all.
>
> He went for the police when Whiting drew his attention to the heap of remains, and on his way met two gentlemen ... He thought they were students, and told them of the discovery. They returned with him, one remarking, 'It's a female's head.' After talking with each other a few minutes the two gentlemen walked off in the direction of St. Thomas's Hospital.[25]

Those two medical students, possibly from the nearby St Thomas' Hospital, remained unidentified. They took a professional interest in the remains before walking on. Invited by the coroner to describe the men, Cox provided the court with a comedy turn:

Asked what the men were like, witness with outstretched finger pointed to one of the reporters, who, he said, bore a remarkable resemblance to one, and to another of the reporters, who was like the other.

**The Coroner:** Were either of these gentlemen there?

**[Cox]:** I couldn't say it was them, but they are very much like. One of them was just the build of this gentleman.

**[Cox]** continued strongly to emphasise the likeness, though the Coroner smilingly reassured the pressmen that he did not think the police would keep an eye on them.[26]

Cox caused further amusement by saying that, after reporting the discovery of the body to a policeman he called 'Ginger', he crossed Waterloo Bridge and hurried to the offices of *The People* to sell his story. It was published in an extra special edition with 'a detailed account of the gruesome discovery' from Cox.[27]

The 1911 census records Cox as living at 17 Albert Embankment,[28] a building located between the pottery works and the river. But he cannot be traced in Vauxhall's 1901 census, which features dozens of Doulton's workers: potters, moulders, pottery hands and boys, kiln men, packers, labourers, carters, any of whom might have killed a woman and dumped her remains in Salamanca Place. A series of watermen emerges, including bargemen and watchmen on steamers, but without reference to James Crick as a stray river worker or lodger.

George Henderson, a lamplighter, testified that he extinguished the lamps in Broad Street at ten past three on Sunday morning, and then went through Salamanca Place, but noticed nothing. Doctor Henry was then recalled to brief the details of the post-mortem examination that he had carried out with Professor Pepper:

> The body had been subjected to moist heat until the flesh could be stripped off easily. To bring home to the jury the conditions under which this had been done the doctor used the illustration of an overboiled fowl, reduced to a consistency which allowed the bones and flesh to be separated by a fork. Some of the limbs had been boiled for some hours probably, then stripped of flesh, and roasted ...

The mutilations and cooking took place soon after death. A clot of blood in the nose led the medical men to suppose that death was probably caused by suffocation, but apart from this there was no evidence to show how death took place.

The mutilations showed no anatomical knowledge whatever, nor could they have been caused by surgical instruments. The lower extremities had been removed by an irregular circular sweep round the hips and then wrenched off. Only a saw and knife had been used for dismemberment. The saw was probably an ordinary carpenter's saw. Of course, the mutilation might have been done by a person with surgical knowledge desirous of hiding the fact.[29]

Detective Inspector McCarthy gave evidence about the results of the police investigation to date:

[He was] called to Salamanca-alley shortly after the discovery, and [made] a complete search in the adjoining potteries for further human remains. A house-to-house inquiry within a half-mile radius had been made to see whether anyone was missing, and photographs had been circulated throughout the Metropolitan Police district, but so far without result. All cab-yards, bakehouses, and butchers in Lambeth and Vauxhall had been visited, but so far without any information being obtained.

A great number of people had come forward, but so far six out of seven missing women had been accounted for. As a result of inquiries made at hospitals where dissection was going on it was found to be absolutely impossible for a corpse to be removed without the knowledge of the treasurer or secretary. As [he] was anxious to make further inquiries with reference to the seventh woman, he would like another adjournment.[30]

The inquest was therefore adjourned until Wednesday, 2 July. On 24 June, as preparations for the coronation by the palace, military and police were intensifying, the King developed an abdominal abscess that required urgent surgery. On the original coronation date, in place of the ceremony itself, a solemn service of intercession for the monarch's life was held at St Paul's Cathedral.

When the inquest resumed, Detective Inspector McCarthy again took the stand to inform the court that, despite much effort, little progress had been made since the adjournment:

> The police inquiries had been continued, but so far without any result. The scope of their investigation had included the barges going up and down the river, and those lying alongside at Lambeth.[31]

Doctor Henry was recalled to reply to a question from the coroner about whether the woman's ears were deformed, as any visible defect might help the police to secure an identification. Henry replied: 'There was no deformity of either of the deceased's ears. One ear was more shrunken than the other by reason of heat.'[32]

In summing up, the coroner made a highly significant reference to the Elizabeth Jackson case:

> There was a case on all fours with the present at Battersea about thirteen years ago, but in that instance, thanks to the careful piecing together of the mutilated remains by Dr. Kempster, the woman was identified.
>
> This case was a very unsatisfactory one by reason of the want of identification of the deceased, but the matter would still remain in the hands of the police.[33]

Taylor's phrase 'on all fours' meant, in legal terms, an identical case that set a precedent for how a later case should be decided. His meaning implied that the same perpetrator had killed Elizabeth Jackson and the woman found in Salamanca Place. The jury returned an open verdict: 'That the deceased was found dead, but there is no evidence to show under what circumstances she came by her death.'[34]

The time of death was not estimated in the inquest hearings. Several newspapers made their own assessment of the killer's motivation to dismember his victim:

> It was the deed of a man in a desperate hurry. As soon as life was out of the poor woman she must have been hacked to pieces for easier removal. Then an attempt must have been made to get rid of the flesh by boiling, and after that there was a hasty endeavour to burn

the bones. Both efforts were only partly successful, and the murderer, collecting the evidences of his crime in a sack, shot them down into the first quiet thoroughfare he could find ... It is an area of desolation that would suggest itself to a man knowing the locality and anxious to unburden himself of the results of a great crime.[35]

Although no more than a newspaper reporter's opinion, the phrase 'in a desperate hurry' fits the murderer's actions. This makes it more likely that he killed within twenty-four hours of the discovery of her body, rather than, as in the Pinchin Street case, when the perpetrator may have stored it for up to forty-eight hours. Deductions reported in the press that might be attributable to a police officer suggested that the murder must have taken place within ½ mile of Salamanca Place:

> It is deemed impossible that any one above the condition of a labouring man could carry the remains in the midnight hours, or even be seen in these small, mean streets and byeways, without being watched. The respectable portion of the community would suspect him and watch him. The disreputable would think the police were 'nosing about on a job', and they also would keep observation.
>
> In the second place, the nature of the mutilation points to the commission of the crime at some place other than a tenement dwelling-house. There are three such places in the vicinity of Salamanca Place.
>
> The first is Doulton's great pottery factories ... where men are employed night and day ...
>
> Then there is Stiff's pottery [on Lambeth High Street], where investigations have also been made ...
>
> The other is the Nine Elms Gasworks – a spot where, if sufficient secrecy could be secured, the part-boiling part-burning of the body would find more easy accomplishment than anywhere else.[36]

It is likely that the killer was a working-class local man, but it is not certain that the dismemberment and cooking took place outside a domestic environment. The killer might have believed that he could wholly dispose of his victim by using a domestic copper and stove. The boiling and burning processes made her unrecognisable, but did not decompose her remains. An uneducated man would not have known that an intense heat of over 1,000°C is required to destroy a human body.

On discovering that the domestic equipment at his disposal had little effect on the remains, he panicked and dumped them. He knew enough about police procedure not to leave the sack nor any trace of her clothing. However, this scenario directly contradicts the thinking of Doctor Henry: that the body might have been boiled whole, the legs were then wrenched off, and the torso and limbs dismembered, and the parts finally roasted. It is hard to specify any environment, domestic or otherwise, where a whole human body could have been treated in that way.

The use of the oven had an unintended benefit for the perpetrator. In a crime committed within days of Salamanca Place, on 27 June 1902, Harry Jackson burgled a house in Denmark Hill. He left a set of fingerprints on a freshly painted windowsill, which were matched to prints held in the Metropolitan Police Fingerprint Bureau. The first man ever to be convicted on fingerprint evidence, that October Jackson was sentenced to seven years' imprisonment.[37] Fortunately for the Salamanca Place killer, the charring of the body and removal of any clothing or covering meant that fingerprints could not be taken.

The assumed date of death was Saturday, 7 June 1902. The weather was gusty and showery with fine intervals. It was two days after a new moon and the day would have been bright after sunrise at 3.46 a.m. The morning high tide was as early as 2.09 a.m.[38] Tidal analysis suggests that the perpetrator missed the first tide. It could be argued that this led the perpetrator to dump on land in a similar style and even a similar time to the deposit at Pinchin Street. But the timing also fits anyone who needed to be rid of the body before people were up and about on a Sunday. Was a relative coming to visit his house, or did he need to go out early to a workplace that operated on the Sabbath?

James Crick's address at the date of his death in 1907 was 6 Perseverance Street, Bermondsey,[39] an hour's walk from Salamanca Place. Previously it was probably with the Sumners at 50 Lucey Road, and it seems reasonable to assume that he lived in Bermondsey continuously after his release from prison. Salamanca Place is 2½ miles from Bermondsey, a long trek by land with a heavy sack, but only ten bridges west by boat. The Lambeth Pottery had its own dock two blocks north of Salamanca Place.

As in the Ripper murder of Mary Jane Kelly, which preceded the Lord Mayor's parade through the City of London, a significant public event took place on the following day. Sunday, 8 June 1902, was the date of the Thanksgiving Service for the end of the South African War at St Paul's Cathedral, attended by the King and Queen. As James Crick took his boat out for sightseers wanting to see the arrival of the Shah of Persia at Westminster, he would surely have done the same for that church service. As the King and Queen's route from Buckingham Palace to the cathedral was inland, passengers were ferried to riverside stairs to make their way on foot to viewing points. The royal return journey, however, partly followed Victoria Embankment, and was visible from the river between Blackfriars Bridge and Horse Guards Avenue.

James Crick could have been on the river that June morning, but it cannot be assumed that he unmoored early to deposit a sackful of remains. Nothing links him to the Salamanca Place murder, and neither the method of rendering the body unidentifiable, nor its dump inland on the south bank fit the signature of the Torso Killer, whether or not he was Crick. By coincidence, Mozaffar ad-Din Shah Qajar, the son and successor of the Shah who featured in the attack on Jessie Miller, visited England shortly after the King's coronation.

The unidentified victim was a serial killer's preferred victim type: vulnerable, poverty-stricken, isolated. More allusions were made in the press to Jack the Ripper's ghastly work than the Torso Killer's. It does not seem possible to identify either McCarthy's 'seventh woman' about whom there is no published information, or, assuming her to be someone else, the victim herself. The police photographs of the victim cannot be located, nor, if one existed, any sketch reconstructing her appearance. She probably did not have a leg injury, but if she did, it might have taken her to Prince's Road Workhouse Infirmary, where Jessie Miller stayed in December 1899. Disappointingly, its online records do not specify what its patients' illnesses or injuries were. A search in the 1901 census for women in the correct age-range with possible Mediterranean lineage, who lived in the Lambeth area, surfaces some Marias and Luisas, of mainly Italian or Swiss origin, all of whom survived beyond June 1902.

One point of speculation is whether the victim might have met her killer at or near one of many local pubs, when he clocked off work on a Friday evening or Saturday lunchtime. He needed private premises to meet her at, or take her to, where the murder, dismemberment and heat treatment of the body occurred. That location must have been inland, on the assumption that he walked towards the river to dispose of his sack, and reached a deserted Salamanca Place first. The embankment was not only too far for him to walk with a heavy load, but was regularly patrolled by police, with a direct line of sight along it and across the river. Dumping on the south bank was atypical of the Thames Torso Murders, with the exception of Elizabeth Jackson, part of whose remains were left in Battersea Park.

The killer had access to an ordinary carpenter's saw and knife, a sack of some sort, and a newspaper described in the press as *Country Life*, a portion of which was found under the remains and another portion 'in Messrs Doulton's yard, and near the entrance gate'.[40] The use of a newspaper as wrapping material is reminiscent of the Whitehall case, as are all of the tools and wrappings. Also a methodical worker, the Salamanca Place murderer placed the remains in a neat pile, with the head inside the pelvis.

The medical evidence lacks the fine detail of the Hebbert report, and Doctor Henry's testimony does not appear to be reported verbatim in any of the press accounts. The torso was divided into three parts, and a total of ten body parts were found. There was no Hebbert-report-style analysis of the cuts at the vertebrae. A journalist who must have viewed the remains at the mortuary stated, 'The backbone is broken up into equal lengths, and the "sides", with their adherent ribs, have been cut up into portions which could easily be put in an ordinary oven.'[41] Each limb was cut in half at the joint and the hands and feet were missing. The head was not disposed of separately, and it is most likely that the body parts were cut up to facilitate their destruction, not their disposal. The removal of the hands and feet, as if to fit into a boiling copper or oven, clearly suggests this.

It is the choice of Salamanca Place as a location to deposit his incriminating sack and the assumption that he had access to cooking facilities in a private premises nearby that indicate that the perpetrator was a local man, and a landlubber. In Salamanca Place, he found the most suitable place near where he lived; a dark passage with high walls, lit only by one lamp at each end, that was quiet in the early hours. The perpetrator probably killed a woman directly connected to him, possibly his partner, meaning that he had to render her body unrecognisable to avoid identification. Her remains showed no firm evidence of violence inflicted while alive. Her teeth were considered to have been broken after her death.

If the same perpetrator were both the Thames Torso murderer and the killer of the Salamanca Place victim, it would take his tally to the same total as Jack the Ripper: six kills, including Elizabeth Jackson's unborn child. But there is insufficient evidence to link it to the Thames Torso series, and both killer and victim remain unidentified. The inquest jury's verdict marked the end of the police investigation, as far as it is recorded. On 26 July, the final mention in the press of Salamanca Place simply stated that Lambeth Council agreed that the alleyway should be 'better lighted' and two new street lamps erected.[42] King Edward VII and Queen Alexandra were crowned on 9 August, and a new era began.

# 10

# A parallel case: the murder of Julia Martha Thomas in 1879, and a reconstruction of the Salamanca Place murder

> It is a capital mistake to theorize before one has data. Insensibly one begins to twist facts to suit theories, instead of theories to suit facts.
>
> Sherlock Holmes, from 'A Scandal in Bohemia' by
> Sir Arthur Conan Doyle

With no existing records, it is impossible to determine to what extent the authorities explored the possibility that the Salamanca Place murder might fit into the Thames Torso Murders series. Of the medical experts involved in those cases, those still available for consultation in 1902 were Battersea's Doctor Felix Kempster and his Whitechapel counterpart Doctor Percy Clark, who examined the Pinchin Street torso. In the previous year, following a long illness, Thomas Bond had died by his own hand. Charles Hebbert had emigrated to North America in the 1890s.

Occurring thirteen years before the Salamanca Place murder, an 1879 case stands as a better parallel than any of the Torso killings, clarifying the type of person who might have committed the 1902 murder, its motivation, and how it was done. It demonstrates how a body could be deconstructed in an ordinary domestic kitchen and disposed of locally. As with the murder of Elizabeth Jackson, it offers an opportunity to validate the accuracy of Thomas Bond's assessments of a victim's age and height against known facts.

The police investigation into what was initially called 'The Barnes Mystery' started on Wednesday, 5 March 1879, at shortly before seven o'clock in the morning, when a wooden bonnet-box was washed up 5 miles downstream on the lower side of Barnes Railway Bridge. Barnes, in South-West London, was over 6 miles from Charing Cross, the centre of London. Henry Wheatley, a local coal porter, spotted the box from his cart and thought it might be the proceeds of a burglary:

> I saw a box in the Thames ... about a quarter to seven. The tide was just ebbing from the top of it, and it was half afloat. There was a cord round it. I cut the cord. I kicked the box and broke it ... The contents looked like a lot of cooked meat. The box was quite full of it.[1]

He left another man in charge of the parboiled human remains while he reported his discovery at the local police station.

On the following Monday, the Coroner for West Surrey George Hull held an inquest into the victim's death at the Red Lion Inn, at Barnes. After the jury viewed the body parts, they heard evidence from the 'finder' Wheatley. Wheatley was followed on the stand by the local police surgeon, Doctor Frederick Adams, who testified that the box contained:

> ... the trunk and other portions of the body of a woman. The heart was in the right cavity of the chest. I found a portion of the right lung, but the left lung was absent. Attached to the trunk was the right shoulder. The upper part of the left arm had been detached, and I found it to be perfect down to the elbow. A portion of the thigh of the right leg and the remainder of the leg down to the ankle was also among the remains. A part of the pelvis was present, as also a small portion of the spine – the rectum was divided. The head was absent.
>
> The woman had been dead about a week, while the remains might have been in the water about two days. From what I can see I should

say that the remains must have been those of a woman of between 18 and 30, and she may have borne children. Her height may have been about five feet three or four inches, judging from the measurement of the parts that were found and making allowance for those that were absent. I think she must have been a dark-haired woman.

In my opinion all the fractures to the bones must have been made after death, and had been made very unskilfully and with very bad instruments. The mutilation must have been a work of time. The bones must have been smashed with a blunt instrument. I see no marks on the remains which could have been inflicted before death or could have caused it.[2]

The inquest was adjourned for a week to enable the police to obtain further evidence, and search for the missing body parts. The press speculated that the police had no leads to follow, as the headless remains could not possibly lead to the body's identification and there were no identifying marks on the box.

On the next day, Tuesday, 11 March, a jobbing gardener found a human foot and ankle buried in a manure heap at Twickenham, near Richmond Upon Thames. By coincidence, Richmond was where the Cross family lived, whose daughter was investigated as the possible Rainham victim. Called in by Scotland Yard to provide expert advice, Thomas Bond compared the body part with the other remains and judged it might have belonged to the same body. A week later, on Tuesday, 18 March, the inquest resumed and concluded. Bond testified that he had examined the remains of a woman in Barnes Cemetery, to which the recently discovered foot had been united. In addition to the description already provided by Doctor Adams, he stated:

The bones had been roughly torn asunder, and the flesh was torn and hacked. [He] placed all the parts together and compared each individual part. He arrived at the conclusion that they all belonged to one body and that of a woman. These remains had not been used for anatomical purposes.

On measuring the arm bone, he found that the woman was of short stature. In all probability she measured, when alive, about 5ft. 3in. The whole of the remains, with the exception of the thigh bone, presented a dark colour and a shrunken appearance. The limbs that were discovered had been boiled or exposed in hot water of a very high temperature. [He] had failed to discover any marks which had been inflicted before death ... [and] could not assign the cause of death.[3]

The gardener, George William Court, testified about finding a foot when loading a manure barrow at Copt Hall allotments at Cross Deep in Twickenham:

His pitchfork struck a soft substance. On making a close examination he discovered that it was a human foot. Not knowing what to do with it he buried it. In the course of the same afternoon he thought he that he had better dig it up again. [He] spoke to a police-sergeant, and he advised him to take the foot to the station-house.[4]

Inspector Rowley stated that 'the place where the foot was found was quite exposed and frequented by many persons'.[5] The foot discovery is interesting because the person disposing of it must have visited that site, unlike the box, which could have been deposited anywhere along the river and washed up at Barnes. That part of Cross Deep, near Holly Road, was easily accessible, being close to Twickenham railway station. As no further evidence was put forward, the jury returned an open verdict of 'Found dead'.

Fittingly, at seven o'clock on that very evening, 3 miles west of Barnes in Richmond Upon Thames, the killer's attempts to conceal their crime started to unravel. At number 2 Vine Cottage, close to Richmond Park, two vans arrived to remove some furniture, dresses and other household effects which publican John Church had bought for £68 from its 29-year-old incumbent. Miss Elizabeth Ives, the leaseholder of that property who lived next door, went out to ask why the furniture was being taken away. Church and his companion Henry Porter called for the putative Mrs Thomas, whom Ives knew as the maid, Kate Webster. Webster came down the stairs and explained in an agitated manner that Mrs Thomas had sold her furniture. Webster said that she did not know where her mistress was and could not provide a forwarding address for her.

The two men overheard this conversation with some surprise. Webster had revived her acquaintance with Porter and his family two weeks previously, after a gap of six years. She had told Porter that her name was now Mrs Thomas and that she was a widow. Her aunt had died and left her a comfortable home in Richmond, which she wanted to sell before moving to Glasgow. Becoming suspicious, Church refused to take the furniture. Fatally for Webster, at her insistence he did take the dresses. Church managed to contact Charles Menhenick, a friend of the genuine Mrs Thomas using the *deus ex machina* of a letter found in the pocket of one of the dresses. Menhenick alerted Mrs Thomas's solicitor, William Hughes, that she was believed to be missing. On Saturday, 22 March, Hughes, Church and Porter went to Richmond police station, where Inspector Pearman took a statement from Church before going to Mrs Thomas's house.

Finding the place in great confusion, Pearman did not carry out a complete search until the following Monday, when he found bloodstains in places as varied as the back bedroom and the pantry, along with some stained brown paper. The laundry copper contained a fatty substance like black grease, and there was a quantity of charred bones under the copper grate. He also found a chopper, razor and table-knife.

Crucial evidence provided a connection to the box of human remains, as Pearman later told a court at the Old Bailey:

> I found under the sink in the scullery the handle of a box, which I produce; it fits the bonnet-box found in the Thames. I found some cord there too. It is of the same kind as that with which the box was tied.[6]

On the evening of the furniture sale, 18 March, Kate Webster picked up her young son from his childminder, and took a cab to Hammersmith station, where they boarded a train to King's Cross. A week later, the police published a 'Wanted' description:

> Wanted for stealing plate, &c., and the supposed murder of her mistress, Kate __, aged about 32; 5 feet 5 or 6 inches high; complexion sallow, slightly freckled. Teeth rather good; prominent. Usually

dressed in dark dress, jacket rather long, and trimmed with dark fur around pockets, light brown satin bonnet; speaks with an Irish accent, and was accompanied by a boy aged five, complexion rather dark [,] hair dark; was last seen at Hammersmith.[7]

Webster had fled to her native County Wexford in the south-eastern corner of Ireland. She was arrested by the Royal Irish Constabulary within six hours of their receipt of a Scotland Yard telegram. Known to the local police, Webster had been convicted for larceny at Gorey Quarter Sessions in December 1864. Her description being recognised, she was arrested at her uncle's farm at Killann and placed in custody at Enniscorthy.[8] Two inspectors from Scotland Yard took her back to England. She consistently denied any involvement in what she called 'the murder', saying, 'It is very hard the innocent should suffer for the guilty.'[9]

The case was first heard before a magistrate at Richmond police court, where publican John Church stood in the dock with Webster, accused by her in a formal statement of the murder. Church was quickly discharged owing to lack of evidence, and crossed the court to testify for the prosecution. Although circumstantial, the evidence against Webster was sufficient to send her for trial at the Old Bailey. There is no record of whether she was considered fit to plead, nor any attempted defence of insanity. She made statements attempting to incriminate Henry Porter as well as the father of her child.

Webster's trial lasted six days from 2–8 July 1879, under High Court Judge George Denman. The Solicitor General Sir Hardinge Stanley Giffard QC and Archibald Levin Smith, a future Master of the Rolls, appeared for the Crown. William Warner Sleigh and Marischal Keith Frith acted for the defence. It was a complicated case for the jury to consider, with fifty-three witnesses to hear. To reach a verdict on the crime of murder, they first needed to establish whether the remains found were those of Mrs Thomas, and whether Mrs Thomas had been murdered or not. The prosecution admitted that there was no proof of her murder. Julia Thomas was last seen alive on Sunday, 2 March, at the evening Presbyterian service at Richmond lecture hall, leaving at 7.30 p.m.

## A PARALLEL CASE: THE MURDER OF JULIA MARTHA THOMAS IN 1879

Childless and twice-widowed, Thomas was not as financially comfortable as she appeared. She was planning to let rooms at the cottage before her disappearance. A small, well-dressed and educated lady, she was sober and religious. The contrast between her and Webster in appearance and demeanour was stark, making the latter's impersonation of the former even less plausible. Webster was a large, strong Irishwoman fifteen years younger than Thomas, and she drank to excess. Her ability to read and write was imperfect.[10]

The leaseholder of 2 Vine Cottage, Elizabeth Ives, who had challenged Church and Porter about the furniture sale, lived next door at number 1 with her elderly mother, Jane Ives. Both women testified at the trial about things they had heard and smelled after Julia Thomas's disappearance. Jane Ives had heard a noise like the fall of a heavy chair in next door's ground-floor hallway before 9 p.m. on the night of Sunday, 2 March. On the next morning, she heard a poking of the copper fire, and saw some clothes hanging out in the back garden of number 2.

On the same morning, her daughter smelled 'a very strange smell like an escape of gas', and over that day and the next, she could hear the fire being lit and a sound of chopping wood on the hearth and the copper fire being poked, audible from the back of her own kitchen range. As in Sherlock Holmes's curious incident of the dog that did not bark in the night-time,[11] on the Tuesday after the murder she heard the audible clue of someone next door touching the keys of the piano to make a sound, although the person was unable to play it. Julia Thomas played competently.

The Ives women were among several witnesses who confirmed that Webster was at Thomas's cottage in the days after the latter's disappearance. A local tradesman, William Dean, was the first to call, at 12.30 p.m. on Monday, 3 March, to ask for payment for a coal account. Webster answered the door, her manner excited and abrupt, and would only say that she did not know when her mistress was likely to be in.

Extraordinary evidence was given about Webster's alleged deposit of two items in the River Thames. Henry Porter's son, 15-year-old Robert, testified that Kate Webster visited his family at their Hammersmith home at around 5.30 p.m. on Tuesday, 4 March. An hour later, she asked his father, 'Would you let Bob come with me to Richmond?'

Porter agreed, and he went part of the way with them, helping to carry Webster's heavy black bag. Not fully secured, it had stood open under the tea table, with a brown paper parcel on view inside.

They all went into the Oxford and Cambridge pub on Hammersmith Bridge Road, then Webster took the bag, claimed that she wanted to meet a friend at Barnes, on the other side of the bridge. A quarter of an hour later, she returned without the bag. After an interval at the pub, drinking and looking at the photographs and rings shown to them by Webster, the Porters walked with her to Hammersmith railway station, and Robert Porter went home with Webster.

On arrival at the cottage, Webster carried a corded wooden box downstairs, saying, 'I want you to help me with this box to Richmond-bridge; I have to see a friend.' The box was missing one of its brass handles, so they carried it clumsily. Young Robert Porter testified as follows:

> We went together, carrying the box. We carried it to Richmond-bridge ... She went into the recess just over the middle of the bridge (Middlesex side) and said, 'Now you be going home; I'll catch you up. Go on.' I came towards the Surrey side ... and stopped. Then I heard a splash, and a gentleman who was coming the same way – a tall gentleman with a high hat – looked round and I looked round. Kate came up and said, 'Come on, Bobby, I've seen my friend.'
>
> ... I was [later] taken to Barnes police-station, and I identified the box.[12]

It was the bonnet-box that contained the remains, and Webster herself identified it as that carried by her and young Porter. Mary Ann Kent, a relative of Mrs Thomas by marriage, identified the box as belonging to her, and the bloodstained best bonnet that was usually kept in it, as did a former houseguest.

A shop assistant from Niblett's jewellers in Hammersmith testified that, on Friday, 7 March, he bought a gold dental plate, with two teeth on each side of it, for 6s. Henry Porter testified that Webster had given it to him to sell on her behalf. A Richmond dentist, George Rudd, testified that on 22 February, he had seen Mrs Thomas at his surgery,

## A PARALLEL CASE: THE MURDER OF JULIA MARTHA THOMAS IN 1879

and made a cast of her mouth. She was not wearing the plate, but the one he was shown in court would fit her lower jaw. She complained that it hurt her. He saw her again on 26 February and 1 March. A letter he wrote to her after that date was returned to him through the General Post Office's dead letter office.

Thomas Bond gave evidence as the expert medical witness, in addition to Doctor Adams, who had conducted the post-mortem examination. He provided a diagram of a human skeleton as an exhibit, 'showing what was found, what was missing, and those portions burnt which would supply the places of those which are wanting'. The judge viewed the diagram, and allowed defence counsel to be shown it, but not the jury, opining, 'It is not desirable to brandish about pictures of skeletons in a murder case ... It is most desirable to avoid anything like sensation in cases of murder.'[13] Bond's use of a diagram of a human skeleton as a court exhibit implied this was his standard practice. The judge's refusal to have it shown to the jury might have limited Bond's future use of such diagrams to his own reference, explaining why they were not produced in court for the Torso Murders inquests.

Bond confirmed that there was no fragment of skull, and that the head would not float by itself in water after death. If placed in a box, the specific gravity of the wood would help to keep it afloat. Having viewed the remains on 12 March, he estimated 'that the lady had been dead about a week, but it might have been a fortnight. No decomposition had taken place.'[14] The weather had been very cold. Bond testified that he had measured the only intact bone, one long arm bone, at 11½in, and he estimated that the woman was 5ft 2in tall. He was sure that it was an older woman 'over 50' with dark hair, as 'there was some short, dark hair under the right armpit'.[15]

The facts matched Bond's estimates. Born in April 1823, Julia Thomas was 55 years old. A witness who had known her said that she was 5ft 3in in height, rather stout for her height, and that her hair was dark. Her date of death was almost certainly 2 March, and was estimated by Bond as being between 26 February and 5 March. This validates the accuracy of the information about the Torso Killer's victims stated in the Hebbert report.

Bond described his analysis of the bloodstains, which included 'great clots of blood' on Mrs Thomas's bonnet, 'as if the bonnet had fallen into blood'. There was 'a big splash' of blood on a piece of the hall wallpaper and 'The quantity of blood would be as much as from 10 to 15 drops. It had apparently struck against the wall and then run down.'[16]

Bond was cool in his responses when strenuously cross-examined by the defence, who considered that Thomas, who suffered from 'convulsive fits', might have died of natural causes:

> **[Defence counsel]:** There was not the slightest means of finding out how she came by her death – whether she died naturally or by violence?
> **[Bond]:** Not at all ...
> **[Defence counsel]:** A woman may die from heart disease ... or apoplexy, or she may burst a blood vessel and die from vomiting or from hemorrhage?
> **[Bond]:** Quite so.
> **[Defence counsel]:** If a woman was excited and burst a blood vessel she would drop down, and there would be a copious flow of blood from the mouth?
> **[Bond]:** Quite so.[17]

At a police court hearing, the defence declared an intention to employ Doctor Joseph Coates, a renowned pathologist, to examine the remains in support of their case.[18] Either that examination did not take place, or it did not result in any useful findings. Bond was also asked if he clearly came to the conclusion that the body had been boiled, replying, 'Yes. It was a difficult problem at first.'[19] As in the Torso series, he rejected the idea that the body had been used by medical students for anatomical examination, adding that he had never heard of any portions of a body being boiled for the purpose of dissection in a hospital.

Despite the efforts of the defence, the judge summed up the case in a series of questions that resulted in Webster's conviction:

> Was any reasonable doubt left that that box was taken from the house, and that the remains were those of Mrs. Thomas? ...
>     Was it conceivable that Mrs. Thomas came to her death by natural causes? ...

Could the remains have been placed in a box without [Webster] being aware of it?[20]

The jury took one hour and thirteen minutes to return a verdict of 'Guilty', and Webster was sentenced to death.[21] Webster responded to her sentence by claiming not only that she was innocent, but pregnant, which would entail a stay of execution. As was the custom, a jury of twelve matrons, meaning married women, was sworn in to hear evidence from the matron at Wandsworth Prison, where Webster was being held. That and subsequent evidence from Bond, who examined Webster in the absence of the prison surgeon, was not reported in detail on grounds of delicacy. Bond declared that Webster 'was not quick with child',[22] and the jury pronounced that she was not pregnant. On Tuesday, 29 July 1879, Webster was executed by hanging at Wandsworth Prison. Her waxwork joined that of other murderers in the London attraction Madame Tussaud's Chamber of Horrors.[23]

On the eve of her death, she made a full confession to her solicitor in the presence of a Catholic priest. Extracts from that confession, in which Webster explained in detail how she carried out the murder, and her actions afterwards, are reproduced below.[24]

## Webster's employment and dismissal

I entered the lady's service in the month of January. At first I thought her a nice old lady, and imagined I could be comfortable and happy with her; but I found her very trying. She used to do many things to annoy me. When I had finished my work in the rooms she used to go over it and point out places where she said I did not clean, thus showing evidence of a nasty spirit towards me. This sort of conduct made me have an ill-feeling towards her, but I had no intention of killing her, at least not then.

One day I had an altercation with her, and we mutually arranged that I should leave her service, and she made an entrance to that effect in her memorandum book.

Julia Thomas's murder made Victorian homeowners question whether their own Mary Jane could be trusted. Webster admitted to an intent to kill her employer with the words: 'I had no intention of killing her, at least not then.' Testimony from Webster's acquaintance Mary Durden, a straw-bonnet and hat maker from Kingston, suggested that the murder was premeditated. Durden testified that Webster had told her on Shrove Tuesday, 25 February, that she was going to Birmingham that afternoon to sell her late aunt's property, furniture, and possessions, which had been left to her in a Will.

## Modus operandi

On the Sunday evening, 2nd March last, Mrs. Thomas and I were alone in the house. We had some argument at which she and myself were enraged, and she became very agitated and left the house to go to church in that state ...

Upon her return from church, before her usual hour she came in and went upstairs. I went up after her, and we had an argument which ripened into a quarrel, and in the height of my anger and rage I threw her from the top of the stairs to the ground floor. She had a heavy fall.

I felt that she was seriously injured, and I became agitated at what had occurred, lost all control of myself, and, to prevent her screaming or getting me into trouble, I caught her by the throat, and in the struggle she was choked ...

I did not murder Mrs. Thomas from any premeditation. I was enraged and in a passion, and I cannot now recollect why I did it; something seemed to seize me at the time ... I cannot account for the awful feelings that came over me from the time Mrs. Thomas came home from church until the murder was completed.

By her own admission, Webster killed Thomas by pushing her over the top of the upper-storey bannisters, running down the stairs to the hallway, and strangling her prone body. Thomas's fall was almost certainly the loud noise heard by Mrs Ives next door. Doctor Adams was incorrect in testifying that the fractured bones were caused after death. Webster's method of disabling her victim was efficient, not requiring significant bodily strength to haul her over the bannisters. Her age, physical size and strength gave her an advantage over her victim. Motivated by financial gain and with an extensive criminal history, Webster's claim that her crime was not premeditated is not credible.

A state of tension and power imbalance between those two individuals could have fuelled Webster's motivation to murder. This case opens up the possibility that the Salamanca Place perpetrator could be, if not a woman, then living in the same household as their victim. A key similarity between the two cases could be that the killer knew their victim well in an intimate domestic setting. An additional motive might have been the childless Julia Thomas's failure to understand Webster's responsibilities as a parent. Webster's friend and childminder Sarah Creese was a character witness at her trial. According to Creese, Webster usually visited her son on a Sunday afternoon, and was expected to return before Thomas left for church. Although Webster might have felt pressurised over the timings of those visits, she did not see her son on the date in question.

The killer's relationship with the victim not only created the need to obliterate the identity of the victim, but also obliged the surviving party to explain the other person's absence, assuming it was noticed. Webster had not crafted a specific excuse for Mrs Thomas's absence, beyond the pretence that she was her aunt, but the Salamanca Place 'husband' might have claimed that his wife had left to nurse a sick relative, or visit her mother.

A comparison of the victim types between the two cases reinforces the fact that the Salamanca Place victim was a very different type of woman, living in poverty. How could her killer have private access to a room, tools and a laundry copper and fire? Was it a reversal of roles, not a servant killing her mistress, but a master his live-in servant or visiting charwoman? Alternatively, like a Jack the Ripper victim, was she a street walker killed by her client?

## Dismemberment

Looking on what had happened, and the fear of being discovered, I determined to do away with the body as best I could.

I chopped the head from the body with the assistance of a razor which I used to cut through the flesh afterwards.

I also used the meat saw and the carving knife to cut the body up with.

I prepared the copper with water to boil the body to prevent identity; and as soon as I had succeeded in cutting it up I placed it in the copper and boiled it.

I opened the stomach with the carving knife, and burned up as much of the parts as I could.

During the whole of this time there was nobody in the house but myself. When I looked upon the scene before me and saw the blood around my feet, the horror and dread I felt was inconceivable. I was bewildered, acted as if I was mad, and did everything I possibly could to conceal the occurrence, fearing the neighbours might suspect something had happened. I was greatly overcome, both from the horrible sight before me and the smell ...

I remained in the house all night endeavouring to clear up the place and clean away traces of the murder ... When [the coal man] called I was engaged in regulating the place, and was in a dreadful state of mind.

Under circumstances that strongly resemble the Salamanca Place murder, Webster dragged her mistress's body into the kitchen and stripped it of all clothing and jewellery, even her dental plate. She dismembered the body by cutting off the head with a razor, and using a meat saw and carving knife to cut up the remainder and remove the internal organs, which she burned. She also used the razor to remove pieces of skin and flesh. What could not be burned was divided up and boiled in the copper, which measured about 40in in diameter and 23in deep.

The Richmond case provides a breakdown of timings for the clean-up actions after the murder. Timing it by the loud noise heard by

## A PARALLEL CASE: THE MURDER OF JULIA MARTHA THOMAS IN 1879

Mrs Ives, Webster killed Julia Thomas shortly before 9 p.m. on Sunday, 2 March 1879. Again, according to the Ives women, a light was on in the back bedroom at six o'clock on the following Monday, and there were sounds like 'the usual process of washing' on a Monday wash-day, including the noise of a brush and a poking of the copper fire. At about eleven that morning, some clothes were hanging out to dry in the back garden. The coal man, William Dean, called to request payment for his account at 12.30 p.m. The Ives women confirmed that the sounds of the lighting of the fire, chopping of wood and poking the fire from next door continued on the Tuesday.

Using her arrival at the Porters' house for the timing, Webster had filled and secured the bag and box, and transported the former to Hammersmith, before 5 p.m. on the second day after the murder. In a rough estimate, the clear-up took a maximum of nineteen hours across that Monday and Tuesday, motivated by Webster's need to make the house presentable before selling items from it.

Those timings make it unlikely that the Salamanca Place killing occurred on the Saturday daytime, when the body was discovered early on a Sunday morning. That murder may have taken place after a Friday night drinking binge. The perpetrator had all day on the Saturday to deal with the remains before taking a sack out for disposal early on the Sunday morning, when for some reason, he needed to have the house clear.

In each case, the dismemberment must have been handled with implements that were readily available. The kitchen copper and household utensils were the only means of erasing the body's identity and breaking it up for disposal. In the Salamanca Place murder, could the killer also have been in a domestic setting without the use of a tradesman's tools?

### Depositing the remains

> I then put parts of the body into the little wooden box that was produced in Court, and tied it up with cord, and determined to deposit it in the Thames ... with the help of young Porter.

> I put the head of Mrs. Thomas into the black bag, and being weary and afraid to remain in the house, I carried it to the Porters ... and disposed of it ...
>
> The foot found in the dunghill ... was placed there by me ...

With the unwitting help of the Porters, Webster dropped the black bag from Hammersmith Bridge, and the wooden box from Richmond Bridge. She disposed of one foot in a manure heap in Twickenham within an easy walk of the railway station. As in the Torso Killer's likely modus operandi, she chose to conceal it on the opposite side of the river to where the murder was committed. Assuming that both the Richmond and Salamanca Place murders were unplanned, the body parts were deposited in places that were easy to get to and unobserved. Webster could do this piecemeal as she had time, whereas the Vauxhall killer was acting under some degree of pressure.

## The avoidance of suspicion

> [I] cleared up the place so that a person coming in might not suspect or see anything irregular, and it was suggested to my mind to sell all that there was in the house and go away; and with that view I went and saw Porter, and introduced the sale of the things to him ... [I] also kept ordering things for the house from tradespeople in order to evade suspicion ...
>
> It is true that I went by the name of Mrs. Thomas and that I wore her gold watch ...

The initial absence of suspicion is interesting. Several visitors came to the cottage in the days after the murder, none of whom suspected any crime had taken place. The next-door neighbours, despite what they heard and smelled, were not unduly suspicious until the attempted furniture sale.

Thomas's brother and sister-in-law had last received a letter from her on 25 February and replied a week later. When they did not hear back, Mrs Batterbee told the press, 'We got a little anxious, but we supposed she probably was off on a visit to some of her friends, and were not much alarmed.'[25] On Sunday, 23 March, Charles Batterbee had a telegram from the police requesting him to go to his sister's house immediately, as something was wrong. If Batterbee had not been notified by the police, it is safe to assume that he would have paid his sister a visit in late March or early April, and then discovered that she was missing.

What would have happened if Webster had not reinvigorated her friendship with the Porters, nor sold locally any items belonging to Mrs Thomas? Could she have got away with murder either by reporting the death as a natural one, or reporting it as a murder that had taken place in her absence, or simply by leaving for New York? By contrast, the Salamanca Place killer did get away with murder.

### The possible discovery of the head

> The deposition of this black bag gave me great uneasiness, as I feared it might be discovered, and the identity of Mrs. Thomas thereby proven, and when I heard that a black bag had been found I was greatly troubled …

Webster stated in her confession that the black bag contained her employer's head, and it may also have concealed the missing half of the pelvis, and a portion of the ribs and abdomen. The meat saw, which was missing from the cottage, might have been used to weight the bag. In an attempt to locate it, the river police dredged the river, and Scotland Yard offered a £25 reward for its return. It was described as a black leather Gladstone or American cloth bag about 15in long and 9in deep. According to Henry Porter, it weighed between 20–25lb, or 9–11kg.

There is no record that a black bag was found. However, a newspaper article dated 26 July 1879 reported the finding of an unrelated skull:

> About a week ago the skull of a woman was found amongst some mud and ballast which had been dredged from the bed of the Thames

near Barnes Bridge, and the remains having been deposited at Hammersmith Police-station, a rumour spread that the head was that of the murdered woman, Mrs. Thomas. There is no ground whatever for this supposition. The skull is that of a much younger person, and it has evidently lain in the water for many months, if not years. There are five teeth remaining in the upper jaw, whereas Mrs. Thomas, it was shown at the recent trial, had none. The lower jaw is missing. There are no vestiges of hair or flesh remaining on the skull.[26]

It was also widely reported in the press that on Friday, 17 October 1879, a female skull was found in the Thames near Lambeth Bridge.[27]

In October 2010, a skull was recovered in the back garden of the famous naturalist Sir David Attenborough, during building work. Coroner Alison Thompson recorded a verdict of unlawful killing and the cause of death as asphyxiation and a head injury. She concluded that all of the evidence presented to her pointed to the body being that of Mrs Julia Martha Thomas, murdered in 1879.[28] Attenborough's garden was in the immediate vicinity of Thomas's home. Although it would not have changed its outcome, the head was discovered 131 years too late to assist the murder investigation.

## Review of the Salamanca Place murder

All of the crimes covered in this book are considered as 'how-dunits', with the method of the killing providing the best clues as to the perpetrators' profiles. They also raise the question of how far the killers could transport the bodily remains of their victims. The distances that human remains could be carried by hand is demonstrated in the 1879 case. After the murder of Mrs Thomas, Kate Webster was able to dispose of the bag and box containing most of the remains in two trips, and only with the unwitting help of the aptly named Porters. With assistance, she was able to carry the box from Park Road to Richmond Bridge, a distance slightly less than 1 mile, or 1.3km. Swanson's estimate of the distance that one man carried the torso found at Pinchin Street was less than a quarter of that. In an estimate of the so-called 'region of theory' for the Pinchin Street murder, a route devised by the author from London

Docks' Western Dock to Backchurch Lane takes three and a half minutes to walk.

Transposed onto the 1902 murder, four minutes' walk eastward from Salamanca Place stood Prince's Road Workhouse. It might have been excluded from Scotland Yard's house-to-house enquiries, and also from the Yard's visits to local businesses. A credible hypothesis suggests that a workhouse employee killed an inmate, dismembered, boiled and roasted her body using its extensive kitchen facilities, and dumped the sack containing her remains within a local factory's premises. Frequented by Jessie Miller and Ripper victim Polly Nichols, that workhouse might have been the place where the Salamanca Place victim, while seeking refuge, lost her life.

This theory takes the murder away from a purely domestic setting, while explaining the power imbalance between the killer and his victim. Placing the kill at the workhouse explains how the perpetrator had private access to cooking facilities which enabled him to destroy the identity of a woman who was recognisable, with a direct connection to him. The workhouse kitchen was unused from the late evening onwards, as the main meal of the day was served at lunchtime, with only 6oz of bread and butter, and a pint of tea, for supper. If he killed his victim on Friday evening, he would need to work through the night to reduce her body into manageable parts. He would process the remains for several hours before morning, before storing them somewhere safe. Overnight on Saturday, he would have further time to reduce the body parts to unidentifiable pieces. In the early hours of Sunday morning, he might dispose of the remains within a short walk, to be back on duty in time to prepare breakfast.

A list of the names of male employees at Prince's Road Workhouse in the 1901 census does not result in any matches to criminal records. Nor can any disappearance of a female inmate be deduced from the workhouse's admission and discharge register. Its inmates were transients who came and went casually, and it was not unusual for someone simply to walk out of 'the spike' without being formally released.

This theory is similar to propositions from other researchers that Jack the Ripper was a workhouse employee or mortuary attendant, with easy access to destitute women and the facilities to dispose of them. The Salamanca Place killer removed his victim's clothes that, like those of Polly Nichols, were marked with the workhouse's name, and could have led to her identification. Assuming that he was neither the Ripper nor the Torso Killer, we will never know whether he had killed before, or would kill again. But it is possible to create a speculative re-run of what he did on that fateful weekend.

### Reconstruction of the Salamanca Place murder

*My assumptions are that:*
- *the date of the murder was Friday, 6 June 1902;*
- *the perpetrator was a workhouse employee and resident, who was able to secure private use of the workhouse laundry and kitchen facilities in the late evening and overnight, and to store items for a period of time;*
- *his victim was a workhouse inmate;*
- *the perpetrator walked eastwards towards the river to deposit the remains, but failing to reach it, deposited the sack in Salamanca Place;*
- *the sack was deposited shortly before it was found.*

It is late when he corners her in the kitchen, where she happens to be alone. Petite and attractive, she knows what he wants, ducks under his outstretched arm, yet is caught by it. He deliberately swings for her head, above the hairline, where no marks from his blows will be seen. Despite his superior size and strength, she puts up a fight to avoid what will become rough, painful advances. He takes hold of her throat and squeezes it until her struggles stop. Having gone too far this time, he checks her breathing, curses, and tries to think beyond his panic. He has until five o'clock tomorrow morning to cover his traces.

Working methodically, he stokes up the oven, fills a large copper with water, and only then takes a knife to her. He burns what he can, including her clothes marked as Prince's Road Workhouse property, and dozes in between batches of cutting, boiling and roasting. Time is running out, so he empties the hot pieces into one sack, with some leftover remains of flesh and bones pushed into a second sack. He drags the sacks back into the storeroom for their contents to cool. After he cleans and mops the kitchen, he is satisfied with his work, and reflects: *It wasn't that clean in the first place.*

## A PARALLEL CASE: THE MURDER OF JULIA MARTHA THOMAS IN 1879

He is on guard for the rest of Saturday, keeping helpers away from the storeroom. After supper, he boils whatever needs further reduction, and lays those last pieces into the top of the first sack, which is now full to the brim. Avoiding the Saturday night revellers on the streets, he sets off at daybreak on the Sabbath. Although it is heavy, he manages to walk at pace with the largest sack over his shoulder. He won't make it to the river, but if he can dump its contents on the far side of the railway bridge, the pottery workers will be in for a shock. As for the second sack, he cannot risk another outing. At a quiet time on the day of rest, its bony shards and fleshy remnants will be emptied into the infirmary's receptacle of waste from the sick wards. Once sprinkled with chloride of lime, nobody will look at it, let alone touch it.

# 11

# Why not Jack the Ripper?

He feared neither God, nor devil, nor man, nor wind, nor sea, nor his own conscience.

From *The Shadow Line* by Joseph Conrad

A crucial question recurs throughout the Metropolitan Police Whitechapel Murders files: is *this* murder the work of Jack the Ripper? Whitechapel's police surgeon Doctor Phillips, who, like Bond, was regularly consulted on that issue, coined the phrase 'the one man theory' when discussing the murder of Alice Kinsey (who was also known as McKenzie). A 44-year-old street walker, Kinsey was murdered after midnight on Wednesday, 17 July 1889, on Castle Alley, a narrow thoroughfare which led between Wentworth Street and Whitechapel Road. Unlike Bond, Phillips did not consider that Kinsey's murder, despite being that of an 'unfortunate' with stab wounds, and occurring close to Whitechapel Road, was a Ripper kill, and, in an extension of that thinking, she was also not a victim of the Torso Killer:

> After careful and long deliberation I cannot satisfy myself on purely anatomical & professional grounds that the Perpetrator of all the 'WhChl. [Whitechapel] murders' is one man.

I am on the contrary impelled to a contrary conclusion. This noting the mode of procedure & the character of the mutilations & judging of motive in connection with the latter.

I do not here enter into the comparison of cases neither do I take into account what I admit may be almost conclusive evidence in favour of the one man theory if all the surrounding circumstances & other evidence are considered.[1]

Phillips validated the concept that the Ripper's mutilations were done for his gratification whereas the Torso Killer's dismemberment served a mainly practical purpose. But the question is compelling: were two serial killers operating side by side in the period 1887–89, in central London, or could the Thames Torso Killer be Jack the Ripper?

In my re-examination of the Ripper case, *One-Armed Jack*, a serial killer active in the East End was identified by police but never prosecuted owing to insufficient evidence. Between August and November 1888, Jack the Ripper murdered six vulnerable women, 'unfortunates' who resorted to sex work to pay for their food and lodgings: Martha Tabram, Polly Nichols, Annie Chapman, Elisabeth Stride, Catherine Eddowes and Mary Jane Kelly. Although he killed by cutting their throats, the signature of his crimes developed with the escalation of violence across his victims. In at least two cases, he was interrupted and unable to complete his objective of disembowelling his victims, and removing their internal organs, some of which he took away as trophies. He always left the dead women lying where he had assaulted them, mostly on the street, although Kelly was killed in bed at her private lodgings.

The Ripper was seen with nearly all of his victims, and the police logged dozens of eyewitness descriptions. The murder of Annie Chapman, the third in the Ripper's canon of six, was the first where a man with distinctive physical characteristics and an unusual gait was seen running from the scene of the crime. He was in his mid-30s, of average height and weight, and broad-shouldered, with brown hair and a moustache. He favoured dark clothing that appeared 'shabby-chic', and spoke colloquial English. In the author's analysis, local cigar maker Hyam Hyams was Jack the Ripper, a man with physical and mental health issues whose severe epilepsy triggered episodes of violence. He had a stiff left arm following a broken elbow, and walked with a peculiar gait characterised by bent knees and asymmetric foot dragging. Eyewitnesses also described a similar man seen with the next three victims: Elisabeth Stride, Catherine Eddowes and Mary Jane Kelly. Eddowes's was the only murder in the series where potentially useful physical evidence was left on the killer's route home: a corner cut from her apron alongside some scrawled words in chalk on a doorway.

Despite interviewing dozens of suspects, and receiving a huge volume of information from the public, the police were unable to make an arrest. The Ripper's crimes ended as suddenly as they began, in November 1888. Hyams was detained by the authorities from late December 1888 almost continuously until his death in 1913 at Colney Hatch Lunatic Asylum. However, like Crick, Hyams committed acts of violence during 1889, in his brief periods of liberty, in the months of April and September. He was arrested for assault in early April and readmitted to Stepney Workhouse on the grounds that: 'In attempting to strike his wife with a chopper he seriously injured his mother on the head.'[2] In early September, he was arrested for stabbing his wife, and spent the rest of his life in secure medical facilities.[3] Hyams was diagnosed as suffering from epileptic mania and insanity.

There are notable similarities between the Torso and Ripper series:

- It is extraordinary that two serial killers were operating in broadly the same area at the same time, with the Torso Murders overlapping the Ripper's by less than a year on either side.
- The date of the discovery of the Whitehall torso was two days after the 'double event' when the Ripper killed Elisabeth Stride and Catherine Eddowes within two hours of each other in the early morning of Sunday, 30 September 1888.
- The date of the Pinchin Street murder was estimated by police to be 8 September 1889, exactly a year after the Ripper murder of Annie Chapman.
- Pinchin Street was close to the Ripper's area of operation, in particular to Berner Street where Elisabeth Stride was killed, and to Swallow Gardens, where Frances Coles had her throat cut, although in the author's opinion the latter was not a Ripper murder.

- Both killers were believed to be right-handed.
- The signature of their crimes indicates that both men were sexually motivated, harbouring a pathological hatred of women. The Whitehall victim and Elizabeth Jackson had their uteri removed, which was a Ripper signature and arguably a significant source of sexual gratification for both killers. Jack the Ripper removed the breasts of Mary Jane Kelly in an act of sexual violence exceeding his previous mutilations.
- It is highly likely that both men experienced an escalation in their mania, and an increase in violence, starting with non-fatal attacks on women. The extent of the violence inflicted on Mary Jane Kelly's body towards the end of 1888 strongly suggests that the Ripper was becoming so mentally incapacitated that it would affect his ability to operate, and also be apparent to other people. Hyam Hyams was arrested as a 'wandering lunatic' suffering from *delirium tremens* (acute alcohol withdrawal syndrome which could cause hallucinations) in December 1888. There is an assumed escalation in the Torso series from rape to murder.
- Both murderers ran out of time after killing their victims. The Ripper was interrupted by people approaching after the murders of Polly Nichols and Elisabeth Stride. The Torso Killer arguably abandoned his dismemberment of the Whitehall and Pinchin Street victims owing to the need to start work in the early morning.
- Each killer removed one or more finger rings from the bodies of his victims, in the Ripper's case Annie Chapman and in the Torso Killer's Elizabeth Jackson. The rings might have been taken as trophies, although it is possible that they were used as gifts, pawned or sold.
- Both killers arguably left physical evidence behind them. On the night of the 'double event', when he killed two women in forty-five minutes, the Ripper left two pieces of physical evidence in a doorway at Goulston Street. That location was on his escape route from Mitre Square, where he killed Eddowes, to his lodgings. He dropped a corner cut from her apron under a 'graffito', some scrawled words in chalk on a doorway lintel. The Torso Killer deposited physical evidence in the form of the women's remains, pieces of their torn clothing, and other wrapping materials that were in his possession.

- All of the women attacked by the Ripper, and, with the possible exception of the Rainham and Whitehall victims, the Torso Killer, were probably casual prostitutes, making them vulnerable to attack and attractive to sexually motivated perpetrators.
- Both murderers had extensive local knowledge of the areas in which they operated. The Ripper made his escapes through back alleys and cut-throughs that only a local man would know. The Torso Killer was highly familiar with the River Thames and its riverside and canal-side areas, in addition to building sites and trade yards within easy reach of the water. His extensive local knowledge enabled him to deposit two torsos on land; one inside a fenced-off building site at Whitehall and the second in a remote railway arch in Whitechapel.
- Both serial killers either escaped detection or, as in the author's analysis, Jack the Ripper could not be prosecuted for murder owing to a lack of evidence.
- If the Ripper were Hyam Hyams, and the Torso Killer James Crick, both men were investigated by the authorities for non-fatal attacks, which led to their detentions. Hyams was detained in medical facilities for hitting his mother with a chopper whilst attempting to assault his wife. Crick assaulted his wife, and was first charged with the attempted murder and assault of Jessie Miller. At Crick's Old Bailey trial on similar charges for an attack on Elizabeth Sarah Warburton, he was sentenced to a period of imprisonment.
- Police surgeon Thomas Bond produced the first-ever criminal profile when asked to review the Ripper murders by CID Chief Robert Anderson. Bond also provided the basis for the Hebbert report, which included estimates of the type of work the Torso Killer might be engaged in. Both series of murders were sexually motivated.

However, the differences between the two series of cases are compelling:

- The Thames Torso Killer attacked and killed on the river, not inland, forcing police to think differently about his unusual approach and methods of disposal.
- It is highly likely that the Torso Killer's crimes were sexually motivated, and he might have raped some of his victims. Although similarly motivated, the Ripper did not rape his victims.

- With the exception of Martha Tabram as a possible inclusion in the canon, the Ripper victims were killed by the severance of their carotid arteries, often following a partial suffocation. The Torso Killer may have used more than one method of killing, such as throat-cutting or blunt trauma to the head. Bond ruled out suffocation as the cause of death for the Whitehall victim.
- Unlike the Ripper, who tried and failed to decapitate at least two of his victims, but had some anatomical knowledge, the Torso Killer had butchery skills and was able to decapitate and cut up all of his victims. The previously quoted unnamed East End detective commented publicly: '[Jack] could not get the knife further than the vertebrae of the neck ... [and] as skilful as Jack may be with the use of the knife, I don't think that he is the man to use a saw.'[4]
- The Torso Killer must have had the time and a safe location to carry out his murders and butcheries. The quoted press article was wrong in placing those activities 'inside a house'. They probably took place on board a boat, or multiple boats even in a single attack. By contrast, the Ripper lacked secure premises and conducted non-fatal attacks at lodging houses, while killing all but one of his victims on the street. The last, Mary Jane Kelly, was killed at her private lodgings, and he spent several hours mutilating her body.
- Both Commissioner Monro and Doctor Phillips publicly compared the Ripper murder of Mary Jane Kelly to the Pinchin Street murder, resulting in the conclusion that the two murders were carried out by different men.
- The primary motivation for the Torso Killer's mutilation of the bodies was their easy disposal, while for the Ripper this was his main gratification. In the author's opinion, both men derived gratification from post-mortem mutilations.
- Each man used different techniques to remove his victims' organs. Where the lungs and heart were missing, in the Rainham and Battersea cases, the Torso Killer had removed them from the top end, leaving the diaphragm intact. In the Ripper murder of Mary Jane Kelly, Bond reported an approach from below the ribcage: 'The Pericardium [membrane enclosing the heart] was open below & the Heart absent.'[5]
- Neither man had use of a private indoor or outdoor space where a woman might be killed and her dead body buried – for example, in

a backyard. Unlike the Ripper, who abandoned his victims' corpses where they lay, the Torso Killer was organised and methodical in disposing of the body parts by river and land.
- All of the Ripper victims were identified, as they lived and worked close to where they were killed. Owing to his deliberate dismemberments and disposals, only one of the Torso Killer's victims was named by the authorities.
- The two killers' ideal victim types arguably differed with respect to their poverty. The Ripper preyed upon destitute street walkers in the East End of London. At the time of her death, Annie Chapman was ill and her body showed signs of great privation, and Catherine Eddowes was visibly undernourished. By contrast, the Torso victims were plump and well nourished, with a better standard of clothing and grooming than the Ripper victims.
- Unlike the Ripper, the Torso Killer is likely to have used accomplices.
- The Ripper was seen by eyewitnesses who reported their sightings to the police, facilitating descriptions to be circulated in the press and the holding of identity parades. In the Torso series, nobody reported a man behaving suspiciously, either in the presence of a victim, or alone. The non-identification of most of his victims also helped him to escape notice.
- The lack of proof that the Torso Murders were part of a series and the absence of sightings of the Torso Killer meant that, unlike his nicknamed counterpart, he did not enter the public imagination. There was no public awareness that he was in fact a serial killer as dangerous as the Ripper, and therefore none of the resulting hysteria or pressure to neutralise him as a threat. Ironically, the police focus on the Ripper may have helped the Torso Killer to evade justice.
- A dog was used unofficially, then semi-officially, to find further body parts in the Torso series. Under Metropolitan Police Commissioner Sir Charles Warren's direction, police experimented with the use of bloodhounds to track murderers and locate body parts. The so-called canine sleuths were not used for the Ripper case, although police delayed forcing an entry into Mary Jane Kelly's lodgings in the hope of their arrival.
- The Ripper was a disorganised killer, while the Torso Killer was organised. Their different approaches helped police to separate the two sets of crimes.

The terminology of the level of an offender's organised behaviour originates from the American Federal Bureau of Investigation (FBI). Jack the Ripper was 'a disorganized offender', as his crimes were 'committed suddenly with no set plan of action for deterring detection. Facial destruction and sexually sadistic acts performed after the murder are typical. Disorganized offenders usually leave the victim in the same position in which he or she was killed and make no attempt to conceal the body.'[6]

The Torso Killer was, by contrast, an organised offender, whose characteristics include:

> ... a high birth order, inconsistent parental discipline, average or above average intelligence, and poor work performance. The organized offender is socially adept and usually living with a partner. He may report an angry state of mind prior to the murder and admit to being calm and relaxed after the crime. The crime scene of the organized murderer shows a semblance of order before, during, and after the offense. The victim frequently is a stranger and may be targeted because he or she is in a particular location or has certain characteristics. Obsessive, compulsive traits surface in the organized murderer's behavior and crime scene patterns.[7]

The FBI profile is intended for use against living suspects, and although helpful, parallels to the historical case of the Torso Killer cannot be made in an evidenced way. Yet the concept of him frequently targeting strangers in a particular location or because she has certain characteristics correlates well with what we know of Crick's modus operandi, as would a methodical approach to tidying up the crime scene and dealing with the remains. In terms of having a high birth order, Crick was the oldest child of his mother's second marriage. His father's death would have disrupted his family life and might have contributed towards a lack of discipline at home.

If the Torso Killer had been seen acting suspiciously, and if he were a lighterman like James Crick, he could have been distinguished by his clothes. A man of that trade described the lighterman's unique garb in his reminiscences:

> I could tell a lighterman anywhere, Sunday or day clothes apparel. The important articles of dress were good boots and good overcoats.

Boots were pegged [with tacks attaching the upper to the insole] or sewn, a glance at a man's boots would tell who was the builder. Every riverside district had its shoemaker, this caused heated arguments as to the merits of each.

The essential quality of an overcoat was to be warm and almost waterproof, a good test was to have about 8 hour's rain on a coat then to stand it up alone. I have seen this done, just a little dampness underneath the arms otherwise dry underneath. I believe the cloth used was either box cloth [a heavy felt-like woollen cloth] or Melton [a similar cloth woven in a twill form]. This garment was also our blanket when turned in to rest in the cabin; this accounts for the number of men seen with coats on the arm at all seasons of the year.

The training in those times gave the lighterman an important sense of command; he was in charge, no one to appeal to, the river often presenting problems which called for a decision with only one answer ... I am sure that it is this sense of 'I'm in charge' that makes lightermen appear to be hard headed and cocksure.[8]

The description of a man who was hard-headed and cocksure rings true for the Torso Killer. By the standards of the day, a lighterman had a good regular income. By contrast, the Ripper came across as a mild-mannered clerk, who dressed in a 'shabby-genteel' dark jacket and trousers.

Many officials worked on both the Torso and Ripper series of cases, and the majority considered them completely separate from each other. The best men of the Metropolitan Police investigated both series of murders, while the City of London Police were only involved in the Jack the Ripper case. They were brought into the Ripper investigation by the murder of Catherine Eddowes in Mitre Square, within the City's 'Square Mile'.

Only one City of London official was involved in both series, Coroner Samuel Langham. He handled the inquest of Ripper victim Catherine Eddowes in the autumn of 1888. In the Torso sequence, he had in 1887 refused to conduct an inquest on the Rainham thigh, and years later presided over the inquest into the accidental death of Jessie Miller. His minimal involvement with the Rainham case precluded him from making any comparisons to Jack the Ripper.

Commissioner James Monro, in his report to the Home Secretary, considered that, despite the similarity in date to the Ripper murder of Annie Chapman, this murder was not characterised by the five attributes of the Ripper's 'signature'. Most strikingly, he observed the Torso Killer's methodical approach: 'There was plenty of time at the disposal of the murderer, there is no sign of frenzied mutilation of the body, but of deliberate & skilful dismemberment with a view to removal.'[9]

Chief Inspector Donald Swanson in his own report shared the commissioner's belief that the Pinchin Street killer had sufficient time to mutilate his victim's body. Yet it is possible that the killer ran out of time. Although it would certainly take less time to remove a woman's intestines than to cut her torso into three parts, the incomplete dismemberment of the torso implies that he had to abandon it. Any removal of abdominal organs might have been intended to prevent the body from floating.

At the inquest into the death of the Pinchin Street victim, Doctor Phillips was recalled and asked to compare this murder with that of Mary Jane Kelly on 9 November 1888. His analysis reads as follows:

> There was not such a similarity between the manner in which the limbs were severed in this and in the Dorset-street murder as would convince him that both crimes were the work of one man, but the division of the neck and the attempt to disarticulate the bones of the spine were very similar in each case. The savagery shown in the mutilations in the Dorset-street case was far worse than in that now under consideration. In the former the mutilations were most wanton, whereas in the Pinchin-street crime he believed they were made in order to dispose of the body.
>
> These were the points that struck him without any comparative study of the Dorset-street case, except such as was afforded by partial notes which he had with him. He believed that in this case there had been greater knowledge shown in regard to the construction of the parts composing the spine, and on the whole there had been a greater knowledge shown of how to separate a joint.[10]

Kelly had been found with her throat cut, horribly mutilated, wearing only a thin bloodstained chemise. It was the only Ripper case with extreme mutilation, the skin on one of her thighs removed down to the bone. Several of her internal organs were removed, but her body was not dismembered. Doctor Phillips's reference to the joint separation might be explained by a sentence from Bond's post-mortem report on Kelly: 'The neck was cut through the skin & other tissues right down to the vertebrae the 5th & 6th being deeply notched.'[11] The clumsy hacks to the vertebrae, in which the Ripper tried and failed to separate Kelly's head from her body, indicated that the Torso Killer, who did this successfully at least four times, was more skilled with a knife.

The author's prime suspect as Jack the Ripper, Hyam Hyams, was at liberty for all of the Torso Murders, possibly including the last at Pinchin Street. Violent towards his wife, whom he accused of sleeping with his brothers, he was committed to infirmaries and lunatic asylums intermittently from late December 1888 until 7 September 1889, after which he was permanently detained.

Hyams first came to the attention of the authorities on 29 December 1888, when H Division Constable Edward Walker found him behaving erratically in Leman Street. Hyams went before Franklin Lushington at Thames Magistrates' Court on the charge of being a 'wandering lunatic'. He was sent to Whitechapel's Baker's Row Workhouse Infirmary, where his cause of admission was recorded as *delirium tremens*, meaning severe alcohol withdrawal symptoms.

Franklin Lushington is one of the personalities who link the author's Ripper suspect Hyam Hyams and her Torso suspect James Crick. In this instance, his decision to send Hyams for medical treatment as an in-patient eventually led to his permanent removal from the streets of London. He, along with his colleague Saunders, was responsible for granting James Crick bail when on remand for the assault on Jessie Miller.

Lushington's connections are of historical interest. He was a close friend of artist and poet Edward Lear, and his first cousin, Godfrey Lushington, was involved in the Home Office's oversight of the Jack the Ripper investigation. Lushington reported directly to the Home Secretary from 1886 to 1895, creating what CID Chief Robert Anderson termed 'fatal friction' between the Home Office and the key senior officials it managed. That friction contributed towards the removal from their posts of both Metropolitan Police Commissioners

Sir Charles Warren and James Monro. In his published memoir, Anderson was blunt in his criticism of Lushington: 'With his many excellent qualities Godfrey Lushington's intervention and influence as Under Secretary were generally provocative, and his manner was irritating.'[12]

Franklin Lushington's order regarding Hyam Hyams kept him off the streets for less than two weeks, as he was released once his symptoms ended. In late March or early April 1889, he was in more serious trouble after committing a non-fatal attack: 'in attempting to strike his wife with a chopper he seriously injured his mother on the head'. On 15 April 1889, Hyams was transferred from Baker's Row Workhouse to Colney Hatch Lunatic Asylum in a straitjacket, and admitted as a 'very violent and threatening' man suffering from epileptic mania.

Surprisingly, owing to an onset of improved behaviour, Hyams was discharged from Colney Hatch on 30 August 1889. At the end of what would prove to be his single week of freedom, he was arrested for stabbing his wife. Hyams was admitted to the City of London's Homerton Workhouse on Bow Road from 7–9 September. From there, he was sent to the City of London Lunatic Asylum at Stone near Dartford, 'as a person of unsound mind'. After almost four months at Stone, on 7 January 1890, Hyams was readmitted to Colney Hatch, where he spent the rest of his life.[13]

The police estimate of the date of the Pinchin Street murder as recorded in Police Commissioner Monro's report to the Home Secretary was the evening of Sunday, 8 September 1889. He wrote: 'The state of the body itself showed that death took place about 36 hours or more previously [to the morning of Tuesday, 10 September].' He placed the probable time of death 'on Sunday night, the 8th September'. Swanson estimated it to be twenty-four hours before the finding, meaning the early hours of the Monday morning. Hyams was admitted to Homerton Workhouse on Saturday, 7 September.

Monro also conjectured that the body was concealed between the murder on the night of Sunday, 8 September, until dawn of Tuesday, 10 September, when it was transported to the place where it was found. The place of concealment, where the murder and dismemberment were also assumed to have occurred, was 'probably in the house or lodging of the murderer'.

Hyams was living at an address that was either 26 or 36 New Street, Gravel Lane,[14] over ½ mile away from the Pinchin Street arch. Lodging as he did with his wife and children, it is highly unlikely that he could have committed a murder at his home address and stored a body there afterwards. Even if he could have secured premises for concealment, he was not at liberty to deposit the torso under the archway in the early hours of Tuesday, 10 September 1889, prior to its discovery at 5.25 a.m.

In the Whitehall case, the bloodhounds taken by Sergeant George Rose to the New Scotland Yard basement form a direct connection to the Ripper investigation. Following the 'double event' when two Ripper victims were killed on the same night, Commissioner Charles Warren had paid a Mr Edwin Brough of Scarborough to come to London and demonstrate tracking by scent, using his bloodhounds Barnaby and Burgho. Warren had even participated in one of the trials at Hyde Park. An innovation in hunting down criminals, it was met with a degree of scepticism in the press: 'In Whitechapel we need not say that ten minutes after a dead body is discovered in the streets the scent is "foiled" [contaminated] by cross-trails in all directions.'[15]

Sergeant Rose probably took Brough's bloodhounds to the site of New Scotland Yard. But the commissioner failed to make a firm decision to use them in future cases. As they returned with their owner to Scarborough, the police were issued with a standing order not to disturb any future murder scene, but to wait for the dogs. This led to a delay of hours in police entering 13 Miller's Court after the murder of Mary Jane Kelly, waiting for the bloodhounds that never came. The last murder in the Ripper series led Sir Charles Warren to resign, and the killer was never brought to justice. Warren did not see out the Torso series of murders, as he was only in place for the Rainham and Whitehall murders.

Warren's successor James Monro had extensive knowledge of both the Torso and Ripper murders, holding several police and Home Office roles between 1884 and 1890. In contradiction to Monro, Inspector Henry Moore, who had formerly worked under Abberline on the Ripper investigation, considered that the Pinchin Street murder was part of the Ripper series, and that the perpetrator 'was a mad foreign sailor, who paid periodical visits to London on board ship. He committed the crimes, and then went back to his ship, and remembered nothing about them.'[16] It is the dismemberment, and the fact that the body was stored elsewhere for at least twenty-four, if not thirty-six, hours previously, that categorise it as a Torso murder. Like his mutilations, the Torso Killer's storage of the corpse served not only a practical purpose, but delivered gratification by extending his control over his victim.

The following paragraphs compare and contrast the interactions of each perpetrator with their targets, on this occasion seeking to answer the question: *Why not Jack the Ripper?*

## First sighting and accosting

Both killers targeted lone females, aged between their 20s and 40s. They differed in terms of their physicality, as the Torso Killer preferred plump, bustier women. For each man, their ideal victim type might have resembled their own wives.

The Ripper consorted with destitute street walkers, who were often unwell or undernourished. The Torso victims were better fed, and might have been in regular work, although the Pinchin Street victim was classified by police as a prostitute, as was Elizabeth Jackson. They were probably working class, apart from the Whitehall victim, who could have been lower middle class in her aspiration to follow fashion. Bond and Hebbert considered the Rainham victim 'lower class', as she had a mark on her leg below the knee as if from wearing a garter. However, as Jackson's right calf and foot was tied by a piece of string below the knee, it is possible that the mark on the Rainham victim came from the posthumous tying of a ligature.

The US Federal Bureau of Investigation has defined characteristics which link the victims of serial killers, all of which apply to both the Ripper and Torso series:

> An offender selects a victim ... based on availability, vulnerability, and desirability.
>
> *Availability* is explained as the lifestyle of the victim or circumstances in which the victim is involved, that allow the offender access to the victim.
>
> *Vulnerability* is defined as the degree to which the victim is susceptible to attack by the offender.

*Desirability* is described as the appeal of the victim to the offender. Desirability involves numerous factors based upon the motivation of the offender and may include factors dealing with the race, gender, ethnic background, age of the victim, or other specific preferences the offender determines.[17]

The Ripper arguably targeted his victims on the street, or in a local pub. The Torso Killer did the same, with the additional advantage of his boat, which provided an easy method of transporting and isolating them. The Torso Killer offered free drinks and a free ride, while the women in receipt of his largesse did not stop to think what the payback would be. The Ripper was likely to have bought a few drinks while offering to pay for sexual services, before going with them to a secluded place.

## Seasonality and periodicity

The known Ripper murders took place in a three-month period between August and November 1888, counting Martha Tabram as the first victim followed by The Five. For whatever reason, the Ripper was taken out of action by the end of that year.

All of the known Torso Murders took place in the watermen's summer seasons, which ran between Easter and October. The same can be said of Crick's assaults on Jessie Miller and Elizabeth Sarah Warburton. Whoever he was, the Torso Killer was active from 1887–89, a period of two and a half years. Only one known Torso murder took place in 1887, and one again in 1888. In 1889, there were two further murders. If including the attacks against Miller and Warburton, the periodicity between those four crimes ranges from just under a month to just over two months. Those timings indicate an escalation in his activity and a corresponding mental decline.

## Transfer to the place of attack

Both perpetrators killed at a place away from where they first picked up their victims. The Ripper took them somewhere dark and quiet, did not have sex with them, but cut their throats and mutilated them for his gratification. The Ripper and his victims stopped at the first suitable place they came to, with the exception of Mary Jane Kelly, who was persuaded to take him home with her. That means that each woman was accosted within two to three minutes' walk of the place where she was killed.

The Torso Killer probably killed on his own boat, or one made available to him on an ad hoc basis. Crick, if he were the Torso Killer, was personable and manipulative. He used his mother and his mates to offer false reassurance, and to help him in moving his victims around. The Ripper did not use accomplices, but did use false reassurance in a remark to Mary Jane Kelly. When accosting her, he confirmed, 'You will be alright for what I have told you',[18] possibly referring to a promise of money. He also gave her his handkerchief.

## Attacks and murders

The locations of the Ripper murders were all on the street, except for that of Mary Jane Kelly. The locations of the Torso Murders are more likely to have been under cover, probably inside a boat, barge or steamer cabin. He was able to kill, dismember and dispose of his victims' bodies unobserved. The Torso Killer was a sexually motivated criminal whose violence escalated to murder. None of the police doctors could firmly state a cause of death for his victims. The police view was that he dismembered their bodies for purely practical reasons, to dispose of their bodies.

It is impossible to be certain about the number of murders committed by the Torso Killer. The method of disposal of the bodies means that any number might have gone undetected. Like the Ripper, his violence could have escalated until murder became the usual outcome of his congress with a woman.

Although sexually motivated, the Ripper did not rape his victims. Police surgeons examined them for signs of intercourse, and concluded that there were none. He derived his gratification from mutilating their bodies and, when he had the time, removing their internal organs.

In terms of their signatures, meaning their distinctive methods of killing and deriving satisfaction from that act, the two perpetrators are radically different. The Torso Killer was gratified by sex and violence when his victims were alive. The Ripper wanted a quick kill and carried out as many posthumous mutilations as time permitted. His aim was to remove his victims' uteri, first pulling out their intestines, with some removals of other organs such as a kidney and a heart, gratuitously cutting the face and ears of Catherine Eddowes, and gouging out Mary Jane Kelly's right thigh down to the bone.

The clothes of the Torso victims were removed apart from the Pinchin Street victim's chemise. The Ripper victims were fully clothed apart from Mary Jane Kelly, who was stripped to her chemise. That final Ripper case was different from the others, because the killer could spend hours with his victim, in the privacy of her own bedroom. This is where the similarities to the Torso kills become stronger, as that killer stored his victims' bodies throughout the dismemberment and disposal processes.

### Use of alcohol and possible use of drugs

It is likely that both perpetrators used alcohol to some extent as a device to socialise with their victims and reduce their ability to defend themselves. The possible use of sedatives by the Torso Killer was raised inconclusively in the Battersea and Pinchin Street cases. Some commentators have speculated that the Ripper drugged his victims. This theory does not feature in Bond's largely accurate criminal profile of the Ripper, and is unsubstantiated.

### Depositing the remains

The Ripper left his victims' bodies where they lay. When he had time, as he did for the murders of Annie Chapman, Catherine Eddowes and Mary Jane Kelly, he placed them in a specific pose with their legs open, one straight, one bent at the knee. Their arms were also left in asymmetric positions, one bent at the elbow across their chests, one lying long at a slight angle from their side. He took care with the placement of their intestines, if removed, and when laying out the contents of their pockets beside them.

By contrast, the Torso Killer spent hours cutting up their bodies, neatly parcelled up their dismembered parts and scattered them to the winds. It was only the dumps on land, at New Scotland Yard and Pinchin Street, that were potentially incriminating, as they placed him as being in a distinct location at a known date and timeframe. If he were illiterate, or semi-literate like James Crick, it explains his inattention to the name marked on underwear worn by Elizabeth Jackson, which helped to identify her. Jack the Ripper was literate, as demonstrated by his chalked graffito after the murder of Catherine Eddowes.

## Discovery of the remains

The Ripper victims were found by passers-by, apart from the body of Mary Jane Kelly, which was seen through a window by her rent collector. Those men were questioned by police, and several have been considered suspects by later commentators.

Unlike in the Ripper case, the 'finders' in the Torso series were at considerably less risk of being investigated as suspects. The time-lapse between each murder and any discovery, and in addition the geographical disparity between the murder locations and whether the body parts were found, were considerable.

## Conclusions

In 1879, Warner Sleigh's defence of Kate Webster argued that: 'It was not shown that a murder had been committed, nor that the human remains found were those of Mrs Thomas.'[19] A Devil's advocate might apply that thinking elsewhere: *What if the unexplained deaths in the Thames Torso series were not murders?* It is a purely theoretical view, based on the open verdicts in the first two inquests. Only in the later cases of Elizabeth Jackson and at Pinchin Street did the juries declare a verdict of murder.

The case of Rose Mylett, which features in the official Whitechapel Murders files as a possible Ripper attack, shows the difficulty in attributing a sudden death to either natural or unnatural causes. A 29-year-old prostitute, the discovery of her body in the early morning of Thursday,

20 December 1888, at a yard in Poplar, occurred several months after the Whitehall torso case. Bond and CID Chief Robert Anderson overruled the autopsy's conclusion that she had been strangled or garrotted, opining that she had fallen awkwardly and suffocated herself through pressure from her jacket collar.

A few feasible reasons can be constructed as to why someone might decide to dismember a dead body. In Victorian times, suicide, or attempted suicide, was a criminal offence, and suicides were denied a Christian burial. A family member keen to avoid the associated discredit might conceivably try to conceal the body afterwards. Similarly, a death which occurred as part of a sex game, or under disreputable circumstances, might be covered up. Another plausible hypothesis might involve a significant financial incentive requiring, say, the payer of an allowance to appear to be alive, although for the Torso Killer, that motive would need to stretch across four victims.

The Torso Murders were unexplained deaths in the sense that the causes of death could not be determined. The Rainham case had two inquests, both of which returned open verdicts, the second concluding, 'after hearing the medical evidence [the jury] were of opinion that there was not sufficient evidence to show as to how or by what means the said woman came by her death'.[20] Doctor Callaway and Mr Bond were the medical experts who did not speculate about the cause of death.

In the Whitehall case, Bond and Hebbert provided the medical evidence, and Bond went further towards offering a cause of death, opining, 'It was not a death by suffocation. It was more likely death from haemorrhage …'[21] The Coroner for Westminster, John Troutbeck, did not follow that lead. In his summing-up, he stated, 'How the deceased came by her death there was no evidence to show, but much pointed to the probability of a violent death …'[22] However, he concluded by directing the jury to return an open verdict. It is possible that those early verdicts disrupted the police investigation by reducing the crimes from murders to unexplained deaths.

The Battersea case, like Rainham, had two inquests. Coroner Wynne Baxter's inquest on two body parts returned the verdict of 'Found Drowned'. It was an inaccurate description, as no drowning had been proved, although it may have meant only that a body or body parts had been found in the water. The main inquest was held by Braxton Hicks, taking medical evidence from Doctor Kempster and Mr Bond. Bond was not able to state the cause of death, listing the body parts which, if not missing, might have evidenced a death by poison, suffocation (also meaning drowning or strangulation) or a cut throat. Despite the lack of evidence, Braxton Hicks directed the jury that: 'It was a case in which a woman had died under circumstances that were excessively suspicious, and to the mind of ordinarily reasonable persons it would suggest that whatever the cause of death it was the result of some unlawful act on the part of someone.'[23] The jury duly returned a verdict of 'Wilful Murder'.

Doctor Callaway had been called in to view the body and make comparisons to the Rainham case for the benefit of the police. The police continued in seeking consistent expert opinions across the cases, which they now recognised as linked. In the Pinchin Street case, Bond and Hebbert were again consulted for their medical expertise, as were Doctor Phillips, a stalwart of the Ripper case, and his assistant Doctor Clark. The two latter doctors provided the medical evidence at the inquest.

Clark conducted the post-mortem examination of the torso assisted by Doctor Frederick Gordon Brown, the City Police surgeon who had conducted the post-mortem examination of Ripper victim Catherine Eddowes. Clark testified that there was no arterial spurting visible on the remains of the chemise, while Phillips stated his belief 'that death arose from loss of blood'. This suggests that the woman might have died from a brain haemorrhage as a results of blows to the head. The verdict was 'Wilful murder by some person or persons unknown'.

Although the Torso cases can only have been murders, their causes of death are questionable. Some of the women might have been strangled or had their throats cut, and others killed by blunt trauma to the skull, as suggested by Swanson of the Pinchin Street victim. The killer might not have had a knife immediately to hand in certain situations, which further differentiates his signature from that of Jack the Ripper, who invariably cut his victims' throats within the initial minutes of any attack.

The uncertain nature of many aspects of the Torso Murders caused them to slip from the public imagination. Primarily, the lack of identification of most of the victims and how they were connected to their killer, and the inability to locate him in any particular place, meant that he did not take shape as a distinct personality. Unlike Jack the Ripper, who was a silent and terrifying marauder on the streets of Whitechapel, the Torso Killer posed a threat that might be termed 'non-specific'. His murders were termed as equally grisly and horrific, targeting vulnerable victims that included a pregnant woman and her unborn child, yet their perpetrator did not form a lightning rod for the nation's fear. If the Torso Killer had been recognised more widely as another serial killer active in the metropolis, he might have eclipsed Jack the Ripper as the nineteenth century's 'worst Briton'.[24]

## 12

# A final analysis of the Torso Killer

> A man doesn't alter because you find out more about him. He's still the same man.
>
> From *The Third Man* by Graham Greene

River detective John Regan was the only police officer who worked not only on the Thames Torso and Ripper series, but also on the criminal cases brought against James Crick. Like several of his Metropolitan and City of London Police counterparts, on his retirement Regan spoke to the press about key cases in his career, including the Torso Murders. His reminiscences, *Tales of the Thames*, were serialised in *Lloyd's Weekly Newspaper* in four parts from 16 July 1911. At that time, he had been retired for over ten years, and had moved from Stepney to Camberwell, where he was living with his wife Catherine and their four younger children. A photograph accompanying the first article depicts Regan, aged 60, pale and serious-looking, with a receding hairline counterbalanced by a magnificent twiddle moustache.

A former steam crane driver and goods packer, Regan applied to join the police in the same year as my police ancestor Harry Garrett, and signed the attestation book two months before him. Based at Wapping river police station, the Thames Police headquarters, as a new constable he was on 'ordinary duty' of six hours on, twelve hours off, patrolling the river between East Greenwich and Cannon Street with an inspector and two constables to each boat. Within six months, he joined the detective force with a focus on crimes committed on the river. He served for nearly twenty-seven years until his retirement in 1900.[1]

Regan commented about the vigilance of the river police in what was James Crick's home turf:

> Bermondsey and Horselydown, on the Surrey side, were noted places for smuggling. Whenever we saw a boat row in, and we had an idea that we could not catch it on the water, we would turn to the nearest stairs, pop ashore, and meet the passengers in the street.[2]

This suggests that the Torso Killer would have found it difficult to dispose of body parts in the Bermondsey and Horseydown areas. In addition, as a result of the Fenian bombing campaign during the 1880s, Tower Bridge wharf and the stretch of the river between Chelsea and London Bridge were more strictly patrolled, with one boat reserved to protect the Houses of Parliament. The busyness of the Thames and the fact that he was a bona fide river worker did, however, provide sufficient cover for the Torso Killer to carry out his criminal activities.

Keen anticipation about Regan's commentary on the Thames Torso investigation can only go disappointed. His was briefer and less accurate than Macnaghten's, as he only mentioned one of the murders, in which he concatenated the Rainham and Battersea cases:

> [A] Thames mystery in which I was engaged in trying to solve was, I am bound to say, never satisfactorily cleared up.
>
> One day what was decided on examination to be a fragment of a woman's body was found in the river, off Bermondsey, and brought to the Wapping Police Station. The divisional surgeon conjectured that it was a portion of the arm of a woman who was fully developed, but not old. Soon afterwards another gruesome relic was found, this time at Battersea. This, the surgeon said, was the hip of a fully grown woman. After this second discovery the Coroner for the East End and

the Coroner for Battersea arranged that the inquest on these remains should be held at the court in whose jurisdiction the largest part was picked up.

In the course of the next week or so nearly all the missing limbs were found, in widely separated parts of the river. It was a distressing business, as my readers may suppose, to put these together. At last all was complete, with the exception of the head, and that was never found. It was then seen that the surmise of the surgeon was right, and that the body was that of a well-grown woman.

Many people whose wife or sister had disappeared came forward and tried to identify the remains. The one who got nearest to it was a woman who said that her sister had a deep wound in the lower part of her right leg. There was such a wound, but the doctor decided that it was inflicted after death.

No clue was ever discovered that threw any light upon this extraordinary find.[3]

Regan's commentary is inaccurate, and he does not even name this unsolved crime as a murder, let alone place it in a series. It does not fuel any speculation about whom he suspected to be the Thames Torso Killer.

CID Assistant Commissioner Melville Macnaghten, whose police report referencing the Pinchin Street murder is quoted in an earlier chapter, reminisced about the Elizabeth Jackson case in his memoir, published in 1914. His employment by New Scotland Yard commenced on Saturday, 1 June 1889, meaning that the first murder to appear on his desk was the 'Battersea Mystery'. He made a slight mistake regarding dates, as the remains were first discovered on the morning of Tuesday, 4 June, not the day before:

Reaching office on the Monday morning, I found that two telegrams had just been received – the first from Battersea, stating that the left thigh of a woman had been found on the foreshore of the Thames, near the Albert Bridge, and the second from Horselydown, reporting the finding of a piece of the pelvis. Both of these portions were sewn up in what looked like bits of an old ulster coat. This pointed to murder most foul, and I spent the rest of the day on the river in company with the officer who had been entrusted with the charge of the case [Detective Inspector John Bennett Tunbridge].

Within the next week many other remains were found – some in the river, some in Battersea Park, and the rest on foreshores as far remote as Limehouse and Fulham. The head of the woman never came to light, and the case, in many respects, seemed on all fours with those of the Rainham mystery in 1887, and the Whitehall mystery in 1888. In both of these cases, portions of a woman's body, skilfully disarticulated, were found in various places, for the most part adjacent to the river, but in neither case did the head turn up, nor were the bodies identified.

In the 1889 case, which was commonly called the 'Thames mystery', a scar on the wrist led to the identification of the remains as being those of one, Elizabeth Jackson, an unfortunate, who had resided a few weeks before at a common lodging-house in Turks Row [sic], Chelsea, and who had been in possession of an ulster similar to that in which most of the remains had been wrapped up. A working stone-mason [Faircloth], who, some weeks before, had been living with Jackson, was traced to Devonshire and there detained, but he fully satisfied the police as to his whereabouts at the time of the murder, and was discharged.

Now this murder was of a very peculiar character. The woman, who seems to have been one of the dregs of humanity, must have been done to death somewhere on enclosed premises, and the process of disarticulation must have occupied many hours, and, when this was completed, the murderer must have taken several journeys before he could have disposed of all his ghastly burdens. One of the last portions of the body which turned up was enveloped in a curious piece of white cloth, such as is used by certain students engaged on a particular kind of work. But nothing ever came of police inquiries in this, or any other direction, and the Thames mystery has remained an 'undiscovered' murder in the fullest sense of the word.[4]

It is interesting that 'Mac' referred to the Torso Killer's use of enclosed premises, with 'the process of disarticulation' taking many hours, followed by 'several journeys' to dispose of 'his ghastly burdens'. He did not conjecture that such premises might include a boat, although the number of journeys that were needed might suggest that the perpetrator had his own transport. The 'certain students engaged on a particular kind of work' pointed to medical students. Like Regan's, his commentary can be put to no practical use.

River policeman John Regan's memoir concludes with a modest statement of his own achievements:

> Perhaps I may be permitted to add, without seeming conceited, that during my service in the Force I received 126 commendations and rewards from magistrates, coroners, and judges, and one, which I specially treasure, from the late Sir William Harcourt, when he was Home Secretary, at the time of the dynamite outrages.[5]

On 19 March 1883, Regan, then a sergeant, was temporarily posted to CID's Central Office in response to the ongoing Fenian bombing campaign on the British mainland. He was directly involved in a surveillance operation in the Gallagher dynamite case, in which four men including Doctor Thomas Gallagher were found guilty of treasonable acts and sentenced to penal servitude for life, while a further two were exonerated.

Robert Anderson, who like Regan would work on both the Torso and Ripper cases, was a key figure in the newly formed Special Irish Branch, gathering intelligence about the various Fenian groups and their operations. He commented about the challenges of such work: 'any highly trained Police ought to be able to thwart organised crime, whether the project be treasonable or fraudulent. But to catch a criminal who works alone and keeps his own counsel is a far higher test of skill. And in the case of dynamiters, it may also be a severe test of nerves.'[6]

In a surveillance operation leading to the arrests of the Gallagher gang, Regan had observed them targeting Scotland Yard, while 'in their luggage was found enough dynamite to blow all London up'.[7] Yet the attacks on the British mainland continued. On 30 May 1884, the CID HQ was the target of a Fenian bomb. That incident was one of the factors, alongside the remaining term on its lease, and the expansion of CID and the force in general, which led to the building of New Scotland Yard. The project was a work in progress in the summer of

1888 when the Whitehall torso was placed there. In early 1891, the new building was in occupation by the Intelligence and CID Departments. It was 'exteriorly handsome ... internally entirely "up to date" in fitment of every description'[8] and had space to muster 3,000 men on its ground floor. Notably, it had its own generating plant, meaning that the Yard was the first large public building to be lit entirely by electricity, ensuring uninterrupted telegraphic communications.

Regan's special duty in CID extended to a posting at the port of Gravesend, which lasted until March 1889, when he was promoted to inspector. Within three months of his return to London, he was assigned to the Battersea Torso case, followed by the Pinchin Street case, which occurred between the assaults on Jessie Miller and Elizabeth Sarah Warburton. At that time, Regan was living at 147 Oxford Street,[9] today's Stepney Way. His period of residence overlapped with that of Hyam Hyams, who briefly lived at nearby Jubilee Street.[10]

My police ancestor Harry Garrett, then a Whitechapel sergeant, had rented accommodation at 4 The Circus, Minories, within seven minutes' walk of the Irongate wharf opposite Horsleydown Old Stairs, and twelve minutes from the Pinchin Street railway arch. In around 1890, he moved to 177 Oxford Street[11] on the same side of the road as Regan, with eleven houses and a church between them. Garrett would have passed Regan's house on his way to and from work at Leman Street police station. Garrett was also a contemporary of Inspector Francis Knight of Thames Division, who was involved in the investigation into Elizabeth Jackson's murder. Garrett and Knight joined the Metropolitan Police on the same day, and went through their new entrants' training together at Lambeth. Their warrant numbers, awarded alphabetically by surname, were eight numbers apart.[12]

While Regan's memoir of events on the great silent highway is equally silent on the identity of the Thames Torso Killer, it produces a piece of information which supports his profile as a bargeman. As late as the 1880s, despite the efforts of the river police, the lower reaches of the River Thames between Wapping and Erith were 'quite a happy hunting-ground for sheep-stealers'.[13] A crime typically committed by passing bargemen, sheep-rustling aligns to Charles Hebbert's conjecture that the Thames Torso Killer was a butcher or hunter, and 'a man accustomed to cut up bodies quickly in somewhat large pieces'. It also fits Swanson's use of the verb 'jointed' when assessing the Pinchin Street mutilations, and the variation in how the separation of the leg at the kneecap was handled, with the patella variously attached to either the thigh or the lower leg.

A sheep's carcass was worth a hefty 50*s* on the black market, sold to any butcher who would not enquire about its provenance. Before sale, thieves would butcher it and remove its fleece with the telltale smit marks of coloured dye that identified its owner. In his memoirs, Regan described how this crime was carried out and the police response:

> A man would go ashore on a dinghy and take a large sheep. He would turn it legs up and put it into the dinghy [and take it back to the barge]. On the barge the sheep would be killed and the skin thrown into the water. The sheep was then sold to the butchers in the neighbourhood, who were glad to get a supply of cheap mutton, or else the carcase [*sic*] was divided up amongst the men.
>
> Several arrests were made when we discovered what was being done, but in most cases the men got only a couple of months' imprisonment for 'unlawful possession'. We knew where the sheep were stolen from, but, as the skins were removed, the owners could not identify the animals. But at last we got a man actually convicted for the offence of sheep-stealing, which is a serious one, and that pretty well put a stop to the practice.[14]

Three cases heard at the Old Bailey throw further light on the methods used to dispatch the animals and dispose of their carcasses. In an 1893 case, three bargemen stole a ewe from a butcher's paddock overnight, and brought it back alive onto their barge. When on deck, one of them killed the sheep by hitting it on the head with a chopper. The animal's butchery was not recorded, and the case concluded with the culprits receiving between two and six months' penal servitude with hard labour.[15]

In an 1879 case, a hay-binder killed a sheep with a knife in a farmer's field: 'He cut its throat – he skinned it and threw the skin and entrails into the ditch, then cut the sheep in halves with an axe which he took with him, and put half in each bag ...'[16] Then as now, best practice for butchering a lamb involves carving its torso into three parts: the shoulder, rib, and loin. This type of butchery fits neatly with the analysis of the Hebbert report when commenting on Elizabeth Jackson's remains:

> The system of division of the parts gave evidence of design and skill, – the design probably being for the purpose of concealment of the crime and easy carriage of the parts; the skill not showing the anatomical knowledge of a surgeon, but rather the aptitude learnt by a butcher, horse-knacker, or other person used to deal with dead animals and to readily separate limbs at the joints.[17]

There are sufficient similarities to the Torso Killer's method of cutting up and bundling the remains to form the supposition that he learned those skills from sheep-stealing, transferring his knowledge as a sheep-thief and a lighterman to the crime of murder. Any sight or smell of bloodshed on board the boats he used could be explained away as a spot of sheep butchery. He knew what weight he could physically carry, and what would sink or float, and made up his bundles accordingly. The use of ligatures was a sensible extension of his skills in containing the goods he transported for his trade.

One of Regan's acts of heroism was not officially recognised, as the policeman responsible for bringing James Crick to justice as a violent rapist. Arrogant and self-serving, did Crick's acts of rape and coercive control turn to murder? He was twice charged with attempted murder, but those charges were dropped. His motivation for the attacks on his wife, Miller and Warburton was arguably the same as that of the Torso Killer: coercive control of women whom he perceived as, used and disposed of like pieces of meat. Crick had a history of committing sexual offences in a similar area and his modus operandi fits how the Torso Killer would have operated.

Like the Torso Killer, Crick was a mobile, opportunistic risk-taker, without full control of all of the vessels he used during his assaults. He was criminally active while working, as seen in the attack on Miller which stretched into a free evening, and had the flexibility to take weekdays off, as seen in the attack on Warburton, when he went to the police court in the morning and the pub after that. The Torso Killer probably carried out his dismemberments during non-working hours between dusk and dawn and on Sundays, in the summertime. His work pattern forced him to dispose of the body parts in the early mornings.

From his trade, Crick had access to canvas sacking, sacks, cord and newspapers, but not in large quantities. A lack of available materials made the Torso Killer also use victims' clothing as wrappings. He may always have carried a knife, and it is assumed that a saw formed part of most vessels' on-board repair kit. He worked in a confined space, in a methodical and practical manner, meaning that he first removed his victims' legs to allow greater manoeuvrability. He artfully tied ligatures on body parts to reduce their bleeding.

Significant information gaps and a lack of any evidence, however circumstantial, preclude any identification of James Crick as the Torso Killer. A detailed physical description of Crick when convicted in 1889 itemised his tattoos and moles, yet there is nothing to compare it to without a single sighting of the Torso Killer. In the absence of any photograph or physical description of his known victims Miller and Warburton, we cannot match his ideal victim type to the Torso victims, who tended to have curvy figures. His mental health during and after the attacks was not recorded. The periodicity of the Torso Murders was irregular but escalating, but it is difficult to map that pattern onto Crick's crimes, not least as many either went unreported or lacked the necessary evidence to enable police to charge him. He cannot be connected to the Torso victims, nor any of their possessions that were taken as trophies. No physical evidence survives to enable the analysis of his knife cuts, butchery style, or method of wrapping and tying the remains into bundles.

Despite those constraints, working on the hypothesis that Crick was the Thames Torso Killer, it is possible to reconstruct a plausible modus operandi from his first sighting of his victims to his final disposal of their remains.

## First sighting and accosting

The vantage point of his pitch at Horsleydown Old Stairs next to the Anchor Brewery building overlooked Shad Thames and any passing female. At high tide, the brown river water washes up the lower flight of steps and splashes bystanders at its top. From this place and others close to the river, Crick targeted lone females, busty and mostly brunettes, who appeared accommodating, although appearances can be deceptive. Despite the slightly elevated social standing of the Whitehall victim, he may have been actively looking for women who were vulnerable because they were down on their luck, of the type labelled as unfortunates, who occasionally sold sex. He wagered that any accusation of rape from a woman like that would not stick. His victims were handled violently, and it is assumed that the majority of them escaped with their lives.

He deployed a range of approaches to women. If he fancied a woman he saw on the street, he would persuade her to come for a drink with him. Or, when inside a pub, it was easy to find a woman at the bar. Alternatively, he might chat up a passenger or persuade a woman as his non-paying guest onto a boat laden with other passengers. When whiling away the late afternoons in his skiff, waiting for the last paying customers of the day, he might spot a lone woman on the embankment and hail her over. If sleeping as a watchman on a river barge, he could invite her on board.

His banter sought sympathy, and offered reassurance followed by fun. His mother and his mates helped him out, reassuring the women, making them tea, and supplying the use of their skiffs, barges and steamers. Crick's mates were not rapists, killers or disposers of body parts, but the Miller and Warburton cases demonstrated that a minority were conscious accomplices who enabled him to subdue the women, detain them against their will, and rape them. His mother was chief among those willing to give false evidence on his behalf, and guilty of criminal collusion.

It is useful to compare the locations where he picked up the women whose movements are known. Elizabeth Jackson was most likely accosted at Battersea Park, where she intended to sleep rough, although bargemen also moored up on the Chelsea side of the river. Jessie Miller was picked up on what is assumed to be the southern end of Westminster Stairs, and Elizabeth Sarah Warburton on Tooley Street. All of those locations are on the south bank of the River Thames in a range between ½ mile and 4 miles of Crick's plying place at Horsleydown. The likely disparity between where the other women lived, and the scattergun locations where their headless body parts were found, makes it impossible to identify them. They must have been picked up at, or near, the riverside, not least because that was where Crick lived and worked.

## Seasonality

All of the known murders took place in the watermen's summer season, which ran between Easter and October, as did his assaults on Jessie Miller and Elizabeth Sarah Warburton. Even in the Rainham case, Easter Sunday in 1887 was 10 April and the murder took place after that, circa 27 April. It begs the question of what he did in the wintertime, when he was not using his skiff to pick up passengers? He could still chat women up in pubs and on the street. His tally of rapes could have been high. He is likely to have demonstrated behaviour consistent among serial rapists, targeting strangers and sex workers

The escalation of Crick's crimes can be tracked from early 1887, with the domestic abuse of his wife and the Rainham murder, to 1889, when he attacked Miller and Warburton. If the Torso Killer, in four months he attacked Elizabeth Jackson, Jessie Miller, the Pinchin Street victim and Elizabeth Warburton. He used extreme violence and was highly controlling, without mercy or remorse.

## Transfer to the place of attack

It is an assumption that, for the Rainham murder, the killer only used a barge or lighter. After his win in August 1887, Crick was in sole possession of a skiff, the *Ally Sloper*. He also had ad hoc access to a barge when on contract work. As was usual within the brotherhood of watermen, his mates let him use their rowing boats, barges and the steamer *Alert*. Many of them were simply doing him a favour, unconscious of his intent. Others were knowing accomplices.

The attack on Jessie Miller demonstrates that, with an accomplice, Crick could commit rape in the bottom of his skiff. He used his body weight to keep her down and, when finished, knelt on her. If she had not jumped from the rowing boat, it is possible that he might have transferred her to a barge or steamer and carried out further assaults, with or without Ruffeit. The case of Elizabeth Warburton proves his ability to transfer his victims between vessels, including larger craft such as a barge and steamer, with the privacy of a cabin, hold or wheel-room.

## Rape, sometimes followed by murder

Crick's objective was to carry out multiple rapes. He used as much violence as he needed to as he hit and kicked the women, tore their clothes off, and violated them. The bruises on their arms, legs and backs demonstrate the extent of his brute force. When in the skiff, he kneeled on their prone bodies to keep them down as he rowed on. If they put up a strong defence, he fought to subdue them, as he did with Elizabeth Warburton, seizing her by the neck. If the struggle continued, it is arguable that he subdued some of them by partial strangulation, which might lead to murder.

Owing to the decomposition of the bodies, the medical experts were unable to determine an exact cause of death. He could have rendered them unconscious by partial strangulation or thumping them before the fatal act of cutting their throats. Alternatively, given the police surgeons' ambivalence about throat-cutting as the cause of death, throttling or blunt trauma to the head could have killed them.

When the women he raped did not resist him, he might pay them off or buy their silence with threats. The fortunate survivors could have been put back on his skiff, and let off at a deserted stairway, somewhere full of drunken sailors like Ratcliffe or Limehouse, where violent assaults were a common occurrence. He bargained that many would not trouble the police, and that those who did would have little but bruises to show for it. Many of them would not know his name, or plying place, although any 'Ally Sloper' branding of his boat would be memorable.

## Use of alcohol and possible use of drugs

Crick used alcohol to befriend his victims and make them less able to defend themselves. He might have used his cargoes to provide himself with a primer of alcohol before going out. But did he also use sedatives to ensure their unconscious compliance? Jessie Miller claimed that, when Crick and Ruffeitt gave her a drink on board the skiff, 'immediately after partaking of the liquor she became dazed'. The possible use of sedatives was raised in the Battersea and Pinchin Street cases. Bond testified that he was unable to examine Elizabeth Jackson's body for drugs, as her intestines were missing.

An informal briefing to the press about the Pinchin Street postmortem examination stated:

> On opening the stomach there was found a small quantity of fluid, which, from its appearance, gave an impression that the unfortunate woman had been stupefied by some drug, or that she had even met her end by poison. For this reason it is not unlikely that Dr. Stevenson, the toxicological expert, will be called upon to make an analysis of the viscera and contents of the stomach, which have been carefully preserved ... There was a small amount of internal inflammation, the cause of which could not be ascertained.[18]

Doctor Thomas Stevenson was a forensic analyst for the Home Office, who acted as an expert witness in several famous poisoning trials. He advised on the case of potential Ripper suspect George Chapman, also known as Severin Klosowski, who was hanged for the murders of three women by poison. Chapman has been considered a suspect for one or more of the Torso Murders.

The Hebbert report does not confirm the hypothesis that the Torso victims were drugged or poisoned in either the Pinchin Street or the Whitehall case, when the victims' stomach contents were examined. Both contained partly digested food, identified in the former as plums. Narcotics such as chloral hydrate, laudanum and bromide of potassium were readily available from chemist's or grocer's shops. They could be used as date-rape drugs, making a woman unconscious at the time of any assault, and unable to testify about its specific details afterwards. It can be noted in passing that, in 1881, on Southwark Park Road, Arthur Crick lived next door to a herbalist. The fact that both the Pinchin Street torso and Elizabeth Sarah Warburton had defence wounds suggests that sedatives were not used. There is no evidence that tea-maker Benjamin Turton slipped a 'Mickey Finn' to Warburton. By Jessie Miller's own account, she drank so much beer that she passed out, and Crick appears to have deliberately plied her with alcohol.

## Dismemberment

The killer's rationale for dismemberment, instead of simply putting the women's intact bodies overboard, must have been to avoid identification of his victims, and any connection to himself if seen with them. As a waterman, Crick would know about the customary 'finder's fee' for any body fished from the water and reported to the authorities. He could not have risked an early retrieval by someone he knew. In May 1883, an Irish lighterman simply referred to as 'Regan' was commended by a coroner for having pulled an unidentified body from the Thames, having 'in the course of his career as a Thames lighterman, recovered 19 other bodies under the same circumstances, and saved the lives of 25 persons from drowning'.[19] It has not been possible to identify the public-spirited lighterman, as several Regans of that trade were based on the stretch of the south bank between Horsleydown and Rotherhithe.

Bodies could also be dredged from the riverbed, as in the case of 18-year-old servant Sarah Grant, who in December 1886 went missing from an address in Bayswater. Her body was accidentally retrieved from the River Thames in the following February, and identified from a locket she was wearing, that contained a photograph of her fiancé. At the inquest into her death, held by Coroner Langham, evidence showed that she planned to kill herself after a broken engagement. The jury returned a verdict of 'Suicide whilst temporarily insane'.[20]

The circumstances of Grant's disappearance and discovery were reported as follows:

> She left home in the afternoon of December 12 to meet her sweetheart at 4 p.m. at a given spot, but failed to put in an appearance. The young fellow, Fox by name, finding she did not come, made inquiries, which led to her being reported by the police as missing.

> The family have been in a great worry ever since as to her whereabouts, and it is probable nothing would ever have been heard of her but for the dragging up of the body by a dredger named Passfield, who says it was so buried down in the mud and sand at the bed of the river that, but for his dredging apparatus laying hold of her, she would never have come to the surface.[21]

Passfield was dredging off Battle Bridge Stairs, near London Bridge station, only five minutes' walk from Horsleydown Old Stairs. Sarah Grant's story not only demonstrates one of the many ways that a body could resurface from the Thames, but also how easy it was to disappear. Were it not for her locket, she would not have been positively identified after two months underwater.

Driven by the need to erase the identities of his victims, because he knew them or was seen consorting with them, the Torso Killer must have had suitable premises to carry out the dismemberments. If he were the murderer, Crick must have used a barge, or his skiff if there was no alternative, to dismember the bodies, using butchery skills learned from stealing sheep. The Warburton case demonstrates his ability to use accomplices to assist him, regardless of how much they knew about his illicit activities.

The type of knife he used might have been a sailor's knife, rigging knife, hunting knife or domestic carving knife. He could have borrowed a fine-toothed saw from his carpenter brother-in-law. The process of dismemberment took several hours, and included the efficient packing and tying of the remains, with the occasional use of cord as ligatures. Packing and transporting were skills used by Crick in his day job as a lighterman. For a highly controlling personality, the dispatch of the body into its constituent parts and their neat bundling must have been gratifying. He used the materials he had to hand: cord and canvas, sacks and torn pieces of his victims' clothing and bindings, even their bootlaces. The cord might have been a similar width of strong cord or twine to Venetian blind cord, of a type used by lightermen. Although only publicly described in the Rainham case, the knots were not sailor's knots, but as if done by a layman.

The killer needed to clean up after himself following the kill and subsequent dismemberment. The bloodied chemise in the Pinchin Street case demonstrates that sufficient blood was spilled to require a thorough clean-up job. It was considered that the Pinchin Street torso had been washed. He may have rinsed the remains, and certainly cleaned the decks, and his hands, with river water using whatever buckets, brushes and soap were available. Bloodstains would have been easier to shift when wet. He might have laid out a piece of canvas on which to carry out the dismemberments, and slung it over the side of the boat to wash it afterwards.

## Depositing the remains

His preference was to deposit the remains in the river, following the warped logic of his daily working life, when rubbish would be thrown overboard. Tidal analysis proves that, on occasion, his need to dispose of remains coincided with inconveniently slack tides. When he failed to synchronise with the tide, and ran out of time, he stored the remains for a period of days. If he lost use of the barge or steamer, he moved the remains onto his skiff. But that meant that he made fewer cuts and was forced to dump the partly intact torsos on land, as in the Whitehall and Pinchin Street cases, when he probably killed on a Sunday night. When he dumped on land, he placed the items down as carefully as if they were the goods he handled every day, for which he was liable. Although his choice of those locations was directed by his work, they also signified his attitude towards the women he killed. They were disposable objects to be used and discarded in places where rubbish might be tipped.

To reduce the risk of detection, the dump sites needed to be distanced from Horsleydown, and, with the exception of the item thrown into Battersea Park, were consistently north of the river. The women's clothing and boots were similarly disposed of, when not used as absorbent wrappings to bundle up their body parts. He could not risk taking them to pawn shops.

There is a connection between the dumping grounds and the brewing trade. The perpetrator attacked and killed opportunistically, meaning that his disposal of the body parts had to fit around his pre-planned work activities. Horsleydown Old Stairs adjoined the Anchor

Brewery, which received its supplies of malt, coal, timber and forage for horses by river. It delivered its barrels of beer by horse and cart, as many of its publican customers were located inland. Properties on both Horsleydown Lane and Gainsford Street were owned by Courage brewers, suggesting that the Cricks might have had company housing when they lived there. And the brewing industry connects many of the sites where body parts were discovered.

Several of the Rainham victim's body parts were found in the Regent's Canal. The canal ran past the Camden Town Brewery precisely by Camden Lock. It was possible to return by turning around at Regent's Park Basin or continue on to Paddington, going past Regent's Park where other body parts were found. The finding of the first body part in the Whitehall murder case was riverside of Ward's Deal Wharf underneath a sluice from the neighbouring Thames Bank Distillery. It is impossible to say whether the tide took it there or the perpetrator dropped it nearby. Regarding the Elizabeth Jackson case, there was a malt house on Church Lane close to Battersea Park. Pinchin Street hosted a whisky distillery, and at its eastern end, two sugar refineries.

## Avoiding detection

The Torso Killer was able to avoid being prosecuted for the Thames Torso Murders by distancing himself from those crimes. Only one of his victims, Elizabeth Jackson, was identified, owing to the fact that she was local to the area where her remains were scattered. Up to and including the Whitehall case, police made the error of seeking missing women in the area where the torso was found. Owing to his mobility, their killer could have picked them up anywhere within walking distance of the River Thames.

Although he kept their bodies for as long as a day or two, he was able to store them privately, and clean up after the kills. It was a common practice to discard rubbish in the river, meaning that no explanation was needed if seen distributing his 'parcels'. Another way he avoided detection was by stopping his crimes, assuming that the Pinchin Street murder was the last in the series. As elucidated by the FBI:

It has been widely believed that once serial killers start killing, they cannot stop. There are, however, some serial killers who stop murdering altogether before being caught. In these instances, there are events or circumstances in offenders' lives that inhibit them from pursuing more victims. These can include increased participation in family activities, sexual substitution, and other diversions.[22]

There is no record of any further criminal charges being brought against Crick after his period of imprisonment, nor any hint of his subsequent relationships with women. Sexually motivated, if he were the Torso Killer, his crimes had escalated from rape to murder. Crick was an opportunist sex attacker, who did not pre-plan when rape would turn to murder. If a woman was likely to create a scene, or report him, he would kill her. His ultimate objective was her silence. A 'Jack the Lad' with a brash personality, he was well known on the river and its embankment, and he was seen with the women whom he killed. In a parody of his day job, he worked with their body parts as he might bundle goods in manageable weights, unload and deliver them. He used his sheep butchery skills and knives to cut up their bodies, and boats owned by himself and his workmates as premises for all of his illicit activities.

Like the Ripper, he was not as clever as might be surmised. His depositing of the Whitehall torso in the foundations of New Scotland Yard was a matter of convenience, not a jibe at the police, yet it increased scrutiny and public awareness of that crime. The work-related sacking that he used to wrap some body parts might have led to his identification, if marked with a trade name. One of his mates, or even a family member, might have turned him in. Unlike that of his victims, his own luck held.

# Conclusion and true crime reconstructions of the Thames Torso Murders

The existing information about the Thames Torso Murders forms pieces of an incomplete jigsaw, like the bodies themselves. The positive identification of the killer's third victim, Elizabeth Jackson, assisted police in understanding his victim type and, to some extent, his modus operandi and movements. Yet no description of the killer existed that could be matched to a convicted criminal such as James Crick, who was known to the police, with his personal details recorded for posterity. Unlike the Ripper case, when police officers of the day commented on the Torso series, their accounts were sparse and inconclusive. Our most useful sources of information derive from the inquest reports and, importantly, the medical analysis by Charles Hebbert and Thomas Bond. Regrettably, Bond was not tasked by the CID to profile the Torso Killer, as he did to useful effect with the Ripper.

John Faircloth was the only officially named suspect, with a history of theft and violence, yet out of London at the time of Jackson's murder. Other potential suspects covered by my research were far from fitting the Torso Killer's profile: Jack the Ripper suspects including Portuguese cattlemen, slaughterers and butchers; a myriad of river workers and barge builders; inquest witnesses who discovered body parts, in particular builders and carpenters; employees at metal foundries and factories including distillers, oil refiners and colourmen; labourers and travelling tradesmen; itinerant stonemasons and mill-workers like Faircloth; Faircloth's brother Samuel, who lived in the East End; homicidal squaddies; random doctors and medical students, with hunters proving to be almost untraceable; two men who nearly drowned a woman in Battersea Park's lake in 1888; and a disgruntled former soldier and groom at a horse depot based in Battersea.

If the Torso murderer were James Crick, his series covered four kills and two known rapes. As suspects go, Crick is previously undiscovered and arguably the best yet. One hundred and thirty-five years later, it is likely that no better will be found. If not Crick, the Torso Killer was a man very like him; highly mobile and skilled, a river worker based on the south bank and operating in central London. As bold as brass, he chatted up lone women, offering them free drinks and a river trip. If they were on the game, would he jingle the coins in his pocket and invite them to push a hand in and pull something out?

To deflect from any police investigation near to him, he deposited the body parts that he could not otherwise dispose of at sites on the north bank that he knew from his work. He probably worked as a lighterman for a brewer or as a coalie. His crimes were sexually motivated, demonstrating coercive control, and his victims were mere playthings to him, patchwork dolls to be torn apart and thrown away. He displayed his distinctive 'signature' in how he dismembered his victims' bodies.

In forensic science, every contact leaves a trace. His handling of human remains left traces that were undetectable in the Victorian era, and, although not a stranger, the Thames Torso Killer's presence failed to imprint itself onto the familiar streets and great river of London. Unlike Jack the Ripper, whose reconstructed movements offer a feeling of knowing the streets that he haunted, the Torso Killer was never seen consorting with the women he murdered, nor disposing of their body parts. Even Elizabeth Jackson, who was local to Chelsea and kept bumping into friends and relatives, much to her embarrassment when pregnant, was not connected to this man by anyone she knew. He cannot have been the Turk's Row lodgers' navvy, and the rough sleepers at the Pinchin Street railway arches were too drunk and incapable to notice him.

My four true crime reconstructions of the Thames Torso Murders are speculative, attempting to recreate the interactions between the perpetrator and his victims, including his movements and escape routes. Although written with an intent to be neutral about the killer's identity, they draw on the aspects of Crick's modus operandi which illuminate the case. All of the speech attributed to the killer and the women he attacked is fictitious, apart from a final use of Crick's exhortation for his victim to stay silent, or be settled. Following the timings of the attacks on Miller and Warburton, all of the murders are represented as evening-into-night occurrences.

I make the following assumptions about the locations where the women were accosted and murdered:

- Owing to speculation that the Rainham remains were scattered from a barge, I have the killer guarding his cargo overnight on a dumb barge moored at Limehouse Docks. He picked up his victim at a local pub, having left his cargo unattended, and either walked her back onto the barge, or used a skiff or dinghy.
- Owing to Crick's connection to the Old Swan pub, pier and stairs, as the starting point of Doggett's race, I have linked the Whitehall murder to a pleasure cruise that started and finished at that pier near London Bridge. Following the methodology used by Crick when assaulting Elizabeth Sarah Warburton, I have the killer picking her up in his skiff and transferring her to a barge.
- I envisaged Elizabeth Jackson being accosted in Battersea Park when attempting to sleep rough, and lured onto a nearby barge.
- Again following what happened to Elizabeth Sarah Warburton, the Pinchin Street victim is considered to have been accosted on the South Bank, at a pub on Tooley Street, and taken via skiff to a barge.

A standing assumption is that the perpetrator always carried a knife, and that he had easy access to a saw as part of most vessels' on-board repair kit.

## Reconstruction of the Rainham murder

*The Rainham murder might be the first rape that turned into a killing. Owing to the decomposition of the body parts, we know little about the victim. Aged between*

*25 and 35, she was short, fair-skinned and dark-haired. Her physique was petite yet muscular, with some subcutaneous fat. Owing to the lack of a wedding ring on her ring finger, or any remaining indentation, Hebbert and Bond thought she was unmarried. The only distinctive markings on her body were varicose veins on the fronts of her legs and indentations that might have been left by suspenders. Unusually, no signs of bruising were detected on her body other than at the cuts made on her body after death.*

*My assumptions are that:*

- *the date of the murder was Wednesday, 27 April 1887, based on the early high tide at 4.13 a.m. and the unusually high water levels;*
- *the perpetrator was working a night shift on a barge, giving him continuous use of it;*
- *Doctor Bond correctly judged that all of the body parts were disposed of on the same date;*
- *the body parts discovered on land were deposited from a barge.*

He is meant to be guarding his cargo overnight, on the dumb barge he has brought upstream to Limehouse Docks. But there's nothing to stop him from leaving it and walking across the barges moored next to his, to get onshore. He spots her walking down the street, short, dark and attractive, willing to smile at a passing stranger. *Just the ticket.*

She falls in with his suggestion of a drink, and he buys her a gin. Perhaps she thinks she can make a go of it with this fellow, who fancies her, and, unlike her last, has silver in his pocket. She agrees to walk with him somewhere quieter, just the two of them together, and, reaching the riverside, acquiesces to boarding his boat. He is laughing and joking as he gets her across the first two barges, and grinning harder as she steps onto his. He kindles the lamp that he left on deck, lighting her way down into its cabin below deck, pitch-black and stinking.

He is rough with her, tearing at her clothes and knocking her down. She knows she has made a mistake to go with him, and lies quietly, waiting for it to be over. After the first time, as he keeps going, her discomfort becomes pain. His right forearm is heavy over her neck, obstructing her airway. Her own arms are weighted down by his body, and she struggles in vain, gasping: *I can't breathe!* As he starts to laugh, she knows she is in real trouble. She bites into his flesh, and that does for her. Cursing, calling her a bitch and a whore, he takes her neck in his hands and throttles her until she is still.

He pulls off her clothes and grabs his tools. He cuts up her body in the way that he would butcher a stolen sheep, removing the limbs and dividing the legs at the knees and the torso into three sections. He has plenty of time, enough to carry out a full dismemberment and utilise his well-honed trade skills to prepare the items for dispatch. Each part is neatly wrapped in canvas and secured with cord, materials that are lying on deck. He pulls the laces from her boots to tie up the last package, containing her clothes weighted by her boots. When it is done, he can rest.

Sunrise and high tide get him moving at 4 a.m., an hour before his working day usually begins. He throws most of the bundles overboard before the other bargemen come on deck. As soon as the docks open, he does a drop-off and pick-up. His cargo's delivery takes him up the Regent's Canal. He scatters her limbs where he deposits his load.

He does not himself know who the woman was or where she came from. According to the coroner's court, she is not the daughter of Mrs Cross from Richmond, nor is she Mrs Carter from Lambeth. She has disappeared from the streets of London, yet nobody notices that she has gone.

## Reconstruction of the Whitehall murder

*The Whitehall murder is counted as the second in this series, but it could be the third or more. At the height of almost 5ft 9in, the victim was strikingly tall and well-built, with a shapely figure and dark brown hair, and at around 25, in a similar age bracket to the previous victim. Distinguishing features included her statuesque build, her long, tapering hands with manicured nails and her black brocade bodice and skirt with its previously fashionable bustle. Her grooming and dress demonstrated a higher social status than that of the other women targeted by the Thames Torso Killer, which might have made her harder to get close to. She was single.*

*This reconstruction is based on newspaper articles about the saloon steamer Alexandra's moonlight cruise to Gravesend and back, from Old Swan Pier west of London Bridge, on the evening of Thursday, 23 August 1888. The cruise included* a late supper, which fits with the fact that the unknown woman's stomach contained about an ounce of partially digested food, indicating that she died within two to three hours after eating. It also makes sense of her dressing up for the occasion, and taking a boat ride home with her killer, after the cruise ended at Old Swan Pier. The Alexandra ran aground and sank shortly after the Pinchin Street murder.

Such cruises were social occasions, so she must have gone with a friend or admirer who did not accompany her home. Her absence may have been reported, without any connection being established between her and this murder.

My assumptions are that:

- the date of the murder was Thursday, 23 August 1888, and that while disposing of the body the perpetrator picked up a copy of the Echo dated Friday, 24 August;
- the perpetrator had use of his skiff, and temporary use of a barge, where he carried out the dismemberment and from which he dropped the arm found at Pimlico and the remaining undiscovered body parts into the river;
- he missed the early tide at 3.32 a.m., and ran out of time before his working day started, failing to cut the torso into three parts and being left with a large item that was too noticeable to be put into the river;
- he stored the torso and leg remains on his skiff for at least twenty-four hours until Friday night, or some time over that weekend, when he disposed of them at the same time at the unmanned building site;
- his bizarre choice of the foundations of New Scotland Yard to dump the body parts was a simple coincidence.

In these dog days of summer, the steamboats run popular moonlight trips. He likes the idea of attending an upmarket customer, with ready money to hand, needing to get home late from Old Swan Pier. He rows his skiff up to the next bridge, a mere ½ mile west of Horsleydown, and across the river.

He spots her on the pier, a statuesque woman with curves in all the right places. *Just the job.* She is alone, having separated from her friend. Part of her is still revelling in the night she has had, dancing to the music of the Masonic Band, and marvelling at the fireworks. She may be intending to walk home, but when the waterman calls out to her, quoting a low price, it is too convenient for her to refuse.

She is his shortest-ever fare. He rows straight up to the barge, which is moored off the pier. She expresses surprise that verges on dismay: *I only want to go home.* He threatens to throw her overboard, into the dark waters, if she resists. Too shocked to scream, she is aware of him pushing her up onto the barge and then down into its cabin.

She defends herself ferociously in the darkness, her height and weight working to her advantage, while shouting, *No!* He has to silence her, there is no alternative: *She asked for it*. Although she is dead, she pays the ferryman, with the money that he takes from her purse. He does as much cutting as he can before daybreak, when his fellow bargemen will start work. Catching the early tide at around 3 a.m., he dumps her head and limbs over the side, like damaged goods, before bundling the torso and left calf in parts of her skirt and transferring them onto his skiff, where he covers them with canvas. He cleans up behind him, then rows away fast. A few hours of sleep are all that he needs.

He is committed to work that day, and something delays his return from the docks to the skiff. He no longer has access to a large secluded space where he could finish the dismemberment, but he does have a couple of newspapers, some sacking and pieces of string to wrap up the torso and last remains. He also uses some black tape from the waist of the woman's skirt. Once his bundles are neat and ready, he is good to go.

For months, he has seen the open gate onto a building site behind Westminster pier, with dozens of workmen and lightermen carrying materials to and fro. In the quiet early morning, he rows his skiff to the pier, moors up, and takes out his sack, dragging it where he can. The pier is directly opposite Derby Gate, the approach road to the new building's main entrance. He drops his burden over the hoarding and climbs up after it, sliding down a conveniently placed pile of concrete on the other side.

He finds his way into the basement, although he needs to strike a few matches to locate the 5ft mound of rubbish at its rear that suits his purpose. He tips his parcels out of his sack, kicks earth over them and treads it in. With his empty sack in hand, he is fast to retrace his steps. Nobody can identify the body, not even the 'tecs at New Scotland Yard to whom it was accidentally delivered.

## Reconstruction of the murder of Elizabeth Jackson, between approximately 6 p.m. and 10 p.m. on Monday, 3 June 1889

*This reconstruction is based on Jackson's known movements on the night of her murder. I place the perpetrator as a night watchman on a barge moored near Battersea Park Pier. It is tantalising to speculate that her killer might have been the 'navvy' last seen with Jackson, and that navvy might have been a river worker, not a construction worker. However, in this reconstruction I treat the case like that of Ripper victim Mary Jane Kelly, who was seen with another man on the night of her murder, two hours before she met her killer.*

*My assumptions are similar to those in the Rainham case, that:*

- *the perpetrator had continuous use of a barge, and that the body parts discovered on land were deposited from a boat;*
- *he was working a night shift on the barge, giving him time and the means of transport to dismember and dispose of the body.*

It is a chance early-evening meeting outside the Royal Hospital Tavern on Franklins Row. Lizzie is with her navvy, on their way southbound, when two girls walk up from her sometime lodging house on Turk's Row. Jenny is smirking as Eliza says to Lizzie, *I suppose you're going to Battersea?*

Lizzie is not best pleased to be seen with a paying client, or to be called out for it. She puts on a bold front, replying, *That's just where I am going*, and moves her fellow along. They walk slowly, at her pace, down Royal Hospital Road and Cheyne Walk and over Albert Bridge. They go down the stairs to the wharf, and step over a low railing into Battersea Park. It is quiet and still light as they walk out of any onlookers' sight. When their business is complete, the man leaves her at the waterfront, where she intends to stay the night.

As Lizzie is sitting on a bench looking across the river, wrapped in a carapace of other women's clothing, a man calls to her from a barge moored near the pier. He looks nice enough, all teeth and muscles. *Come onto my boat, flower! Come along with me and let's get you warmed up, eh?*

She is not averse to a warm shelter, or company, and, as she stands up stiffly, he notices her condition. She walks along to the pier and accepts his help to cross onto his boat. He goes ahead of her into the cabin, and leans around her to shut out the daylight. He is too close, and his eyes are not smiling. He turns rough, and Lizzie fights him, more fierce for the sake of her unborn child than for herself. Far stronger than she is, he pulls her clothes up, and rapes her. She will not lie still, won't stop struggling and wailing. Holding her arms down, he knees her in the belly to shut her up. She screams with pain as the wetness comes, her waters broken, or is it blood?

He abandons the idea that she is easy meat, and reaches for his knife to settle her. His capable hands are givers of death for the woman and her baby. Her clothing and boot-laces come in useful to make up the bundles. He uses oddments of string and cord to make up the shortfall. They will all go overboard in the early hours, when he wakes for work. All that is left to be done is to lower a bucket into the river and wash down the decks, and himself.

The morning high tide is at 4.31 a.m., perfect timing to dispose of most of the remains in the river. As he is sailing downstream as free as a gull, he throws out one parcel over the park railings to his right, and another to his left, which drops satisfyingly behind the railings of a smart house on Chelsea Embankment. *Somebody else's problem.*

But the problem resurfaces, too close for comfort, as close as Horsleydown itself. And several bundles are discovered at Battersea, although mistakenly believed to be dropped from Albert Bridge. For once, the police assumption that the victim was a local woman holds good, and she is identified. But he still has the luck of the devil. As the father of her child, Jack Faircloth is the prime suspect, and the last person believed to see her alive was an untraceable navvy.

## Reconstruction of the Pinchin Street murder

*The unidentified victim was aged around thirty-five, a short and busty brunette, who did not do rough manual work. The only clothing left to her was a torn, bloodied white chemise, London-made. Neither married nor a mother, she must have earned her living somehow, perhaps by working in a factory or shop. As with the other murders in that series, she was neither killed nor dismembered where her torso was found.*

Both Jack the Ripper and James Crick were at liberty for this murder, when they should have been behind bars. Crick was not only a free man, on bail for the assault on Jessie Miller, he was also temporarily out of work. He would have downed tools for all or part of the Great London Dock Strike from 14 August to 16 September 1889, when the watermen and lightermen came out in support of the dockers' demands for better pay and conditions.[1] The strike prevented Crick from working, but not necessarily from entering a dock close to Pinchin Street such as St Katharine's or, even closer, the Western Dock.

In November 2021, I walked a route of my own devising, from Penning Street, representing the nearest corner of the now-defunct Western Dock, to Pinchin Street taking the most direct way via Wellclose Square. Timed with a stopwatch, the short uphill route took three and a half minutes. A strong man carrying a sack could have done it in a similar time.

If continued northwards, that route leads to the Salvation Army food depot at 272 Whitechapel Road, where striking men and their families were given handouts. If continued southwards, it leads over the river to St Saviour's Dock, five blocks east of Horsleydown Old Stairs.

My assumptions are that:

- the date of the murder was the evening of Sunday, 8 September 1889, based on the police estimate stated in Commissioner Monro's report;
- as in the Whitehall case, the perpetrator had full use of his skiff, and temporary use of a barge for storage through to Tuesday morning;
- Doctor Phillips was correct in his assessment that there was no evidence of recent sexual intercourse;
- the perpetrator was involved in strike action on the Monday, and ran out of time to dismember the torso;
- the early, low tides made it impossible for him dispose of the torso in the river;
- he walked northbound up Backchurch Lane, turned into Pinchin Street and deposited the torso in the first arch on his right, as the nearest and most convenient place that he already knew;
- he did not borrow a hand-barrow.

He has spent a long day on the dockers' protest march from Canning Town through to Hyde Park, where speeches were made from four platforms. Strike leader and socialist firebrand John Burns asked the assembly if they would accept the terms offered by the dock companies, and was met by a roar of *No!*

It is thirsty work, protesting, and he soon finds himself standing next to an attractive brunette in a pub on Tooley Street, who is eyeing up potential punters. He is also on the hunt, and likes the look of her, although she could do with a wash. A quick drink, and into his skiff, as simple as that. His routine is as slick as petroleum, and it excites him to know how their coupling will end. Does he feed her his usual line, *Keep silent, and you will be safe*, as he kneels heavily on her to subdue her, bruising her back? He forces her down into the barge's cabin and holds her down. As she starts screaming, his response is to shut her up, and he thumps her head repeatedly, above the hairline, until she is still. He rolls off her, panting and unsatisfied.

He has had too much to drink, and he sleeps after the kill. When he wakes, he has a scant hour to do what he can; cutting off her legs to get them out of his way. He has to cover her with a canvas, and leave her. His fellow pickets are expecting him, and if he doesn't show up, he'll be labelled a blackleg and never work again.

On the second night, he is lit by a bright full moon. His first task is to remove her head and throw it in the river, wrapped in canvas and weighted with a stone. Her legs soon follow, bundled and weighted with whatever he has to hand. But high tide is early, at half-past midnight at London Bridge, and he has run out of time. He cannot throw the torso overboard and row away, as it will float and give him away. He needs to dump it on land, and he knows a place. He draws up a bucket of water to wash the torso, and the deck. He puts the single heavy mass of flesh into a large sack, wrapping a piece of rope around its open end and back around the torso's waist, creating a makeshift handle. Then he takes his skiff to the Western Dock, mooring it as far inland as he can row.

It is five o'clock in the morning when he alights with the sack on his back. He walks from the dock across Upper East Smithfield and halfway around Wellclose Square to its far side, where Wilton's Music Hall is. He cuts across Cable Street, turning left onto Backchurch Lane and then right into Pinchin Street to deposit his load under the first railway arch, against its western wall.

By chance, he misses Constable Pennett, who has continued up Backchurch Lane northbound on his way to knock up a man. Under the dark railway arch, the killer carefully lowers his heavy sack, takes out the torso and places it on the ground. He cannot leave the sack behind, as it is marked with the name of a warehouse owner. He walks quickly back to his boat, the empty sack rolled under his arm, blending in with other men who are out and about on their separate ways to work. For him, too, new day's work can begin.

# Epilogue

Reflecting the difficulties posed by this case, I close with a comment from the fictitious yet acute Doctor John H. Watson: 'A problem without a solution may interest the student, but can hardly fail to annoy the casual reader.'[1] The series of Thames Torso Murders ended in Pinchin Street, three months before James Crick was imprisoned for the rape of Elizabeth Sarah Warburton. Her case, and that of Jessie Miller, illuminate the possible modus operandi of the Torso Killer. Yet 135 years later, it is not possible to name James Crick with any degree of certainty as the killer of the four Torso victims. No surviving evidence or testimony exists to enable a more definite identification.

Despite my consideration of the Salamanca Place murder, Crick did not reoffend between his release from prison in 1898 and his death on 29 June 1907, aged 44, at Bermondsey Infirmary. On his death certificate, his cause of death was listed as tuberculosis and his occupation was still that of a lighterman.[2] He was buried at Tower Hamlets Cemetery.[3] Ten weeks later, his estranged wife Rosina married her long-term partner Robert Marler.[4]

Two questions are left floating here: was James Crick the Thames Torso Killer, or a violent rapist who paid his debt to society? And, if *Arm of Eve* argues a sufficiently convincing hypothesis, to what extent was justice done in his lifetime? The case against Crick is derived from the charges relating to Miller and Warburton, and his fit to a profile. Two women survived his attacks and testified against him. When challenged in court, he went straight to victim-blaming, viciously undermining anyone who stood up to him. He accused them of being drunken whores, and, in a classic reversal of the truth, of attacking him. As an intimidation tactic, he warned, '*Keep silent, and you will be safe.*' Thanks to the courage of Jessie Miller and Elizabeth Sarah Warburton, he was charged with his offences. Once convicted for the rape of Warburton, he served nine years of a fifteen-year sentence.

A marauding rapist turned murderer, the Torso Killer evaded the justice he deserved. I believe that his crimes were prolific: he raped hundreds of women, and killed at least four of them, and in addition Elizabeth Jackson's unborn child. If brought to account for the Torso Murders, he would either have been hanged or held at Broadmoor as a criminal lunatic, at the monarch's pleasure.

The extent of the violence used in the Torso Murders is sickening. A malignant narcissist, the killer got his kicks from rapes, beatings and murders. He cynically accosted his victims, viciously assaulted them, and, if they offered sufficient resistance, did not hesitate to kill. Next came his workmanlike dismemberment, a gratifying task which he conducted with expertise. The Thames and Regent's Canal were watery chutes for the disposal in batches of their remains, while a building site and railway arch were his rubbish tips. Baffling the police investigations, his mobility saved him from the gallows.

Survivors of abuse know how violent abuse silences you, erodes your identity, and conditions your responses. When severe and prolonged, it deconstructs your personality and can destroy you. In the Thames Torso cases, the women's physical annihilation was complete. All but one of his victims were unidentified, leaving their families with unresolved grief, unable to mourn for them. There may have been others who simply disappeared without any trace, never to resurface. As for *him*, the river was his hunting ground, and the scene of his crimes was always in front of his eyes.

# Acknowledgements

Part of my inspiration for this, my second book, came from former river police officer Robert Jeffries, who introduced me to the history of Thames Division. He established the Thames Memorial at All Hallows-by-the-Tower Church for those who have lost their lives in the River Thames, which has meaning for me as a remembrance of the *Marchioness* disaster. I owe him and many others my thanks. Among my family and friends, Michael Chambers and Mai-Ling Savage were a great support, while Ruth Al Sadie boosted me with her kindred enthusiasm for family history and historical research.

I would not be a published author without old friends' belief in me and the decision by my literary agent Andrew Lownie to take me on. Producing a book is a team effort, and I thank my commissioning editor Mark Beynon and everyone involved at The History Press. Louise Dixon and Lucy Stewardson at Michael O'Mara Books steered my first book, *One-Armed Jack*, to a success beyond my imagining, alongside the excellent publicist Alison Menzies.

I take this opportunity to express my sincere gratitude to the Whitechapel Society and members of what might be called the Ripper community for their expertise and encouragement over a period of years, in particular Keith Skinner, Paul Begg, Adam Wood, Lindsay

Siviter, Debra Arif, Sue Parry and Steven E. Blomer. I am also grateful to Justine Solomons at Byte The Book, and to colleagues at the Society of Authors, the Crime Writers' Association and the Welsh crime writing collective Crime Cymru. Again, I thank staff at the London Metropolitan Archives, The National Archives and the British Library for their professional assistance.

# Timeline

| Day | Month | Year | Event |
|---|---|---|---|
| 2 | March | 1879 | Murder of Julia Martha Thomas by Kate Webster |
| 11 | May | 1887 | Discovery of the Rainham torso, the first in the Thames Torso Murder series |
| 12 | May | 1887 | Rosina Crick brought a case of assault against her husband, James Crick |
| 10 | January | 1888 | The author's great-great-grandfather Harry Garrett was transferred to H Division's Leman Street police station on promotion to sergeant |
| 7 | August | 1888 | Possible Ripper murder of Martha Tabram |
| 31 | August | 1888 | Ripper murder of Polly Nichols, the first of the 'canonical five' series |
| 8 | September | 1888 | Ripper murder of Annie Chapman |

| Day | Month | Year | Event |
|---|---|---|---|
| 11 | September | 1888 | Arm found at Pimlico, and subsequently a torso found at Whitehall, the second in the Thames Torso murder series |
| 30 | September | 1888 | Ripper murders of Elisabeth Stride and Catherine Eddowes |
| 9 | November | 1888 | Ripper murder of Mary Jane Kelly |
| 9 | November | 1888 | James Monro succeeded Charles Warren as Metropolitan Police Commissioner, on the latter's resignation |
| 10 | November | 1888 | Police surgeon Mr Thomas Bond produced a criminal profile of Jack the Ripper |
| 20 | December | 1888 | Death of Rose Mylett |
| 29 | December | 1888 | The author's prime suspect as Jack the Ripper, Hyam Hyams, was arrested as a 'wandering lunatic' and admitted to Baker's Row Workhouse |
| 9 | April | 1889 | After a period of liberty between 11 January and early April, Hyams attacked his wife and mother, and was temporarily readmitted to the workhouse |
| 15 | April | 1889 | Hyams was transferred to Colney Hatch Lunatic Asylum |
| 4 | June | 1889 | Remains of the third Torso victim, Elizabeth Jackson, began to surface |
| 1 | July | 1889 | Non-fatal attack on Jessie Miller by James Crick |
| 17 | July | 1889 | Murder of Alice Kinsey, also known as McKenzie |
| 6 | August | 1889 | James Crick was bailed after being charged with the attempted murder and rape of Jessie Miller |

# TIMELINE

| Day | Month | Year | Event |
| --- | --- | --- | --- |
| 30 | August | 1889 | Hyams was discharged from Colney Hatch Lunatic Asylum |
| 7 | September | 1889 | After a brief period of liberty, Hyams assaulted his wife and was admitted to the City of London Workhouse, followed by Stone Lunatic Asylum |
| 11 | September | 1889 | Discovery of the Pinchin Street torso, the fourth in the series; police estimated the murder date to be 8 September 1889 |
| 23 | October | 1889 | Non-fatal attack on Elizabeth Sarah Warburton by James Crick |
| 18 | December | 1889 | James Crick was sentenced to fifteen years' imprisonment for the rape of Elizabeth Sarah Warburton |
| 4 | January | 1890 | Hyams was transferred to Colney Hatch Lunatic Asylum for the second time, where he died in 1913 |
| 13 | August | 1898 | James Crick was granted early release from prison |
| 22 | January | 1901 | Death of Queen Victoria |
| 8 | June | 1902 | Discovery of dismembered human remains at Salamanca Place, Vauxhall |
| 9 | August | 1902 | Coronation of Edward VII and Queen Alexandra |
| 29 | June | 1907 | Death of James Crick, aged 44 |

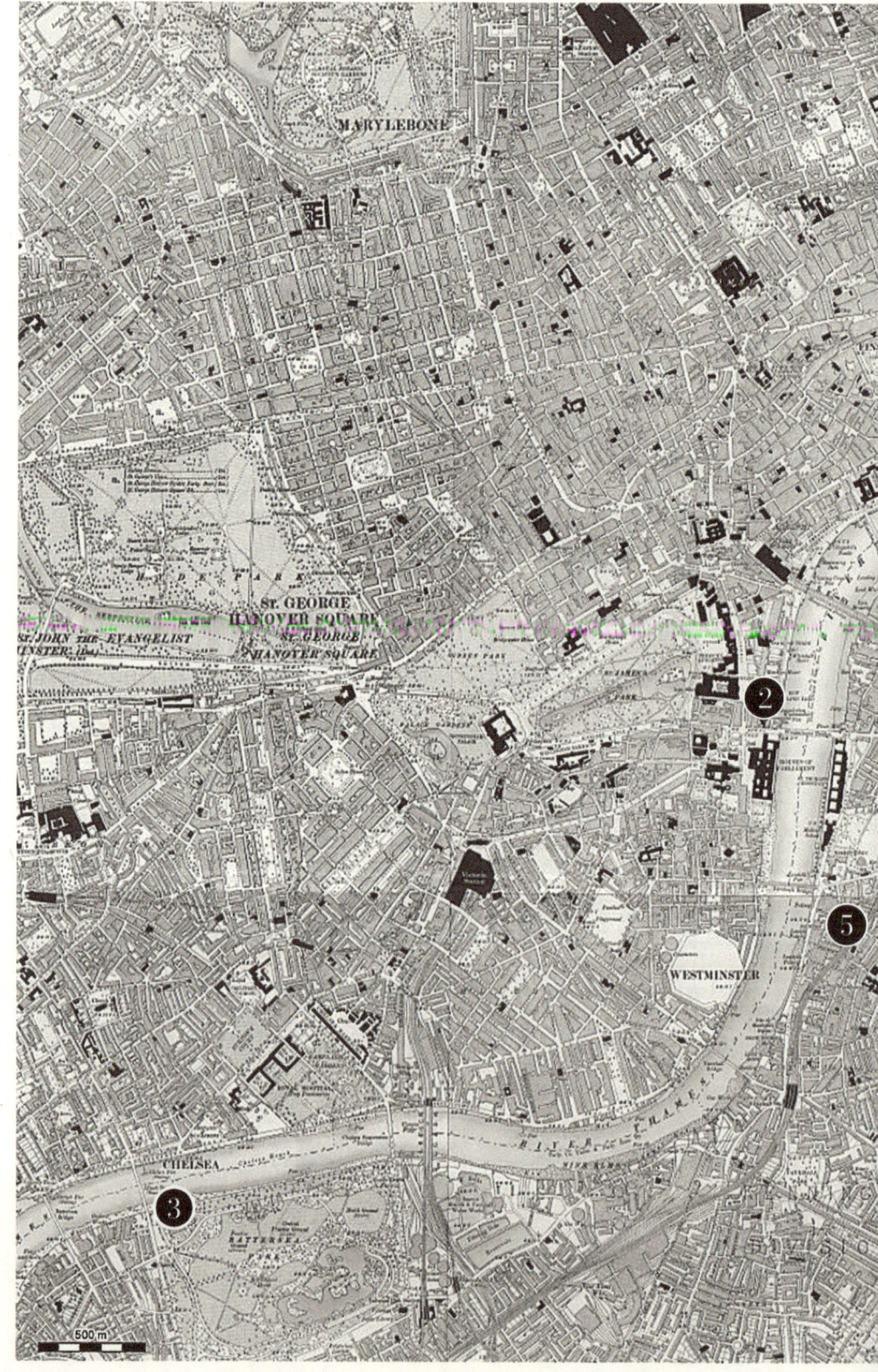

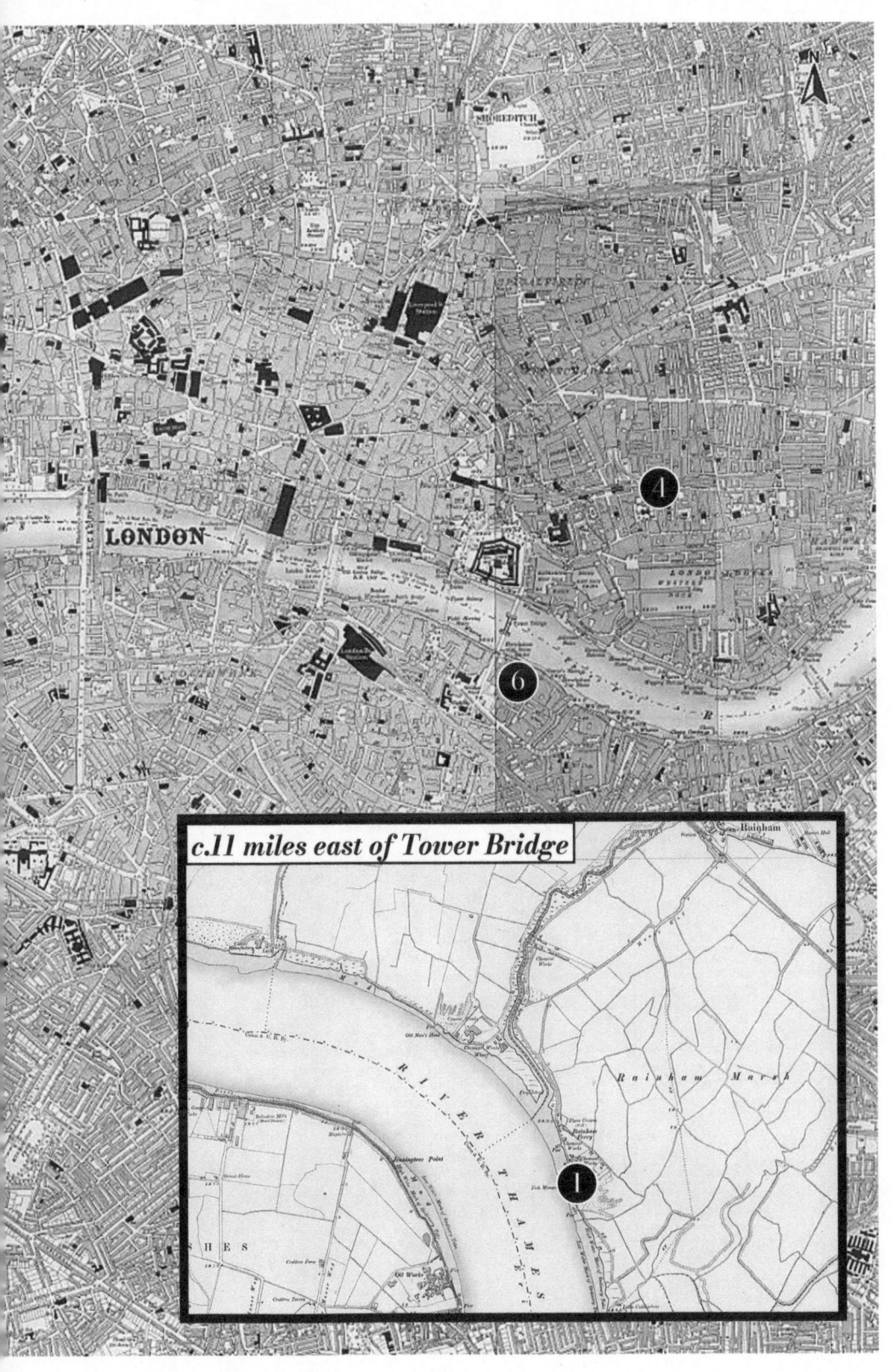

c.11 miles east of Tower Bridge

| | Map Key |
|---|---|
| 1 | **Rainham Ferry**, where a partial torso was discovered on 11 May 1887 |
| 2 | **New Scotland Yard, Whitehall**, where a torso and leg were discovered as the foundations were being built on 2 October 1888 |
| 3 | **Battersea foreshore, near Albert Bridge**, where the first part of Elizabeth Jackson's dismembered remains were discovered on 4 June 1889 |
| 4 | **Pinchin Street railway arch, Whitechapel**, where the Pinchin Street torso was discovered on 10 September 1889 |
| 5 | **Salamanca Place, Vauxhall**, where a sackful of remains were discovered on 8 June 1902 |
| 6 | **Horsleydown Old Stairs, Shad Thames**, where James Crick plied his trade |

All locations approximate; base maps are extracts from the Ordnance Survey 6-inch 2nd Edition Series of England, Wales, Scotland and Ireland, 1888–1915, which have been reproduced with the permission of the National Library of Scotland.

# Select bibliography

Every reasonable effort has been made to trace copyright holders.

## Abbreviations

British Library (BL)
British Newspaper Archive (BNA)
City of London Police (COLP)
General Register Office (GRO)
Home Office (HO)
London Metropolitan Archives (LMA)
Metropolitan Police (MEPO)
Ordnance Survey (OS)
The National Archives (TNA)

## Select Bibliography

Sarah Bax Horton, *One-Armed Jack* (Michael O'Mara Books, 2023)
Paul Begg, Martin Fido and Keith Skinner, *The Complete Jack the Ripper A to Z* (John Blake Publishing, 2010)

Paul Begg and John Bennett, *Jack the Ripper: The Forgotten Victims* (Yale University Press, 2013)

Stewart P. Evans and Keith Skinner, *The Ultimate Jack the Ripper Sourcebook* (Robinson, 2001)

R. Michael Gordon, *The Thames Torso Murders of Victorian London* (McFarland & Company, Inc., Publishers, 2002)

Drew Gray and Andrew Wise, *Jack and the Thames Torso Murders: A New Ripper?* (Amberley Publishing, 2019)

Christer Holmgren, *Cutting Point: Solving the Jack the Ripper and the Thames Torso Murders* (Timaios Press, 2021)

Philip Sugden, *The Complete History of Jack the Ripper* (Da Capo Press, 2002)

M.J. Trow, *The Thames Torso Murders* (Wharncliffe, 2011)

# Notes

When quoting sources, some adjustments have been made to the punctuation and text to aid readability.

## Introduction

1. Paul Begg, Martin Fido and Keith Skinner, *The Complete Jack the Ripper A to Z* (John Blake Publishing, 2010), p.59.
2. *Penny Illustrated Paper*, 22 September 1888.
3. W.H. Allchin, M.B.Lond., F.R.C.P.; George Cowell, F.R.C.S.; and C.A. Hebbert, M.R.C.P. (eds), *The Westminster Hospital Reports, Volume IV* (J. & A. Churchill, 1888), Chapter VI. Charles A. Hebbert, M.R.C.P., 'An Exercise in Forensic Medicine', p.49.
4. Octavius Sturges, M.D.Cantab., F.R.C.P.; and George Cowell, F.R.C.S. (eds), *The Westminster Hospital Reports, Volume V* (J. & A. Churchill, 1889), Chapter XI. Charles A. Hebbert, M.R.C.P., 'An Exercise in Forensic Medicine, Part II', p.152.
5. W.H. Allchin, M.B.Lond., F.R.C.P.; George Cowell, F.R.C.S.; and C.A. Hebbert, M.R.C.P. (eds), *The Westminster Hospital Reports, Volume IV* (J. & A. Churchill, 1888), Chapter VI. Charles A. Hebbert, M.R.C.P., 'An Exercise in Forensic Medicine', p.49.
6. Octavius Sturges, M.D.Cantab., F.R.C.P.; and George Cowell, F.R.C.S. (eds), *The Westminster Hospital Reports, Volume V* (J. & A. Churchill, 1889), Chapter XI. Charles A. Hebbert, M.R.C.P., 'An Exercise in Forensic Medicine, Part II', p.151.
7. The author has used the modern spelling of Horsleydown except when quoting sources using an alternative spelling.
8. *East London Observer*, 24 September 1892.

## 1: The first murder: Rainham, May 1887

1. Ancestry.com: Library and Museum of Freemasonry; London, England; Freemasonry Membership Registers; Description: Membership Registers: London B 90–198 to London C 201–813; Reel Number: 2.
2. Ancestry.com: TNA: Metropolitan Police Pension Registers, 1852–1932, Number 16,908 of 1 November 1906.
3. *Illustrated Police News*, 21 May 1887. The author's account of the witness testimony in inquest hearings is neither comprehensive nor strictly chronological.
4. *Illustrated Police News*, 28 May 1887.
5. *Illustrated Police News*, 21 May 1887.
6. *Chelmsford Chronicle*, 20 May 1887.
7. *Southend Standard and Essex Weekly Advertiser*, 11 August 1887.
8. *Chelmsford Chronicle*, 20 May 1887.
9. Ibid.
10. *Illustrated Police News*, 21 May 1887.
11. TNA: The Anatomy Act 1832 (2 & 3 Will. IV c.75).
12. *The People*, 22 May 1887.
13. *Essex Newsman*, 21 May 1887.
14. W. Lawler, *J Clin Pathol*, 'Bodies recovered from water: a personal approach and consideration of difficulties', first published as 10.1136/jcp.45.8.654 on 1 August 1992 and also published in the *British Medical Journal*.
15. *The Essex Herald*, 17 January 1893.
16. *The People*, 22 May 1887.
17. *Chelmsford Chronicle*, 20 May 1887.
18. *The Globe*, 13 September 1875.
19. *The People*, 5 June 1887.
20. *Southend Standard and Essex Weekly Advertiser*, 9 June 1887.
21. *Express and Echo*, 4 June 1887.
22. *London Evening Standard*, 25 September 1886.
23. Ibid.
24. Old Bailey Proceedings Online (www.oldbaileyonline.org, version 8.0, 30 January 2023), November 1886, trial of William Carter, William Higgins, Charles Richard Harding (t18861122-32).
25. *London Evening Standard*, 5 October 1886.
26. *London Evening Standard*, 25 September 1886.
27. *The People*, 5 June 1887.
28. Ibid.
29. *Lakes Chronicle and Reporter*, 10 June 1887.
30. Paul Begg and John Bennett, *Jack the Ripper: The Forgotten Victims* (Yale University Press, 2013), pp.95–6.
31. *Lakes Chronicle and Reporter*, 17 June 1887.
32. Ibid.
33. *Reynolds's Newspaper*, 3 July 1887.
34. *Shields Daily Gazette*, 4 July 1887.
35. *Hastings and St Leonards Observer*, 13 August 1910.

36 *Hampstead News*, 11 August 1910.
37 Nicholas Connell, *The Annotated I Caught Crippen: Memoirs of Ex-Chief Inspector Walter Dew, C.I.D. of Scotland Yard* (Mango Books, 2019), pp.66–76.
38 Ibid. and *Gloucester Citizen*, 7 January 1930.
39 *Lloyd's Weekly Newspaper*, 17 July 1887.
40 *Dundee Evening Telegraph*, 12 July 1887.
41 *Lloyd's Weekly Newspaper*, 10 July 1887.
42 *Lloyd's Weekly Newspaper*, 17 July 1887.
43 Ibid.
44 Ibid.
45 Ibid.
46 *Essex Standard*, 13 August 1887.
47 MEPO 3/140, f K, quoted from Stewart P. Evans and Keith Skinner, *The Ultimate Jack the Ripper Sourcebook* (Robinson, 2001), p.485.
48 *Essex Standard*, 13 August 1887.
49 *Weekly Irish Times*, 13 August 1887.
50 W.H. Allchin, M.B.Lond., F.R.C.P.; George Cowell, F.R.C.S.; and C.A. Hebbert, M.R.C.P. (eds), *The Westminster Hospital Reports, Volume IV* (J. & A. Churchill, 1888), Chapter VI. Charles A. Hebbert, M.R.C.P., 'An Exercise in Forensic Medicine', pp.52–3.
51 W.H. Allchin, M.B.Lond., F.R.C.P.; George Cowell, F.R.C.S.; and C.A. Hebbert, M.R.C.P. (eds), *The Westminster Hospital Reports, Volume IV* (J. & A. Churchill, 1888), Chapter VI. Charles A. Hebbert, M.R.C.P., 'An Exercise in Forensic Medicine', p.60.
52 *Edinburgh Evening News*, 9 August 1887.
53 *Lloyd's Weekly Newspaper*, 10 July 1887.
54 *Sunderland Daily Echo and Shipping Gazette*, 1 July 1887.
55 W.H. Allchin, M.B.Lond., F.R.C.P.; George Cowell, F.R.C.S.; and C.A. Hebbert, M.R.C.P. (eds), *The Westminster Hospital Reports, Volume IV* (J. & A. Churchill, 1888), Chapter VI. Charles A. Hebbert, M.R.C.P., 'An Exercise in Forensic Medicine', p.50.
56 W.H. Allchin, M.B.Lond., F.R.C.P.; George Cowell, F.R.C.S.; and C.A. Hebbert, M.R.C.P. (eds), *The Westminster Hospital Reports, Volume IV* (J. & A. Churchill, 1888), Chapter VI. Charles A. Hebbert, M.R.C.P., 'An Exercise in Forensic Medicine', pp.53–4.
57 *Southend Standard and Essex Weekly Advertiser*, 9 June 1887.
58 *Lloyd's Weekly Newspaper*, 1 May 1887.
59 *Morning Post*, 27 April 1887.
60 *Sporting Life*, 23 April 1887.

## 2: The Whitehall murder, September 1888

1 *London Evening Standard*, 28 September 1888.
2 *London Evening Standard*, 28 September 1888.
3 TNA: MEPO 2/245.

4   W.H. Allchin, M.B.Lond., F.R.C.P.; George Cowell, F.R.C.S.; and C.A. Hebbert, M.R.C.P. (eds), *The Westminster Hospital Reports, Volume IV* (J. & A. Churchill, 1888), Chapter VI. Charles A. Hebbert, M.R.C.P., 'An Exercise in Forensic Medicine', p.57.
5   *Pall Mall Gazette*, 4 October 1888.
6   *Peterborough Express*, 10 October 1888.
7   *The Globe*, 29 February 1912.
8   *Hull Daily Mail*, 8 October 1888.
9   *York Herald*, 9 October 1888.
10  *Lloyd's Weekly Newspaper*, 14 October 1888.
11  Ibid.
12  Ibid.
13  *The Evening Mail*, 10 October 1888.
14  *London Evening Standard*, 8 October 1888.
15  *Lloyd's Weekly Newspaper*, 14 October 1888.
16  Ibid.
17  *The Scotsman*, 9 October 1888.
18  *Lloyd's Weekly Newspaper*, 14 October 1888.
19  *The Evening Mail*, 10 October 1888.
20  Ibid.
21  Ibid.
22  W.H. Allchin, M.B.Lond., F.R.C.P.; George Cowell, F.R.C.S.; and C.A. Hebbert, M.R.C.P. (eds), *The Westminster Hospital Reports, Volume IV* (J. & A. Churchill, 1888), Chapter VI. Charles A. Hebbert, M.R.C.P., 'An Exercise in Forensic Medicine', pp.55 and 58.
23  *Lloyd's Weekly Newspaper*, 14 October 1888.
24  *The Evening Mail*, 10 October 1888.
25  *West Somerset Free Press*, 13 October 1888.
26  *Penny Illustrated Paper*, 27 October 1888.
27  *Glasgow Evening Citizen*, 22 October 1888.
28  *Lloyd's Weekly Newspaper*, 28 October 1888.
29  Ibid.
30  Ibid.
31  *The Evening Mail*, 24 October 1888.
32  *Lloyd's Weekly Newspaper*, 28 October 1888.
33  W.H. Allchin, M.B.Lond., F.R.C.P.; George Cowell, F.R.C.S.; and C.A. Hebbert, M.R.C.P. (eds), *The Westminster Hospital Reports, Volume IV* (J. & A. Churchill, 1888), Chapter VI. Charles A. Hebbert, M.R.C.P., 'An Exercise in Forensic Medicine', p.59.
34  *Wigton Advertiser*, 27 October 1888. Named in the press as Constable Thomas 'Button', he was probably Metropolitan Police Officer Thomas Lyle Bowden, 1851–1925, warrant number: 58905.
35  Ancestry.com: TNA: 1881 England Census; Class: RG11; Piece: 117; f. 9; p. 12; GSU roll: 1341026.
36  *Lloyd's Weekly Newspaper*, 21 October 1888.
37  *Wigton Advertiser*, 27 October 1888.

38 *Lloyd's Weekly Newspaper*, 28 October 1888.
39 *The Canterbury Journal, Kentish Times and Farmers' Gazette* of 6 October 1888 has 'now that steels are done away with'.
40 *Northampton Mercury*, 6 March 1886.
41 *Echo* (London), 6 October 1888.
42 For example, *Shipley Times and Express*, 6 October 1888.
43 For example, *Lloyd's Weekly Newspaper*, 21 October 1888.
44 *The Globe*, 14 September 1888.
45 *West Somerset Free Press*, 13 October 1888.
46 Ancestry.com: LMA: Church of England Marriages and Banns, 1754–1938; Reference Number: P84/TRI1/007. Marriage date: 22 June 1890.
47 *Dundee Courier*, 31 October 1888.
48 The author consulted the MEPO series of files at TNA.
49 *South Wales Echo*, 31 October 1888.
50 *Brecknock Beacon*, 12 October 1888.
51 *Weekly Dispatch* (London), 21 October 1888.
52 W.H. Allchin, M.B.Lond., F.R.C.P.; George Cowell, F.R.C.S.; and C.A. Hebbert, M.R.C.P. (eds), *The Westminster Hospital Reports, Volume IV* (J. & A. Churchill, 1888), Chapter VI. Charles A. Hebbert, M.R.C.P., 'An Exercise in Forensic Medicine', p.57.
53 Ibid., p.56.
54 Ibid., pp.56–7.
55 *Hampshire Independent*, 6 October 1888.
56 *Lloyd's Weekly Newspaper*, 14 October 1888.
57 TNA: HO 45/9765/B841A.
58 Ibid.

## 3: The Battersea murder, Monday, 3 June 1889

1 *London Evening Standard*, 17 June 1889.
2 Octavius Sturges, M.D.Cantab., F.R.C.P.; and George Cowell, F.R.C.S. (eds), *The Westminster Hospital Reports, Volume V* (J. & A. Churchill, 1889). Chapter XI. Charles A. Hebbert, M.R.C.P., 'An Exercise in Forensic Medicine, Part II', pp.153–4.
3 *Birmingham Daily Post*, 6 June 1889.
4 *Birmingham Mail*, 5 June 1889.
5 *The Shipley Times*, 8 June 1889.
6 *The Portsmouth Evening News*, 13 June 1889.
7 Octavius Sturges, M.D.Cantab., F.R.C.P.; and George Cowell, F.R.C.S. (eds), *The Westminster Hospital Reports, Volume V* (J. & A. Churchill, 1889). Chapter XI. Charles A. Hebbert, M.R.C.P., 'An Exercise in Forensic Medicine, Part II', p.151.
8 *The Portsmouth Evening News*, 13 June 1889.
9 *Birmingham Daily Post*, 11 June 1889.
10 *The Scotsman*, 8 June 1889; *Dundee Courier*, 5 June 1889.
11 *Northampton Mercury*, 15 June 1889.
12 *Western Morning News*, 8 June 1889.

13 *The Scotsman*, 8 June 1889.
14 Wikipedia, quoting *Richmond Herald*, 24 May 1902.
15 *Lancaster Gazette*, 19 June 1889.
16 *Marlborough Times*, 22 June 1889.
17 Ibid.
18 Ibid.
19 Octavius Sturges, M.D.Cantab., F.R.C.P.; and George Cowell, F.R.C.S. (eds), *The Westminster Hospital Reports, Volume V* (J. & A. Churchill, 1889). Chapter XI. Charles A. Hebbert, M.R.C.P., 'An Exercise in Forensic Medicine, Part II', p.155.
20 Ibid.
21 *Hants and Sussex News*, 19 June 1889.
22 *Birmingham Daily Post*, 6 June 1889.
23 Octavius Sturges, M.D.Cantab., F.R.C.P.; and George Cowell, F.R.C.S. (eds), *The Westminster Hospital Reports, Volume V*, (J. & A. Churchill, 1889). Chapter XI. Charles A. Hebbert, M.R.C.P., 'An Exercise in Forensic Medicine, Part II', p.154.
24 *London Evening Standard*, 15 June 1889.
25 A day's pay was often greater than the court's standard compensation for witnesses.
26 *London Evening Standard*, 15 June 1889.
27 Ibid.
28 Its full title is *Frankenstein; or, The Modern Prometheus*.
29 Octavius Sturges, M.D.Cantab., F.R.C.P.; and George Cowell, F.R.C.S. (eds), *The Westminster Hospital Reports, Volume V* (J. & A. Churchill, 1889). Chapter XI. Charles A. Hebbert, M.R.C.P., 'An Exercise in Forensic Medicine, Part II', p.155.
30 *London Evening Standard*, 15 June 1889; *Lloyd's Weekly Newspaper*, 16 June 1889.
31 *Gloucester Citizen*, 10 June 1889.
32 Marked on the 1896 OS map as Honduras Wharf, 74 Bankside.
33 For example, *Sheffield Independent*, 11 June 1889.
34 *South Western Star*, 22 June 1889.
35 *Weekly Dispatch* (London), 23 June 1889.
36 *Birmingham Mail*, 17 June 1889.
37 GRO: Birth Certificate, 1865, 1st Quarter, Chelsea, Volume 01a, p.224.
38 *Evening Star*, 28 June 1889.
39 *The Star of the East*, 28 June 1889.
40 *Weekly Dispatch* (London), 7 July 1889.
41 *The Tewkesbury Register*, 6 July 1889.
42 *Weekly Dispatch* (London), 7 July 1889.
43 Ibid.
44 *Shipley Times and Express*, 6 July 1889.
45 *Thame Gazette*, 9 July 1889.
46 GRO: Death Certificate, 1889, 3rd Quarter, Wandsworth, Volume 01d, p.317.
47 *Evening Star*, 28 June 1889.
48 *Weekly Dispatch* (London), 7 July 1889.
49 Ibid.

50　Octavius Sturges, M.D.Cantab., F.R.C.P.; and George Cowell, F.R.C.S. (eds), *The Westminster Hospital Reports, Volume V* (J. & A. Churchill, 1889). Chapter XI. Charles A. Hebbert, M.R.C.P., 'An Exercise in Forensic Medicine, Part II', p.154.
51　*Weekly Dispatch* (London), 7 July 1889.
52　Ibid.
53　*Whitstable Times and Herne Bay Herald*, 13 July 1889.
54　*The Banbury Advertiser*, 11 July 1889.
55　*Weekly Dispatch* (London), 7 July 1889.
56　*Evening Star*, 4 July 1889.
57　*London Evening Standard*, 3 July 1889.
58　*Evening Star*, 28 June 1889.
59　*Sheffield Evening Telegraph*, 26 June 1889.
60　Evening edition of *The Star of the East*, 5 July 1889.
61　*Cambridgeshire Times*, 28 June 1889.
62　*Western Times*, 9 July 1889.

## 4: A suspect called 'Lancashire Jack'

1　*Lancaster Gazette*, 13 July 1889.
2　*Lincolnshire Free Press*, 16 July 1889.
3　*Cambridge Independent Press*, 12 July 1889.
4　Ibid.
5　*Sheffield Independent*, 28 June 1889; *Cardiff Times*, 29 June 1889, quoting *The East Anglian Times*.
6　Ancestry.com: TNA: England & Wales, Criminal Registers, 1791–1892, General Quarter Sessions of the Peace held at Wisbech, 5 January 1870; *Cambridge Independent Press*, 8 January 1870.
7　*Lloyd's Weekly Newspaper*, 28 July 1889.
8　*Cheltenham Chronicle*, 3 August 1889.
9　*Lloyd's Weekly Newspaper*, 28 July 1889. In fact, Kinsey's was the ninth in the police files.
10　Ancestry.com: LMA: London, England, Workhouse Admission and Discharge Records, 1764–1921, Kensington and Chelsea, Chelsea, England, Admission Date: 12 May 1889.
11　TNA: British Army Service Records, WO 97, Service number 4198, Attestation date: 5 January 1872 at March, Cambridge, Cambridgeshire, England.
12　*Ipswich Journal*, 28 June 1889.
13　Ibid.
14　Ibid.
15　The description of the tools is from: Octavius Sturges, M.D.Cantab., F.R.C.P.; and George Cowell, F.R.C.S. (eds), *The Westminster Hospital Reports, Volume V* (J. & A. Churchill, 1889). Chapter XI. Charles A. Hebbert, M.R.C.P., 'An Exercise in Forensic Medicine, Part II', p.156.

16  *Northampton Mercury*, 15 June 1889.
17  *Dundee People's Journal*, 29 June 1889.
18  *London Evening Standard*, 15 June 1889.
19  *Lloyd's Weekly Newspaper*, 21 October 1888.
20  *Lloyd's Weekly Newspaper*, 10 July 1887.
21  *Weekly Dispatch* (London), 31 July 1887.
22  *Lancaster Gazette*, 17 October 1888.
23  *Eastern Morning News*, 17 October 1888.
24  *Leeds Mercury*, 8 October 1888.
25  *The Grantham Journal*, 13 October 1888.
26  W.H. Allchin, M.B.Lond., F.R.C.P.; George Cowell, F.R.C.S.; and C.A. Hebbert, M.R.C.P. (eds), *The Westminster Hospital Reports, Volume IV* (J. & A. Churchill, 1888), Chapter VI. Charles A. Hebbert, M.R.C.P., 'An Exercise in Forensic Medicine', p.57.

## 5: The Pinchin Street murder, Whitechapel, where a woman's torso was discovered at 5.25 a.m. on Tuesday, 10 September 1889

1   *Ipswich Journal*, 13 September 1889.
2   Ancestry.com: TNA: Metropolitan Police Pension Registers, 1852–1932, Number 10,171 of 9 June 1891; and associated census records.
3   *St James's Gazette*, 11 September 1889.
4   *Reynolds's Newspaper*, 15 September 1889.
5   MEPO 3/140, f. 165, quoted from Stewart P. Evans and Keith Skinner, *The Ultimate Jack the Ripper Sourcebook* (Robinson, 2001), p.557.
6   *Sheffield Independent*, 11 September 1889.
7   HO 144/221/A49301K, ff. 7–8, quoted from Stewart P. Evans and Keith Skinner, *The Ultimate Jack the Ripper Sourcebook* (Robinson, 2001), pp 554–5.
8   TNA: MEPO 4/354/69116; Date of joining: 14 April 1884.
9   *Lloyd's Weekly Newspaper*, 15 September 1889.
10  Ibid.
11  Ibid.
12  Ibid.
13  *Lloyd's Weekly Newspaper*, 29 September 1889.
14  Ibid.
15  Ibid.
16  *South Wales Echo*, 24 September 1889.
17  MEPO 3/140, ff. 166-9, quoted from Stewart P. Evans and Keith Skinner, *The Ultimate Jack the Ripper Sourcebook* (Robinson, 2001), pp.557–9.
18  Octavius Sturges, M.D.Cantab., F.R.C.P.; and George Cowell, F.R.C.S. (eds), *The Westminster Hospital Reports, Volume V*, (J. & A. Churchill, 1889). Chapter XI. Charles A. Hebbert, M.R.C.P., 'An Exercise in Forensic Medicine, Part II', p.159.
19  Octavius Sturges, M.D.Cantab., F.R.C.P.; and George Cowell, F.R.C.S. (eds), *The Westminster Hospital Reports, Volume V*, (J. & A. Churchill, 1889). Chapter XI.

Charles A. Hebbert, M.R.C.P., 'An Exercise in Forensic Medicine, Part II', p.160. The italics are his.
20  Ibid. p.159.
21  *Sheffield Daily Telegraph*, 11 September 1889.
22  *Lloyd's Weekly Newspaper*, 29 September 1889.
23  *Lloyd's Weekly Newspaper*, 29 September 1889.
24  'Ask a P'liceman' by E.W. Rogers and A.E. Durandeau, published in 1888, quoted from Wikipedia.
25  *Lloyd's Weekly Newspaper*, 29 September 1889.
26  Ibid.
27  Ibid.
28  MEPO 3/140, ff. 136–40, quoted from Stewart P. Evans and Keith Skinner, *The Ultimate Jack the Ripper Sourcebook* (Robinson, 2001), pp.531–3.
29  HO 144/221/A49301K, ff. 1–8, quoted from Stewart P. Evans and Keith Skinner, *The Ultimate Jack the Ripper Sourcebook* (Robinson, 2001), pp.545–7.
30  MEPO 3/140, ff. 177–83, quoted from Stewart P. Evans and Keith Skinner, *The Ultimate Jack the Ripper Sourcebook* (Robinson, 2001), p.648.
31  MEPO 3/140, ff. 153–7, quoted from Stewart P. Evans and Keith Skinner, *The Ultimate Jack the Ripper Sourcebook* (Robinson, 2001), p.552.
32  MEPO 3/140, f. 151, quoted from Stewart P. Evans and Keith Skinner, *The Ultimate Jack the Ripper Sourcebook* (Robinson, 2001), p.534.
33  MEPO 3/140, ff. 162–4, quoted from Stewart P. Evans and Keith Skinner, *The Ultimate Jack the Ripper Sourcebook* (Robinson, 2001), p.553.
34  MEPO 3/140, ff. 158–9, quoted from Stewart P. Evans and Keith Skinner, *The Ultimate Jack the Ripper Sourcebook* (Robinson, 2001), p.555–6.
35  MEPO 3/140, ff. 170–3, quoted from Stewart P. Evans and Keith Skinner, *The Ultimate Jack the Ripper Sourcebook* (Robinson, 2001), p.559–61.
36  Octavius Sturges, M.D.Cantab., F.R.C.P.; and George Cowell, F.R.C.S. (eds), *The Westminster Hospital Reports, Volume V* (J. & A. Churchill, 1889). Chapter XI. Charles A. Hebbert, M.R.C.P., 'An Exercise in Forensic Medicine, Part II', pp.160–1.
37  MEPO 3/140, f. 175, quoted from Stewart P. Evans and Keith Skinner, *The Ultimate Jack the Ripper Sourcebook* (Robinson, 2001), p.567.
38  *The Star*, 3 October 1889.
39  Ancestry.com: LMA: London, England, Church of England Marriages and Banns, 1754-1938, Marriage Date: 30 August 1893.
40  TNA: MEPO 3/140, *The New York Herald*, 11 September 1889.
41  MEPO 3/140, ff. 178–80, quoted from Stewart P. Evans and Keith Skinner, *The Ultimate Jack the Ripper Sourcebook* (Robinson, 2001), p.570.

# 6: Profiling the Thames Torso Killer

1  Octavius Sturges, M.D.Cantab., F.R.C.P.; and George Cowell, F.R.C.S. (eds), *The Westminster Hospital Reports, Volume V* (J. & A. Churchill, 1889). Chapter XI. Charles A. Hebbert, M.R.C.P., 'An Exercise in Forensic Medicine, Part II', p.160.
2  *The London Weekly Dispatch*, 11 March 1888.

3   *Saffron Walden Weekly News*, 27 July 1889.
4   *Isle of Wight Times*, 3 October 1889.
5   Octavius Sturges, M.D.Cantab., F.R.C.P.; and George Cowell, F.R.C.S. (eds), *The Westminster Hospital Reports, Volume V* (J. & A. Churchill, 1889). Chapter XI. Charles A. Hebbert, M.R.C.P., 'An Exercise in Forensic Medicine, Part II', p.152.
6   *East London Observer*, 14 September 1889. The company name is from a newspaper drawing.
7   *East London Observer*, 14 September 1889.
8   *Dundee Courier*, 13 September 1889.
9   *South London Chronicle*, 14 September 1889.
10  Jack Gaster, *Time and Tide, The Life of a Thames Waterman* (Amberley Publishing, 2010).
11  *East London Observer*, 23 November 1889. The italics are the author's.
12  GRO: Birth Certificate, 1862, 4th Quarter, St Olave Bermondsey, Volume 01d, p.41.
13  Charles Dickens, *Oliver Twist* ([ebook] Produced by Peggy Gaugy and Leigh Little. HTML version by Al Haines), p.219.
14  Ancestry.com: TNA: Kew, London, England; 1871 England Census; Class: RG10; Piece: 597; Folio: 83; Page: 4; GSU roll: 818905.
15  GRO: Death certificate, 1878, 4th Quarter, St Olave, Volume 01d, p.146.
16  Ancestry.com: TNA: Kew, London, England; 1881 England Census; Class: RG11; Piece: 557; Folio: 69; Page: 14; GSU roll: 1341126.
17  *The Sportsman*, 31 August 1881.
18  An overview is contained in *Daily Telegraph & Courier* (London), 31 July 1905.
19  *Sporting Life*, 2 August 1884.
20  *Sporting Life*, 12 August 1882.
21  Crick's boating challenges were reported in *Sporting Life*, 12 August 1882 and *The Sportsman*, 22 September 1887.
22  Harry Harris, *Under Oars, Reminiscences of a Thames Lighterman 1894–1909* (a pamphlet held at the LMA).
23  *Sporting Life*, 7 November 1888.
24  Harry Harris, *Under Oars, Reminiscences of a Thames Lighterman 1894–1909*.
25  Ibid.
26  Ancestry.com: LMA: London, England, Church of England Marriages and Banns, 1754–1932; Reference Number: p71/js/033.
27  GRO: Birth certificate, 1887, 1st Quarter, St Olave, Volume 01d, p.1956.
28  GRO: Birth certificate, 1888, 2nd Quarter, St Olave, Volume 01d, p.397.
29  *South London Press*, 22 March 1890.
30  Harry Harris, *Under Oars, Reminiscences of a Thames Lighterman 1894–1909*.
31  Ancestry.com: Metropolitan Police Register of Habitual Criminals 1881–1925: MEPO 6; Image reference: 009 0024; Archive piece no: 9. The author has expanded the original abbreviated form.
32  TNA: England & Wales, Crime, Prisons & Punishment 1770–1935, Prisoners Register p.9; Entry P.567.
33  TNA: England & Wales, Crime, Prisons & Punishment 1770–1935, HO 140; Piece 114; Entry 57.
34  Ancestry.com: TNA: Surrey, England, Calendar of Prisoners, 1848–1902; Date of trial: 20 July 1863.

35 *Morning Advertiser*, 14 December 1865.
36 *Surrey Advertiser*, 24 July 1880. The author could not find a subsequent case against Ellen Crick.
37 *East London Observer*, 26 February 1881.
38 *South London Chronicle*, 19 August 1882.
39 *Shipping and Mercantile Gazette*, 26 January 1883.
40 *York Herald*, 24 September 1892.
41 *Weekly Dispatch* (London), 13 November 1898.
42 *South Wales Echo*, 13 May 1887.
43 *Daily News* (London), 9 November 1889.
44 Ibid.
45 Ibid.
46 *South Wales Echo*, 13 May 1887.

## 7: The non-fatal attack on Jessie Miller, Monday, 1 July 1889

1 Wikipedia: Motadel, David (2011). 'Qajar Shahs in Imperial Germany,' *Past and Present*, 213 (1): 193.
2 As pictured in *The Illustrated London News*, 6 July 1889.
3 *The Edinburgh Evening News*, 2 July 1889.
4 Harry Harris, *Under Oars, Reminiscences of a Thames Lighterman 1894–1909*.
5 *The Edinburgh Evening News*, 2 July 1889.
6 Ancestry.com: LMA: London, England, Workhouse Admission and Discharge Records, 17641921, Tower Hamlets (Raine Street), Admission Date: 1 Jul 1889; Discharge Date: 2 Jul 1889.
7 Ancestry.com: TNA: Metropolitan Police Pension Registers, 1852–1932, Number 10,954 of 9 May 1893.
8 Ancestry.com: TNA: 1861 England Census; Class: RG 9; Piece: 1567; Folio: 103; GSU roll: 542832.
9 Ancestry.com: TNA: Metropolitan Police Pension Registers, 1852–1932, Number 10,954 of 9 May 1893.
10 LMA: Thames Police Court registers PS/TH/A/01/013-016 with the hearing dates 30 July 1889; 6 August 1889; 13 August 1889; 27 August 1889.
11 *Morning Post*, 4 March 1890.
12 *East London Observer*, 25 February 1888.
13 *Weekly Dispatch* (London), 21 July 1889.
14 *St James's Gazette*, 9 July 1889.
15 *Weekly Dispatch* (London), 21 July 1889.
16 Ibid.
17 *Woolwich Gazette*, 12 July 1889.
18 *Weekly Dispatch* (London), 21 July 1889.
19 *Daily Gazette for Middlesbrough*, 24 July 1889.
20 *The People*, 28 July 1889.
21 TNA: HO 45/9662/A43067, Police Order of 7 October 1887.

22  *The People*, 28 July 1889.
23  *East London Observer*, 27 July 1889.
24  Ibid.
25  Ibid.
26  Ancestry.com: England and Wales, Criminal Registers, 1791–1892. Class: HO 27; Piece: 213; Page: 258.
27  Central Criminal Court: A Calendar of Prisoners Tried at Assizes & Quarter Sessions, Class: HO 140; Piece: 114. Date of warrant: 27 August 1889.
28  LMA: Thames Police Court registers PS/TH/A/01/013-016 with the hearing dates 30 July 1889; 6 August 1889; 13 August 1889; 27 August 1889.
29  TNA: Home Office: Central Criminal Court Indictments: CRIM 4/1047 dated 16 September 1889.
30  Ancestry.com: England and Wales, Criminal Registers, 1791–1892. Class: HO 27; Piece: 213; Page: 258.
31  *Lloyd's Weekly Newspaper*, 21 July 1889.
32  *Weekly Dispatch* (London), 21 July 1889.
33  For example, *Staffordshire Chronicle*, 13 July 1889.
34  *Woolwich Gazette*, 12 July 1889; *East London Observer*, 20 July 1889.
35  Old Bailey Proceedings Online (www.oldbaileyonline.org, version 8.0, 3 November 2022), July 1889, trial of Samuel Fiford (t18890729-644).
36  GRO: Birth Certificate, 1857, 3rd Quarter, St Olave Southwark, Volume 01d, p.47.
37  Ancestry.com: LMA: Reference Number: P91/LEN/A/01/Ms 7496/60 from London, England, Church of England Births and Baptisms, 1813–1917.
38  GRO: Marriage Certificate, 1875, 4th Quarter, Shoreditch, Volume 01c, p.306.
39  GRO: Birth Certificate, 1876, 1st Quarter, Shoreditch, Volume 01c, p.136.
40  Ancestry.com: TNA: 1891 England Census; Class: RG12; Piece: 167; Folio: 47; Page: 38; GSU roll: 6095277.
41  *Ally Sloper's Half Holiday*, 25 August 1888.
42  *The London Weekly Dispatch*, 21 July 1889.
43  For example, Ancestry.com: London, England, Workhouse Admission and Discharge Records, 1764–1921: Admission Date: 14 December 1899.
44  *Aberdeen Free Press*, 1 September 1888.
45  Ancestry.com: LMA: London, England, Workhouse Admission and Discharge Records, 1764–1930; Reference number: STBG/WH/123/033; Admission Date: 22 November 1899; Discharge Date: 18 December 1899.
46  GRO: Death Certificate, 1900, London City, 1st Quarter, Volume 01c, p.11.
47  GRO: Death Certificate, 1900, London City, 3rd Quarter, Volume 01c, p.21.
48  *The People*, 30 September 1900.
49  *Morning Post*, 15 November 1901.
50  *The People*, 30 September 1900.
51  *Morning Post*, 15 November 1901.
52  Ibid.
53  *Dundee Evening Post*, 15 November 1901.
54  Ancestry.com: England & Wales, National Probate Calendar (Index of Wills and Administrations), 1858–1995, Name: Charles Thomas Edwin Miller; Death Date:

28 Feb 1929; Death Place: Surrey, England; Probate Date: 30 May 1929; Probate Registry: London, England.
55 *The Stage*, 19 November 1908.
56 'I Was In It Comic Song', written and composed by Herbert Cole, arranged by Edmund Forman (White-Smith Music Publishing Co., United States, 1900).

## 8: The non-fatal attack on Elizabeth Sarah Warburton, Wednesday, 23 October 1889

1 GRO: Birth Certificate, 1850, 2nd Quarter, Rotherhithe, Volume 4, p.440; Ancestry.com: LMA: London, England, Church of England Births and Baptisms, 1813–1917; Reference Number: p71/mry/022.
2 Ancestry.com: LMA: London, England, Church of England Births and Baptisms, 1813–1917; Reference Number: p71/jn/014.
3 Ancestry.com: LMA: London, England, Church of England Marriages and Banns, 1754–1932; Reference Number: p93/ctc2/025.
4 Ancestry.com: TNA: 1881 England Census; Class: RG11; Piece: 392; Folio: 49; Page: 38; GSU roll: 1341084.
5 Ancestry.com: LMA; London, England, Church of England Marriages and Banns, 1754–1932; Reference Number: p71/ctc2/015.
6 Fold3: UK, Military Deserters, 1812–1927, Publication Date: 10 May 1875.
7 Findmypast.co.uk: TNA: WO 97; British Army Service Records 1760–1913; Box: 1745; Box record number: 214.
8 GRO: Death Certificate, 1891, 4th Quarter, West Ham, Volume 04a, p.85.
9 GRO: Death Certificate, 1890, 4th Quarter, Shoreditch, Volume 01c, p.109.
10 Ancestry.com: Central Criminal Court: After Trial Calendars of Prisoners, Class: CRIM 19; Piece: 35; entries for 19 November 1889 and 18 December 1889; and TNA: Home Office: Central Criminal Court Indictments: CRIM 4/1050 dated 18 December 1889.
11 LMA: Thames Police Court registers PS/TH/A/01/013-016 with the hearing dates 24 October 1889; 31 October 1889; 6 November 1889; 12 November 1889; 19 November 1889; 26 November 1889; 3 December 1889.
12 *East London Observer*, 23 November 1889. The italics are the author's.
13 *Reynolds's Newspaper*, 24 November 1889.
14 *The Bristol Mercury*, 23 November 1889.
15 *Reynolds's Newspaper*, 27 October 1889.
16 *Reynolds's Newspaper*, 24 November 1889.
17 Ibid.
18 *London Evening Standard*, 20 November 1889. Inspector William Pullen was mis-named 'Pulling' in the press.
19 *Reynolds's Newspaper*, 24 November 1889.
20 *East London Observer*, 7 December 1889.
21 *Liverpool Daily Post*, 3 November 1916.

22  Arthur Francis Day, *John C.F.S. Day: His Forebears and Himself. A Biographical Study by One of his Sons* (Heath, Cranton Ltd., London, 1916), p.113.
23  Quoted from Wikipedia: Bernard Falk, *Bouquets for Fleet Street* (Hutchinson & Co., 1951).
24  Old Bailey Proceedings Online (www.oldbaileyonline.org, version 8.0, 23 September 2020), December 1889, trial of James Crick (25) (t18891216-89).
25  *The East End News and London Shipping Chronicle*, 2 December 1879.
26  *Reynolds's Newspaper*, 22 December 1889.
27  Ibid.
28  Ibid.
29  Ibid.
30  Ibid.
31  Ibid.
32  Ibid.
33  Ancestry.com: TNA: England and Wales, Criminal Registers, 1791–1892; Class: HO 27; Piece: 213; Page: 293.
34  Rosina Crick's occupation is not listed before the 1891 Census, in which it is 'charwoman'. Ancestry.com: TNA: Kew, London, England; 1891 England Census; Class: RG12; Piece: 380.
35  *East London Observer*, 7 December 1889.
36  *South London Press*, 27 August 1887.
37  Ibid.

# 9: The Salamanca Place murder, Vauxhall, where a woman's dismembered body was discovered on Sunday 8 June 1902

1  *Portsmouth Evening News*, 19 October 1899.
2  TNA: Home Office: Criminal Registers, England and Wales, 1805–1892; Class: HO27; Piece 186 dated 19 July 1880.
3  Ancestry.com: England & Wales, Crime, Prisons & Punishment, 1770–1935; Convicts List 1898, Series: MEPO6; Piece 9, for week commencing 10 August 1898.
4  Ancestry.com: Metropolitan Police Register of Habitual Criminals 1881–1925 MEPO 6; Image reference: 009 0024; Archive piece no: 9.
5  GRO: Death certificate, 1898, 2nd Quarter, London, Volume 01d, p.112.
6  *Reynolds's Newspaper*, 24 November 1889.
7  Ancestry.com: TNA: Kew, London, England; 1901 England Census; Class: RG13; Piece: 399.
8  *Morning Leader*, 11 November 1899 has lightermen inhabiting cabins 'for considerable periods at a stretch'.
9  *Dundee Evening Telegraph*, 10 June 1902.
10  *Pall Mall Gazette*, 9 June 1902.
11  *South London Press*, 14 June 1902.
12  *Sheffield Daily Telegraph*, 11 June 1902.

13 *South London Press*, 14 June 1902.
14 Ibid.
15 Ibid.
16 Ibid. Constable James Birtle was also mis-named 'Birton' in the press.
17 Ibid.
18 Ibid.
19 Ibid.
20 *Pall Mall Gazette*, 9 June 1902.
21 *South London Press*, 14 June 1902.
22 *Liverpool Weekly Courier*, 14 June 1902.
23 *Kidderminster Times and Advertiser for Bewdley and Stourport*, 21 June 1902.
24 *Sheffield Daily Telegraph*, 10 June 1902.
25 *Kidderminster Times and Advertiser for Bewdley and Stourport*, 21 June 1902.
26 *South London Mail*, 21 June 1901.
27 *The People*, 22 June 1902.
28 Ancestry.com: TNA: Kew, London, England; 1911 England Census; Class: RG14; Piece: 1985.
29 *Morning Leader* (London), 19 June 1902.
30 *Lakes Herald*, 27 June 1902.
31 *Daily News* (London), 3 July 1902.
32 Ibid.
33 Ibid.
34 Ibid.
35 *Birmingham Weekly Post*, 14 June 1902.
36 *Dundee Evening Telegraph*, 10 June 1902.
37 Old Bailey Proceedings Online (www.oldbaileyonline.org, version 8.0, 5 January 2021), September 1902, trial of Harry Jackson (42) (t19020909-686).
38 *London Evening Standard*, 7 June 1902.
39 GRO: Death certificate, 1907, 3rd Quarter, St Olave Southwark, Volume 01d, p.95.
40 *Aberdeen People's Journal*, 14 June 1902.
41 *Liverpool Weekly Courier*, 14 June 1902.
42 *South London Press*, 26 July 1902.

## 10: A parallel case: the murder of Julia Martha Thomas in 1879, and a reconstruction of the Salamanca Place murder

1 *Daily News* (London), 5 July 1879.
2 *Lloyd's Weekly Newspaper*, 16 March 1879.
3 *Richmond and Twickenham Times*, 22 March 1879.
4 Ibid.
5 *Lloyd's Weekly Newspaper*, 23 March 1879.
6 Old Bailey Proceedings Online (www.oldbaileyonline.org, version 8.0, 11 May 2022), June 1879, trial of Catherine Webster (29) (t18790630-653).
7 *Sheffield Independent*, 29 March 1879.

8   *Dundee Evening Telegraph*, 31 March 1879.
9   *Evening Mail* (London), 7 July 1879.
10  TNA: England & Wales, Crime, Prisons & Punishment, 1770–1935, HO 140; Piece: 47; Date: 30 June 1879.
11  From 'The Adventure of Silver Blaze' in *The Memoirs of Sherlock Holmes* by Sir Arthur Conan Doyle (G. Newnes Ltd, 1894).
12  *Lloyd's Weekly Newspaper*, 6 April 1879.
13  *Lloyd's Weekly Newspaper*, 13 July 1879.
14  *Western Daily Press*, 10 May 1879.
15  Ibid.
16  *London Evening Standard*, 7 July 1879.
17  Ibid.
18  *Bristol Mercury*, 18 April 1879.
19  *Lloyd's Weekly Newspaper*, 13 July 1879.
20  *Northampton Mercury*, 12 July 1879.
21  Ancestry.com: TNA: England and Wales, Criminal Registers, 1791–1892; Class: HO 27; Piece: 184; Page: 131.
22  *Herts Advertiser*, 12 July 1879.
23  *London Daily Chronicle*, 15 October 1883.
24  All extracts are from: Elliott O'Donnell (ed.), *Trial of Kate Webster* (William Hodge & Company Ltd, 1925).
25  *Manchester Evening News*, 29 March 1879.
26  *Southwark Mercury*, 26 July 1879.
27  *Dover Chronicle*, 18 October 1879.
28  BBC News article, 5 July 2011.

## 11: Why not Jack the Ripper?

1   MEPO 3/140, ff. 263-71, quoted from Evans and Skinner, *The Ultimate Jack the Ripper Sourcebook* (Robinson, 2001), p.504.
2   LMA: Whitechapel Infirmary: Porters' Admission and Discharge Register: STBG/WH/123/021.
3   Sarah Bax Horton, *One-Armed Jack* (Michael O'Mara Books, 2023), p.238.
4   *East London Observer*, 14 September 1889.
5   TNA: MEPO 3/3153, ff. 10–18, quoted from Evans and Skinner, *The Ultimate Jack the Ripper Sourcebook* (Robinson, 2001), pp.382–4.
6   R.K. Ressler; A.W. Burgess, 'Crime Scene and Profile Characteristics of Organized and Disorganized Murders', NCJ Number: 99117, *FBI Law Enforcement Bulletin* Volume: 54 Issue: 8 Dated: (August 1985) Pages: 18–25.
7   Ibid.
8   Harry Harris, *Under Oars, Reminiscences of a Thames Lighterman 1894–1909*.
9   HO 144/221/A49301K, ff. 1–8, quoted from Stewart P. Evans and Keith Skinner, *The Ultimate Jack the Ripper Sourcebook* (Robinson, 2001), pp.545–7.
10  *Weekly Dispatch* (London), 29 September 1889.

11   MEPO 3/3153, pp.10–18, quoted from Evans and Skinner, *The Ultimate Jack the Ripper Sourcebook* (Robinson, 2001), pp.382–4.
12   Sir Robert Anderson K.C.B., LL.D., *The Lighter Side of My Official Life* (Hodder and Stoughton, 1910), p.131.
13   Quotations are from: Sarah Bax Horton, *One-Armed Jack* (Michael O'Mara Books, 2023).
14   LMA: Homerton Workhouse: Admission and Discharge Register, 1888–1889: CBG/334/012; City of London Mental Hospital (later Stone House Hospital): Case Book: Male Admissions: CLA/001/B/02/007.
15   *Leeds Mercury*, 8 October 1888.
16   Police Review, 11 July 1913, quoted from Paul Begg, Martin Fido and Keith Skinner, *The Complete Jack the Ripper A to Z* (John Blake Publishing, 2010), p.356.
17   Robert J. Morton (ed.), Mark A. Hilts (co-ed.), *Serial Murder: Multi-Disciplinary Perspectives for Investigators*, Federal Bureau of Investigation Behavioral Analysis Unit, National Center for the Analysis of Violent Crime.
18   TNA: MEPO 3/140, ff. 227–9, quoted from Evans and Skinner, *The Ultimate Jack the Ripper Sourcebook*, pp.418–19.
19   *London Evening Standard*, 8 July 1879.
20   *Sheffield Evening Telegraph*, 8 August 1887.
21   *The Evening Mail*, 10 October 1888.
22   *Lloyd's Weekly Newspaper*, 28 October 1888.
23   *Cheltenham Chronicle*, 3 August 1889.
24   In a 2005 list compiled by academics for *BBC History Magazine*.

## 12: A final analysis of the Torso Killer

1   Ancestry.com: TNA: Metropolitan Police Pension Registers, 1852–1932, Number 14,099 of 19 June 1900.
2   *Lloyd's Weekly Newspaper*, 16 July 1911.
3   *Lloyd's Weekly Newspaper*, 30 July 1911.
4   Sir Melville L. Macnaghten, *Days of My Years* (Edward Arnold, 1914), pp.68–70.
5   *Lloyd's Weekly Newspaper*, 6 August 1911.
6   Sir Robert Anderson K.C.B., LL.D., *The Lighter Side of My Official Life* (Hodder and Stoughton, 1910), p.175.
7   *Lloyd's Weekly Newspaper*, 6 August 1911.
8   *Maryport Advertiser*, 2 January 1891.
9   Ancestry.com: TNA: Kew, London, England; 1891 England Census; Class: RG12; Piece: 304; Folio: 43; Page: 34; GSU roll: 6095414.
10   Ancestry.com: London, England, Workhouse Admission and Discharge Records, 1764–1930, Tower Hamlets, Admission Date: 29 Dec 1888; Discharge Date: 11 Jan 1889: LMA: STBG/WH/123/020.
11   Ancestry.com: TNA: Kew, London, England; 1891 England Census; Class: RG12; Piece: 304; Folio: 53; Page: 3; GSU roll: 6095414.
12   MEPO 4/352 dated 22 September 1873.

13  *Penny Illustrated Paper*, 22 September 1888.
14  *Lloyd's Weekly Newspaper*, 6 August 1911.
15  Old Bailey Proceedings Online (www.oldbaileyonline.org, version 8.0, 12 November 2020), September 1893, trial of James O'Brien (24) Frederick Grucka (28) John William Eyndman (23) (t18930911-834).
16  Old Bailey Proceedings Online (www.oldbaileyonline.org, version 8.0, 12 November 2020), December 1879, trial of Joseph Johnson (57) (t18791215-100).
17  Octavius Sturges, M.D.Cantab., F.R.C.P.; and George Cowell, F.R.C.S. (eds), *The Westminster Hospital Reports, Volume V* (J. & A. Churchill, 1889). Chapter XI. Charles A. Hebbert, M.R.C.P., 'An Exercise in Forensic Medicine, Part II', p.156.
18  *Reynolds's Newspaper*, 15 September 1889.
19  *The Mayo Examiner*, Castlebar, 19 May 1883.
20  *York Herald*, 26 February 1887.
21  *Evening News* (London), 17 February 1887.
22  Robert J. Morton (ed.), Mark A. Hilts (co-ed.), *Serial Murder: Multi-Disciplinary Perspectives for Investigators*, Federal Bureau of Investigation Behavioral Analysis Unit, National Center for the Analysis of Violent Crime.

## Conclusion and true crime reconstructions of the Thames Torso Murders

1  *The Star of the East*, 2 September 1889.

## Epilogue

1  From 'The Problem of Thor Bridge' in *The Casebook of Sherlock Holmes* by Sir Arthur Conan Doyle.
2  GRO: Death certificate, 1907, St Olave Southwark, 3rd Quarter, Volume 01d, p.95.
3  Ancestry.com: LMA: London, England, City of London and Tower Hamlets Cemetery Registers, 1841–1966, Burial date: 6 July 1907.
4  GRO: Marriage Certificate, 1907, St Olave Bermondsey, 3rd Quarter, Volume 01d, p.411.

# Index

Note: *italicised* page numbers denote illustrations

Abberline, Detective Inspector Frederick 12, 18, 89, 214
abortion 55, 59, 70
Adams, Doctor Frederick 182–93
Albert Bridge 53, 54, 60, 61–2, 79, 80, 87, 225, 249
*Alexandra* (saloon steamer) 115, 245–6
*Ally Sloper* (Crick's skiff) 117, 131, 155, 233, 234
Anatomy Act (1832) 20
Anderson, CID Chief Robert 11, 54, 206, 212, 213, 220, 227
Angle, William 44, 46
*Arm of Eve* (Dürer) 9, *157*
Arnold, John (*aka* John Cleary) 104, 105–6
Arnold, Superintendent Thomas 12, 89
Attenborough, Sir David 198

Babington, Joseph 149, 150, 151
bargemen 23, 79, 86–7, 112, 115, 125, 173, 228, 232, 247
Barker, Emily 107
Barnes 182, 183, 184, 188, 198
  see also Thomas, Julia Martha
Batterbee, Charles and Mrs 196–7

Battersea 79, 112, 114, 118, 181, 242
  Rainham victim, remains of 24, 26, 31, 52
Battersea murder (Elizabeth Jackson) 11, 53–71, 72–81, 84, 86, 87, 218, 224–6, 230, 235
  date of murder 60, 114
  inquests 55, 58–62, 63–71, 72–4, 75–6, 219, 220–1, 224–5
  reconstruction 248–9
  uterus removed 85, 205
  *see also* Jackson, Elizabeth
Battersea Park 10, 55–6, 60, 62–3, 75, 79, 87, 179, 226, 232, 239, 242, 243
Baxter, Wynne Edwin 12, 55, 69, 70, 89, 90, 220
Bermondsey 116, 117, 119, 123, 131, 143, 153, 155, 177, 224, 253
Berner Street 88, 204
bigamy 143
Birtle, Constable James 170
bloodhounds 46, 208, 214
Bond, Thomas 11, 82, 83, *159*, 181, 182, 189, 202, 220, 241
  Battersea murder 54–5, 56, 58–9, 220–1, 235

Hebbert report 12, 206
Jack the Ripper 202, 206, 218
Julia Martha Thomas 183–4, 189–90, 191
Mary Jane Kelly 11, 207, 212
Pinchin Street murder 11, 101, 221
profile of a serial killer 11, 206, 218
Rainham murder 27–8, 31, 215, 220, 244
Whitehall murder 34, 37, 40–1, 42, 44–5, 47, 50–1, 82, 207, 220
brewing industry 231, 238–9, 242
Briggs, Detective Sergeant William 60, 62
Brough, Edwin 214
Brown, Charles 36, 37, 38–9, 44
Brown, Doctor Frederick Gordon 12, 221
Burns, James Greville 81
Burns, John 250–1
butchery skills 30–1, 51, 59, 83, 96, 106, 207, 228–30, 237, 240, 241, 245

Callaway, Doctor Edward 20–1, 22, 24, 26–7, 31, 220, 221
Cannon Row 38, 39, 51, 81
Cattermole, Walter 80
Chapman, Annie 9, 33, 55, 60, 99, 138, 203, 205, 208, 211
Chapman, George (*aka* Severin Klosowski) 235
Charley, Sir William Thomas 136
Chelsea 11, 23, 47, 48, 63, 64, 73, 74, 76, 116–17, 224, 226, 232
Chelsea Embankment 23, 60, 104, 249
Chudley, William John 61
Church, John 184, 185, 186
Churcher, Inspector 61–2
Clark, Doctor Percy John 12, 92, 93, 94–5, 100, 106, 181, 221
Cleary, John 104, 105
Coates, Doctor Joseph 190
Cockburn, Lord Chief Justice 121
Coles, Frances 10, 204
Colney Hatch Lunatic Asylum 204, 213
Corpe, Ezra 155
Cox, John 167, 169, 170, 172–3
Crane, Doctor 136
Cream, Thomas Neill 54
Creese, Sarah 193
Crick, Arthur 14, 116, 121, 122, 123–4, 129, 130, 166, 235

Crick, Ellen 14, 116, 120, 122, 130, 145, 148, 149, 151, 152, 153, 154, 166, 232
Crick, James 14–15, 115–25, 165–6, 177, 206, 209, 216, 217, 230–7, 240, 242, 250, 253–4
   alcohol and sedatives, use of 135, 234–6
   competitive rowing 116–18, 127, 131, 155, 233
   and Elizabeth Sarah Warburton 142–56, 233, 253
   imprisoned 152, 165–6, 206
   and Jessie Miller 126–41, 206, 233, 253
   owns skiff 117, 131, 155, 233
Crick, Rosina Caroline (*née* Gorsuch) 119, 124, 128, 133, 153, 154, 166, 253
Criminal Investigation Department (CID) 11, 18, 25, 54, 76, 78, 79, 90, 129, 227–8
Crippen, Hawley Harvey 25
Cross, Miss 22–3, 29, 183

Danford Thomas, Doctor George 25–6, 27, 28–9
Davies, Joseph Evan 55–6, 60
Day, Alfred George 55
Day, John 149, 152, *163*
Denman, George 186
Deuchar, Edward 82–3
Dew, Chief Inspector Walter 25
Dickens, Charles 115
dismemberment 10, 30–2, 203, 217, 220, 236–8
Dobson, Superintendent John 21, 22
Doggett, Thomas 116
Doulton Pottery Works 166, 167, 168, 169, 172, 173, 176, 179
Durden, Mary 192

Eddowes, Catherine ('Kate') 9, 12, 34, 35, 55, 203, 204, 205, 208, 210, 218, 219, 221
Edward VII 166, 178, 180
Faircloth, John ('Jack') 53, 64, 65, 69, 70, 71, 72–9, *161*, 226, 241, 249
Federal Bureau of Investigation (FBI) 209, 215–16, 239–40
Fenian bombings 224, 227
Fiford, Samuel 135–6
fingerprint evidence 177
Fisher, L.E. 57, 74, 86

# INDEX

Fitzrayne, William 155
Ford, Inspector Charles 146–7
forensic science 12–13, 242
Franklin, Arthur 44
Freemasons 18
Freshwater, Alfred 60
Frith, Marischal Keith 186
Froest, Detective Sergeant Frank 12, 25

Gallagher, Doctor Thomas 227
Garrett, Sergeant Harry 12, 17, *159*, 228
Gerard de Grival, Madame Marie 65, 66
Giffard, Sir Hardinge Stanley 186
Grant, Sarah 236–7
Guildford 82

H Division 11–12, 89, 107, 129, 212
Hamerton, Doctor George 24
Hammersmith 112, 185–6, 187, 188, 195, 196, 198
Harcourt, Sir William 227
Hare, Detective Inspector Arthur 18, 24, 26, 27
Hart, Lydia 107
Hawk, Richard 97–8
Hawkins, Detective Sergeant Thomas 37
Hearne, Solomon 61
Hebbert, Charles 11, 30–1, 82, *158*, 181, 228, 241
    Battersea murder 54, 56, 59, 60, 61, 67, 230
    Pinchin Street murder 56, 97, 106, 109, 111, 221
    Rainham murder 29–31, 215, 244
    Whitehall murder 34, 40, 42, 45–6, 47, 49–50, 82, 85, 220
Hebbert report 12–13, 42, 49–50, 59, 60, 61, 67
    deductions about victims 13, 28, 29, 56, 189
    similarities across cases 84–5, 111
    Torso Killer's likely trade 83, 106, 111, 206, 230
Hedge, Ernest 39–40, 43
Hempleman, Frederick Seband 19
Henderson, George 173
Henry, Doctor George Nicol 167, 170–1, 172, 173–4, 175, 177, 179

Hickmott, Thomas 80
Hicks, Athelstan Braxton 24, 25, 58, 59, 62, 72, 75, 220–1
Holborn 24, 139
Horsleydown 115–16, 143, 224, 238
    Butler's Wharf 115, 121, 146
    George's Stairs 54, 55, 60, 128
    human remains 54, 55, 60, 249
    James Crick 14, 116, 119, 128, 129, 145, 149, 153, 232
    Old Stairs 116, 137, 147, 150, *162*, 231, 237, 238–9, 250
Horsleydown Regatta 117
Howard, Detective Sergeant Samuel 123, 129
Hughes, Edward 17–19
Hull, George 182
hunting skills 30–1, 51, 83, 228, 242
Hurley, Jeremiah 98
Hyams, Hyam 14, 122, 203–4, 205, 206, 212, 213, 214, 228

Ives, Elizabeth and Jane 184, 187, 192, 194–5

Jack the Ripper 9–10, 15, 33, 83, 120, 130, 138, *162*, 178, 202–22, 242
    canonical five 9, 33
    dates of attacks 10, 216
    disorganized offender 209
    disposal of remains 208, 218
    'double event' 34, 204, 205, 214
    identity theories 14, 83, 199, 203–4, 214, 235, 241
    method of murder 97, 203, 207, 211, 216–17, 221
    posthumous mutilations 10, 11, 55, 70, 96–7, 203, 207, 211–12, 218
    serial killer profile based on 11, 14
    signature of crimes 203, 205, 211, 221
    similarities with Torso Killer's murders 104, 204–8
    uteri removal 55, 70, 205, 218
Jackson, Annie 63, 65
Jackson, Elizabeth 11, 47, 63–70, 72–9, 152–3, *161*, 215, 219, 239, 242
    *see also* Battersea murder (Elizabeth Jackson)
Jackson, Harry 177

James, Constable William 37–8
Jones, Edward 129, 133

Keefe, Johanna 63, 67
Kelly, Mary Jane 9, 11, 55, 137, 204, 207, 208, 211–12, 214, 217, 218, 219
　location of murder 203, 207
　violence of attack 102, 205, 207, 211–12, 218
Kempster, Doctor Felix 24, 58, 60, 61, 65, 175, 181, 221
King, Sarah Ann 23, 63, 79
Kinsey (*or* McKenzie), Alice 10, 75, 89, 92, 202
Knight, Inspector Francis 61, 228

Lambeth 33–4, 130, 133, 138, 139, 174, 175, 176, 177, 178, 180, 228
　*see also* Salamanca Place murder
Lambeth Poisoner (Thomas Neill Cream) 54
Lane, Harriet 21–2
Langham, Samuel 24, 25, 139, 155, 210, 236
Lear, Edward 212
Lee, Jane (*or* Jenny) 68, 78–9
Leman Street police station 12, 88, 105
Lewis, Charles Carne 18, 21, 23–4, 25
lightermen 14, 23, 58, 86, 114, 118–20, 124–5, *162*, 166, 209–10, 237, 242, 250
Lilley, Sub-Inspector Charles 132
Limehouse 24, 61, 87, 226, 234, 243, 244
London Bridge 31, 82, 83, 114, 115, 116–17, 118, 123, 150, 153, 224, 237, 243, 251
Lushington, Franklin 122–3, 129, 134, 144, 212, 213
Lushington, Godfrey 212, 213

McCarthy, Detective Inspector John 167, 174, 175, 178
McCoy, Doctor Michael 69–70, 132, 147
Macnaghten, Chief Constable Sir Melville ('Mac') 11, 25, 104, 225–7
Marler, Robert 166
Marlow, Charles 61
Marshall, Detective Inspector Henry 43, 46–7, 49, 82
Marshall, Horatio 143–4
Mathews, Charles 'Willie' 149
Matthews, Henry 27, 101, 104

M'Carthy, Patrick 60
Mellor, Claude 60, 105
Menhenick, Charles 185
Metropolitan Police 11
　Register of Habitual Criminals 166
　Thames Division (river police) 12, 18, 61, 62, 89, 129, 132, 146, 228, 255
　Whitechapel murders file 9–10, 104–5, 202, 219
Midland Railway Coal Dock 26, 86–7
Miller, Charles Thomas Edwin 139, 140–1
Miller, George Oliver 137, 139–40
Miller, Jessie 126–41, 153–4, 206, 210, 216, 230, 232–3, 235, 236, 254
Minter, Margaret 66–7
Monkford, George 26
Monro, Commissioner James 11, 27, 90, 99, 101–4, 112, *157*, 207, 211, 212–13, 214, 250
Monsell, Chief Constable Colonel Bolton 11–12, 88–9
Moore, Chief Inspector Henry 12, 89, 99, 106, 107, 110, 214
Mordecai, Abraham 130
Muir, Richard 149
Muntzer, Robert 168, 169, 170
Mylett, Rose 10, 219–20

Nell, Ginger 79
New Scotland Yard 38, *161*, 225, 227–8
　*see also* Whitehall murder
Nichols, Polly 9, 93, 138, 199, 203, 205

O'Brien, Jeremiah 155
Old Swan pub 116–17, 243

Paine, Kate 69, 70, 73, 79
Pattenden, Inspector Josiah 105
Pearman, Inspector 185
Pennett, Constable William 90–2, 98, 252
Pepper, Professor Augustus 167
Persia, Shah of (Naser al-Din) 126–8, 132, 133, 151, *163*
Phillips, Fanny 133
Phillips, Doctor George Bagster 12, 93, 95–6, 106, 107, 202–3, 207, 211, 212, 221, 250
Pimlico arm 33, 37, 41, 42, 246

# INDEX

Pinchin, Johnson and Company 112
Pinchin Street 110, 112, 204, 239, 250
Pinchin Street murder 10, 11, 12, 88–108, 109–15, 156, *162*, 207, 211–15, 219, 228–9, 237–8
    date of murder 102, 115, 204, 213
    inquest 90–9, 211
    reconstruction 243, 249–52
    'region of theory' 198–9
    sedatives 218, 235
    victim 89–90, 107, 109–11, 152
Pinhorn, Inspector Charles 12, 89, 91–2
Pomeroy, Elizabeth 68, 78–9
Pope, Sergeant William 71
Porter, Henry 184, 185, 186, 187–8, 195, 196, 197
Porter, Robert 187–8, 195, 196
Potter, Emma 48
Prince's Road Workhouse 138, 178, 199–201
prostitutes 75, 139–40, 141
    Jack the Ripper 206, 208, 215
    James Crick 141, 147, 232
    Thames Torso Murders 47, 96, 97, 206, 215, 248
Pullen, Inspector William 147

Rainham murder 11, 17–32, 50, 80–1, 84–5, 155, *160*, 233
    date of murder 31, 233, 244
    inquests 18–24, 25–9, 220
    reconstruction 243–5
    victim 27, 28, 30, 152, 215, 243–4
Read, Inspector George 123
Regan, Detective Inspector John 12, 89, 128, 129, 133, 135, 144, 149, 151–2, *158*, 223–30, 236
Regan, John Albert 54, 55, 60
Regent's Canal 24, 25, 26, 27, 31, 32, 80, 86–7, 112, 114, 239, 245, 254
Reid, Inspector Edmund 12, 89, 91–2, 93, 100
Richmond 22, 183, 184–5, 186, 187–8
Robins, Julian 123–4
Rodwell, Charles 26
Rose, Sergeant George 46, 214
Rotherhithe 122, 143, 166
Ruffeitt, Thomas 128–9, 130, 131–2, 133, 134, 135, 154

St Pancras Lock 24, 26, 80, 86
Salamanca Place murder 14–15, 138, 156, *163*, 165–80, 181, 193, 195, 196, 198–201, 253
Saunders, Thomas 129, 130, 134, 136, 144, 147, 149, 212
Scotland Yard 18, 21, 24, 54, 71, 186, 197, 227
Shaw, Norman 52
sheep-stealing 228–30, 237, 240, 245
Sheil, James 124
Shelley House 60–1, 87, 105
Shore, Detective Inspector John 12, 18, 21, 24
Sims, Francis John 121, 130, 144
Slade, Wyndham 123
Smith, Archibald Levin 186
Smith, Emma 9–10
Smith, Rosina Lydia 107
Squires, Joseph 62
Stanton, Edward 61
Stepney 12, 98, 108, 122, 138, 143, 204, 223
Stevenson, Doctor Thomas 235
Still, Robert 150, 151, 154
Stride, Elisabeth 9, 34, 88, 89, 92, 203, 204, 205
suicide 220, 236
Sullivan, James 121
Sumner, Charles 116, 166
Swanson, Chief Inspector Donald 12, 89, 99–101, 105, 112, 198–9, 211, 213, 221, 228–9

Tabram, Martha 9, 203, 207, 216
Taylor, Alfred Swaine 13
Taylor, Doctor Michael 167, 168
Thames Division (river police) 12, 18, 61, 62, 89, 129, 132, 146, 228, 255
Thomas, Julia Martha *164*, 181–98, 219
Thompson, Alison 198
Tilson, Thomas 121
Tooley Street 116, 121, 145, 148, 149, 153, 243, 251
'Tootsie Sloper' 117–18, 131
Torso Killer 216, 223–40
    clothing of victims 53, 86, 89, 154, 205, 218, 231, 237, 238, 249
    dismemberment 10, 11, 111, 203, 207, 211, 212, 219